STICKNEY-FOREST VIEW LIBRARY DISTRICT

3 1803

STICKNEY-FOREST VIEW LIBRARY

W9-BGF-431

DON'T GET ME WRONG!

Mike Ditka's Insights, Outbursts, Kudos, and Comebacks

JIM STAMBORSKI

CHICAGO REVIEW PRESS

Library of Congress Cataloging-in-Publication Data

Stamborski, Jim.
  Don't get me wrong.

  1. Ditka, Mike.   2. Football—United States—
Coaching.   3. Chicago Bears (Football team)   I. Title.
GV939.D57S73 1988   796.332′092′4   88-20238
ISBN 1-55652-040-9

Unless otherwise indicated, all quotes are from the *Chicago Tribune*.

The Buddy Ryan passage appearing on page 64 and dated 7/22/86 is quoted from *Calling The Shots*, ©1986 by Mike Singletary and Armen Keteyian, used with permission of Contemporary Books, Inc., Chicago.

Copyright © 1988 by Jim Stamborski
All rights reserved
Printed in the United States of America
First edition
Published by Chicago Review Press, Incorporated

CONTENTS

FOREWORD

From the time he became head coach of the Chicago Bears, in January 1982, Chicago sports fans have recognized that Mike Ditka is something special. He is a skilled football coach and an excellent motivator. He also is a tough, plain-spoken son of a Pennsylvania steel-worker who speaks from his heart as often as he does from his head. There is no ambiguity with Mike Ditka; something is right or it's wrong. Either way, he will let you know what he thinks, no holds barred.

Mike Ditka has described the Bears affectionately as "his Grabowskis" because the Bears reflect the work ethic, the attitude of a city and a people who aren't afraid to work hard to get ahead and achieve a part of the American Dream for themselves and their families.

This collection of quotes is dedicated to all people, regardless of their ethnic backgrounds, who know what it means to work hard for a living and are fellow Grabowskis.

INTRODUCTION

After 19 straight years of frustration, the Chicago Bears football team had failed to win a championship. Chicago Bears owner George Halas searched for a new head coach who could reestablish the pride and toughness of the glory years when the Bears were considered the Monsters of the Midway. The lethargic Bears needed a head coach who was skilled as a football tactician as well as a skilled motivator, and Halas would not settle for less.

In the Chicago media, speculation as to who the new Bears head coach would be centered around four candidates: George Allen, John Robinson, Mike White, and then-assistant Dallas Cowboys coach Mike Ditka. When contacted by the Chicago media, Mike Ditka said,

> I'm very interested, but I deal in reality. There has been no direct contact between me and the Bears. But I assume they are interested in me because Mr. Halas has indicated to our people [the Dallas Cowboys] that he wants to talk to me. 1/8/82

In the Dallas Cowboys organization, at least one person, General Manager Tex Schramm, knew how badly Mike Ditka wanted the Bear head coaching job. He told Chicago reporters, "His ties are so strong to Chicago I think he'd welcome the opportunity to live with whatever problems there are." 1/17/82

In the previous football season, during a nationally-televised Cowboys game, Mike Ditka, in an act of frustration, threw a clipboard into the air. Reporters asked Ditka if he felt he had the right temperament to be a head coach in light of the clipboard-throwing incident. Ditka shot back,

> I'm 42 years old and I've been in pro football for 21 years as a player and coach. So I threw a clipboard once on national T.V., so what? I've been involved in a lot of football games and I throw one clipboard and it gets written about. 1/8/82

Ironically, years later Jim Dooley, Bears Director of Research and Quality Control revealed that in George Halas' eyes, this incident was a key factor in the decision to hire Ditka. Said Dooley,

> Halas' secretary, Ruth, told me Halas was watching a Bears game at Dallas on T.V. with her when there was a close-up on camera of Ditka, then assistant coach for the Cowboys, storming and ranting on the sidelines. This was in 1981 when the Bears lost to them . . . Halas turned to Ruth and said, "That's my coach, that's who I want." 11/16/86

On January 20, 1982, George Halas announced,

> For some time I have been working out a game plan designed to bring a winning football team back to Chicago. Now with the signing of Mike Ditka as head coach, phase one of that plan is complete. 1/21/82

He added,

> I like his ability to handle himself and other people and I know he'll do a good job getting people to play according to his desires. 1/21/82

In one of Mike Ditka's first press conferences, he displayed his honest and open style in dealing with the media. He candidly assessed his situation as the new head coach.

> I'm excited, yeah, but I'm also realistic. I know that if you don't produce, all these good feelings, all these best wishes, quickly turn sour. 1/24/82

One conviction, first expressed early in 1982, has remained constant. Mike Ditka has always felt that he and the Chicago Bears were destined to be together.

> I believe everyone has a destiny in life, and mine is with the Chicago Bears. I'm going to give Chicago a winning football team, an interesting football team, and a football team that everybody is going to be proud of. 1/21/82

Finally, with typical Ditka candor, he summed up his situation as new head coach. "Now the talking's stopped. Now I've got to do the job." 1/24/82

The reaction to Ditka's hiring around the football league was immediate and positive. Tom Landry, head coach Dallas Cowboys, commented,

> Any time you lose a coach it's tough. He knows your system and he's a part of you. Mike's been loyal and I'm very happy

for him. Mike is ready. . . . If Mike gets a break he'll be OK. 1/20/82

Luke Johnson, Ditka's offensive coach when he played with the Bears, said,

I think it's a good deal. He was always one of my favorites. He won't take any guff from anybody. He had the winning spirit. 1/20/82

Former Packers guard Fuzzy Thurston:

If anybody can work for George Halas, Mike Ditka can. It's a difficult job, but Mike is tough enough to handle it. 1/20/82

Said Tom Brooksheir, former Eagles defensive back and a sports broadcaster,

I went to Lake Forest last summer to watch a Bears workout and I didn't find the same intensity you get when you visit Philly or Dallas. But this will change under Ditka. Absolutely. The players will have to pay to get to the water bucket. 1/20/82

Earl Morrall, former Colts quarterback,

Ditka? Watch out for the Bears, if they've hired Ditka. It means they're going back to the mean old brawling Monsters of the Midway. 1/20/82

And finally, Joe Schmidt, former Lions linebacker:

Ditka will do a great job. If the Bears all play like Mike played, they've got a winner. 1/20/82

1

DITKA ON DITKA

MIKE DITKA, COMPETITOR

I hate to lose. When I was a kid playing Little League baseball, boy I hated to lose. I cried. It just hurt my feelings to lose. I don't like to lose. I'm not proud of that, but I just don't like to lose.   11/17/85

I wasn't a guy who went up and shook hands before the game or after the game.   12/13/85

Would he jump into a preseason brawl as a player?   No question about that.   9/11/86

MIKE DITKA, PLAYER

On his years at Pittsburgh University   I think that's where I understood that the harder you work, the more you get out of life. I became a pretty good football player, not because I was faster or could catch the ball

1

better, but I taught myself to do a lot of things that other guys didn't. Everything was competitive. My whole life was based on beating the other guy, doing better, being equal to, or just showing I could be as good as anybody else. I don't know if that's good or bad.   11/17/85

At Pittsburgh, when a teammate of Ditka's missed a tackle on Herb Adderley, allowing Michigan State to take a 7–0 lead at half-time, Ditka confronted him.   We were coming into the locker room and he said, "Well, we are only down 7–0. It's only half-time." I said, "Seven-nothing? that's bull. It doesn't matter what we're down. You had a chance to make a play and you didn't make it." It was probably wrong to say it, but that's what I confronted him with. I'm sure I hurt his feelings and I'm not saying I was right. I apologized to him the next week.   11/17/85

The Bears made me what I was. The Bears needed a tight end and they found out I could run and catch the ball. . . Mr. Halas knew how to use the tight end. He said, "We'll go to this guy [Ditka] and let him run over some people."   9/8/85

. . . I also hit the bottom in Philadelphia, just a bust-out player with a bad hip and knee and foot, ready to quit until I came to Dallas.   1/24/82

I was told I'd be a backup [at Dallas] and that hurt. And that's what I was, because I didn't do all I could that first year. But the next year I started. I worked harder than anyone else in the off-season. Nobody ever worked harder. I ran in my bare feet to toughen my bad foot. I did everything I could, especially weights and running. I got in such good shape, I could have done anything a 21-year-old kid could do, and I was 30. I dropped my weight 21 pounds until everything was muscle. And I caught more passes the next year than any tight end in Dallas history.   1/24/82

DESTINED TO BE A BEAR PLAYER AND COACH __

You have to be [a Bear] before you really feel it. If they cut Landry open stars would fall out. I'm a Bear.   11/17/84

There was never any question. I wanted to be with the Bears, to be in Chicago and play in the NFL. Then when I left, after fighting over money, I had an empty feeling in my heart over the job that I left undone. Now I've come to feel that I left for a reason, and that there was a reason why I spent 13 years in Dallas. I know there are a lot of people who don't believe that way, but I do.   1/24/82

My personality is the Bears personality, and I saw it when we [Dallas] played them [the Bears] this year [1981]. I saw things that rekindled that old feeling, that old look. The toughness. They really came after us. I really liked what I saw. I didn't like the bad execution in certain areas, but I did like the physical end of it.   1/24/82

Don't get me wrong. I'm a realist. I understand what the situation there is. I understand it's not gonna be the fair-haired son coming home and everything is gonna be beautiful and the sun is going to rise and set on the city of Chicago and the Bears. That's not what I'm saying. I'm saying the opportunity is going to be there and that's where I want to be, that it's been a lifetime ambition to be there.   1/24/82

It's the only thing I've every wanted to do in my life. I'm very happy, and I welcome the opportunity and challenge for three more years. It started when Mr. Halas made the decision and I thank God he made it. I'm sure a lot of people doubted the decision.   1/3/85

COACH DITKA _____

My biggest problem is myself. I think I take coaching too seriously. It's my job. But more than that, it's pride. The main thing to remember is, when you let your guard down, don't get thrown off the track. Just remember what's at the end.   7/14/85

Could Ditka the player have played for Ditka the coach? Yeah. Because I want to win. That's the only thing I want to do. If a player wants to win, he should have no problem. If he wants to be patted on the butt every time he does something wrong, then he'll have a problem.   10/30/85

In 1982, after Ditka threw a tantrum in the locker room following a 10–0 loss to New Orleans Some of the players thought I was nuts, I'm sure.   11/17/85

After he broke his hand punching a steel locker in Baltimore I hit it into a steel cabinet and it broke.   9/27/83

More on the broken hand incident I got my priorities out of whack for the last couple of weeks and it hurt me as an individual. In my case, I've got to relax. And I will. Oh yes, you'll see the most relaxed guy you've ever seen. I can be positive about this. It has to do with what I feel inside.   10/14/83

I wish I could say I'm not going to get excited anymore but that's not my nature. I don't apologize. I wish I could stand out there like [Bud] Grant or [Tom] Landry but I can't do it.   9/27/83

If I fall asleep on the sidelines now, never say anything.   10/14/83

There's no question that when I stand up and talk, a lot of guys say, "Here we go again."   11/17/85

My players play hard because I think they know they have to play hard to stay on the field. There's nobody I wouldn't replace.   11/17/85

Sometimes players feel I don't think they're important to the team. That's not true.   7/17/86

I'm not a tough guy. My God, there's not a coach in the league who bends over backward to congratulate, to build up his people more than I do. But when they're wrong, they're wrong.   11/1/83

On winning the Central Division in 1984   I'm sure I'll be able to express my feelings better someday, but right now I'm happy for the 49 guys in there and for the guy [Halas] that hired me three years ago. 11/24/84

This is the greatest feeling I have ever had.   11/26/84

After Ditka's drunk-driving arrest   It's unfortunate and disappointing. There are rights and wrongs in this life. I'm just a person. It's like anything in life. Sometimes you'd like to change situations, but then you can't change them.   10/15/85

On his feuding with former Bears coach Buddy Ryan   I made it too much of a personal thing. You try to do individual things and that's wrong. We're in a team sport and when I have to start thinking I have to rely on being a genius to win football games, I've got a lot of problems.   9/15/86

ON THE 1986 SEASON _____

I get a little madder [at the 1986 Bears] because we're the world champions and I feel we shouldn't do wrong things, which is a foolish thought. I doubt that it's right, but I doubt I'm going to change. 10/11/86

I'm a little crabbier this year, and I don't smile as much. I dress a little better, but that's about it.   10/11/86

. . . you don't know Mike Ditka if you think success will spoil him. I've been so fortunate. Bud Grant said when I was hired it was not what you know but who you know. I'm just glad Coach Halas knew me.   1/28/86

I like it; we're struggling. You guys [the media] are mad, the fans are angry. Me, I'm calm.   11/19/86

I'm not being bothered by anything the rest of the year [1986], as you'll find out. No more pressure. Pressure's over. I don't worry.   11/2/86

Having fun in the '86 season?   I really am. It's been a struggle this year, but a fun kind of struggle. It's still serious business to me because it's my job and I want to win as much as I can. But I'm having fun. I don't think I've been uptight. I get ticked off on the sidelines. But off the field, I haven't exploded.   12/28/86

It became a little strained at times, and that I don't like. I really feel when it's drudgery to come here in the morning, I wonder. Because I know if we had to go out and work in the mill like my Dad did, that was work. This is not work.   1/5/87 The *Des Plaines Daily Herald*

I took a more businesslike approach and maybe the players took a more businesslike approach, and it wasn't as much fun.   1/5/87 The *Des Plaines Daily Herald*

I guess the major difference in me is that I've learned not to take things so personally. We've come a long way from that first year, but we've come it together.   1/7/86

It's funny to me, it's still a game. Most of us coaches are overpaid as it is.   1/2/87 *Chicago Sun Times*

Would Ditka own an NFL team?   That would be something I would seriously contemplate. There's a lot of ways you can leave a mark in football and society. Coaching is only one of them. Ownership, part of front-office management, I just think there's different ways, and I think somewhere in life you start thinking about them. Not right now, but someday.   1/2/87 *Chicago Sun-Times*

DITKA, JUST AN ORDINARY GUY

I can walk up to any steelworker or any garbage collector in the country and I can sit down and talk life with them. I don't care if I've got a pair of Gucci shoes on or I've got a pair of clodhoppers on.   12/28/86

I can go into any tavern in the city of Chicago, sit down, and have a beer with a guy and be Joe Blow.   12/28/86

On not being voted into the Football Hall of Fame   It doesn't bother me one bit. I owe my whole life to football. Football doesn't owe me one thing.   9/8/85

1988: HALL OF FAME

On February 2, 1988, Mike Ditka was officially voted into the professional football Hall of Fame.   It's not an individual honor. I had coaches. I had teammates. I had a quarterback who threw me the ball. I had a coach who designed an offense that threw the ball to the tight end and changed the look of pro football in the early '60's. It's really nothing I did. I just played the position as good as I could, the way Mr. Halas designed it.   2/3/88 *Chicago Sun-Times*

What the Hall Of Fame means   It means people are going to recognize you in the same breath with Sid Luckman and George Halas and Bronko Nagurski. When you start thinking about all those names, you say, "Hey, this is awfully special." I've been able to do things I once only dreamed about. When I look back and think about all the fun I had playing, to have an honor like this bestowed upon me is mind-boggling.   2/3/88 *Chicago Sun-Times*

I don't think anything I did was great. If I'm going to be remembered for anything, I played hard. I gave it the best I could. I think the people who played against me would vouch for that.

I never asked for anything and I never gave anything. I wasn't a friendly guy. I wasn't a hand-shaker, but I wasn't meant to be. I was trying to beat the other guy. Hand-shaking and butt-patting are things that came in lately.   2/3/88 *Chicago Sun-Times*

I really don't have a private life anymore. I guarantee I signed more autographs in two days [at the Hall Of Fame] than these players signed all week. It's important to take the time to do it, but after a while it becomes hard to do constantly.   2/8/88

2

WITTY MIKE

EARLY SIGNS OF A SENSE OF HUMOR

During Ditka's career as a Bears player, a fan ran onto the field during a Bears-Rams game. Ditka flattened him. In one of his first press conferences with the Chicago media Ditka commented Well, I'll tell you this, if a fan ran onto your desk, where you work, what would you do? 1/21/82

What Ditka calls Dick Butkus Mr. Butkus. I always called him Mr. Butkus and if any of you get as mean as Mr. Butkus I'll call you Mr. too. 2/10/82

Ditka's philosophy on two minute drills Score. What do you think? Give up. 11/8/83

Did Ditka bring anything with him from Dallas to the Bears? Yeah, a few shirts and a couple of slacks. 1/6/85

DITKA'S HOMETOWN ─────────────────────

How tough was Aliquippa? Our definition of quick hands was a guy who could steal hubcaps off a car that was moving.   6/15/87

There was a guy named Pete Maravich, who led the NBA in scoring. Then there was a guy who didn't play sports, but he made some pretty good music. Henry Mancini. Actually, Henry's from West Aliquippa, but after he got famous we moved him into town.   6/15/87

Of course, the most famous football player from Aliquippa is a guy named Tony Dorsett. Ditka, Dorsett. A lot of people liked to compare us. I can understand that. I thought about it a long time. You look at it this way: both of our names started with 'D.' Before I changed barbers, we both had curly hair. We're both Ukrainian. See, Tony's real name was Dorsett-ski. We both attended the University of Pittsburgh. And we've both worked for the Cowboys. I've analyzed this over the years, and let me tell you the differences between Ditka and Dorsett. It's simply 17 years and a million-and-a-half dollars. You figure out who's got which.   6/15/87

It's silly to keep a camera on a coach, especially this coach. Lots of coaches put people to sleep. Put it on me and guys want to go out and buy a gun.   12/17/86

HECKLERS ─────────────────────────

I don't like 'em. I don't like know-it-alls in life . . . We appreciate his 18 bucks.   10/6/86

To a Packer heckler   Aw shut up! Have a quarter. Make a phone call.   9/23/86

To a heckler disrupting a post-game press conference   Jerk! This is your I.Q., buddy. Zero! [turning to reporters] I'd rather talk to him, I know I'm smarter than that S.O.B.   9/29/86

I wasn't trying to be funny with the guy [the press conference heckler] because if I would have got ahold of him, I wouldn't have been funny. It had nothing to do with being funny.   9/30/86

DITKA'S PERSONALITY

We're not going to talk about my personality because I have none. 10/30/86

Johnny Carson: Didn't the players call you Sybil because of your change of personalities?
Ditka: That wasn't the reason. I changed dresses three times a day.   1/21/87 *Chicago Sun-Times*

There's only two; Jekyll and Hyde. There is no third personality. 12/28/86

Let's do this. Forget about who we're playing this week and write about how funny I am and we'll have a good time. Clown around every day. I got magic tricks I'll show you. As much as I smile, I'm not very funny.   9/30/86

IT'S NOT EASY COACHING THE BEARS

After a streaker ran onto the field during the Cowboys-Bears exhibition game in London   I had to look around and see if it was anybody from our bench.   8/4/86

On thinking Walter Payton was sitting out an exhibition game only to find him playing   I didn't hold him out. I assumed he was going to play. Then, before the game, I was told he wasn't going to play, so I changed the starting lineup. Then I see him out there. That's great communications. A lot of guys are saying, "Who's the guy with the tie?"   8/19/85

Thinking ahead to playoff games?   Not me. I'm just a poor Polack. I can't look much past next Sunday in Detroit. *A reporter asked, "Didn't your family come from the Ukraine?*   Same difference, I still can't look past Detroit.   12/16/85

On reversing himself on the reasons why he selected Kevin Butler over Bob Thomas   I lied.   9/3/85

I can tell the players are getting ready when they gripe and complain and get mad at me. I heard it today a little. So we're coming on and making some progress.   8/5/86

I said to the team, "I'd like you to meet Doug Flutie," and a couple of guys threw tomatoes at me, but that's all. I think I heard them saying to him after practice, "Let's have a 7-Up."   10/23/86

Commenting on a picture of himself with a cardboard halo in front of a Platteville, Wisconsin church   I hope it works.   7/18/86

On Bears veterans being late to training camp   I heard five or six guys missed a plane from O'Hare to Dubuque. That's all right. They all have money. They're all multimillionaires. They know how to rent a car. Some probably know how to hot-wire a car.   7/16/86

On the match-up between the 49ers offense, directed by Bill Walsh, and the Bears defense, directed by Buddy Ryan   They're going to put up two signs, "Geniuses at work."   1/6/85

On numerous injuries   I'm expecting some flowers or a sympathy wreath because we are so beat-up.   10/11/85

On being accused of introducing William Perry as a running back against the 49ers to pay back the 49ers for using a lineman in the backfield the previous year   You think I'd do that? I'm not that kind of guy. I wouldn't try to get one-up on people. I just don't forget very easy.   10/14/85

Ditka's 1986 New Year's resolution   To stay off of [interstate highway] 294. [He was arrested there on drunk-driving charges in 1985.]   1/1/86

After the Super Bowl victory party   The party was pretty good if I remember correctly. I'm going to stay off of I-294.   1/28/86

On missing the 1986 NFL best-dressed list's top ten   You can figure that those people aren't really too sharp.   12/31/86

On the Iron Mike music video   There are a lot of long-faced ballplayers because they know they couldn't keep up with me. I know Fencik was sad-faced because he knew I out-danced him.   1/2/87 *Chicago Sun-Times*

It's really embarrassing that I let myself go that much.   1/2/87 *Chicago Sun-Times*

DITKA ON WILLIAM PERRY _____

I don't think we will ever regret this pick. He can have the impact of a Big Daddy Lipscomb. He's going to look good in that navy blue uniform, or two uniforms, whatever it takes.   5/1/85

Why Ditka picked Perry in the draft   Gut feeling.   5/1/85

I once played against a guy who weighed 415 pounds. We ate his lunch.   5/1/85

On giving Perry the ball   I just wanted to see if he could run with it.   10/14/85

On Raider defensive end Howie Long's criticism of William Perry   I never argue with anybody as smart as Howie Long. Or is it Huey Long?   11/8/85

We want him [Perry] around 300 but we don't know what he'll be. He worked out religiously until a week ago and then he went home to South Carolina. That's usually a catastrophe. The chicken population of South Carolina goes down measurably.   7/16/86

He's running twice a day. From the refrigerator to the bathroom. 7/21/87

DITKA ON JIM McMAHON _____

I've never spoken behind sunglasses before, but now I understand why Jim does it. He likes to escape reality.   4/28/87

Why McMahon and Brian Bosworth can't be on the same team   There wouldn't be enough sunglasses to go around.   4/15/87

Does it bother him when Jim McMahon talks about him?   Doesn't bother me. I kinda like Jim. He makes me laugh and I don't laugh that much.   11/14/86

On McMahon's Mohawk haircut   I think it's very nice. I can relate to that. He did it on his own and I tried to do that once in a training camp. Ended up like his Mohawk all over. You can't correct those things once you make the wrong slice.   7/26/85

Is McMahon in Ditka's doghouse?   My dogs aren't even in my doghouse. My dogs are in my house.   8/19/86

This is my sixth year with the Bears. Jim McMahon has been with the Bears six years, too, and people say we don't communicate. That's not true. We've talked four times.   6/15/87

Everybody asks me, "What kind of relationship do you have with Jim McMahon?" I say it's strange and wonderful. He's strange and I'm wonderful.   6/15/87

On roasting Jim McMahon   I'll be as good as anyone up there. It's easy to roast McMahon. I have more material on him than anybody.   4/24/87

What McMahon is doing to rehabilitate his shoulder   He's hitting the 5-iron about 180 yards.   4/24/87

I'm going to tell you one story, and Jim knows I tell this story and he doesn't mind it. 1985 was such a great year for the Bears . . . and you remember one game that I really think was the catalyst. It was the third game, and it was on a Thursday night against Minnesota. You'll probably remember it as the greatest-coached game in the history of the NFL. You're going to remember that I held Jim McMahon out until midway in the third quarter until we got down by nine points. Then I got very smart and put him into the game and he threw three touchdown passes and we won the game. Then we came back to Soldier Field to play the Washington Redskins and we beat them 45–10, and Jim McMahon throws four touchdown passes. He completes 75 percent of his passes and there's no turnovers. This guy, for two weeks he's the best quarterback in football, and nobody can argue that point. Then, you may not remember, but the next week we go to Tampa Bay to play the Bucs, and Jim overthrew Willie Gault for two touchdowns. He fumbled and lost the ball twice, and he threw three interceptions. We're behind by 10 points at half-time. We come into the locker room, and I'm not a guy who minces his words. I walked up to Jim and I said, "You stink." He didn't say anything. But he just kind of looked at me and it made me so darned mad and, of course, he had those stupid sunglasses on. I said, "Jim, can you explain to me how you can be the best quarterback in football for two weeks and now for one half you're the worst?" He never said a word. He just looked at me. I said, "Jim, you're either ignorant or apathetic," and he just kept looking at me. Finally, I said, "Jim, which is it? Are you ignorant or apathetic?" Well, he kept looking at me and then he said, "I don't know and I don't care." 6/15/87

MIKE DITKA, SPORTSMAN

Ditka was invited to go fishing with a group of Chicago-area executives on a charter boat on Lake Michigan. Grudgingly he went along. My dad never raised me with hunting and fishing. Not in a steel-mill town. I've never gone bass fishing or anything like that . . . They tell me about 600 pound marlin off Hawaii, of fighting them for 10 hours. That's nonsense. Why, that's two rounds of golf right there. 5/7/85

The party managed to catch only six fish. Ditka was less than happy. This is great. I was assured we'd be catching 15, 20 fish. You guys must have negative attitudes . . . . I guess I'll be a fisherman when I get to that Great Pond in the Sky.

*A photographer on the dock asked Ditka how many fish he'd caught.
Ditka's response suggests that he might make it as a fisherman.* Two.
He didn't catch any. 5/7/85

A GOLF MATCH _____

*In February 1987, Jim McMahon and Mike Ditka were paired against
John Elway and Dan Reeves of the Denver Broncos in a charity golf
match.*

Jim McMahon Where did I get to know John? Probably at a golf
tournament. That American Airlines tournament they have every
February. He could always hit the ball far, but he didn't have control.
He'd hook one, and slice another. Now, he's a lot better. Look at last
summer. Elway's a 7 handicap now.

John Elway I'm a 9, not a 7. And we had a nice even match for
charity out here last summer. My coach, Dan Reeves, is a 7 and Jim's
coach, Mike Ditka, is a 6. Jim's a 10. So it was perfect, and we went
down to the last hole. I made par, and Denver beat Chicago. I think
the two coaches were more serious about winning than Jim and I,
though.

Jim McMahon Naturally I birdied the first hole and then
disappeared. Mike wasn't too happy with me. I wasn't much help. I
suppose we'll do something like that again, but I don't know if Ditka
will want me to be his partner again. 11/16/87

*The match was even up until the 18th hole. After Ditka hit a six-iron
over the green, he told McMahon to hit a seven-iron* But he wouldn't
listen. The way he hits it, he probably could have hit an eight-iron.
But I don't think it will happen again. He knows now he can rely on
me through thick and thin. 11/16/87 *Chicago Sun-Times*

Jim McMahon I lost a little money. But Mike was betting everybody
at the restaurant the night before. 11/16/87 *Chicago Sun-Times*

MIKE DITKA, WATERBOY _____

At the Daytona Speedway Mike Ditka was to serve as a pit crew assistant for NASCAR driver Kyle Petty.   I'm really looking forward to working on Kyle's crew. I've always been a big fan of NASCAR racing. From what I've heard so far, my main duty will be passing a cup of Gatorade to Kyle during pit stops. They give me this long stick that holds the cup, and I have to pass it to Kyle through the window. That might not sound like that much, but it could be pretty tough.   2/3/88 *Chicago Sun-Times*

On NASCAR driving   It's a lot like professional football in a lot of ways. These guys are tough. My kind of guys.   2/3/88 *Chicago Sun-Times*

I'm very impressed. I don't think most people understand the teamwork and coordination that goes into this sport. There's a lot of discipline in this and that's No. 1 with me.   2/16/88

Does Ditka have the courage to be a professional race car driver?   I've done a lot of crazy things in my life, but I don't think I could have done this.   2/16/88

THE 1987 SEASON _____

Does he look forward to the Platteville team picnic each year during camp?   The picnic is the highlight of my whole summer. The only thing that can beat that is a hole-in-one, back-to-back. I'm looking forward at the picnic to the good pork. It won't be as good as the pork chops at Ditka's restaurant, 223 West Ontario. Nor will the entertainment be as good as the Grabowski Shuffle. But at $19.95, pick up your own copy and take a look at it. I got all my commercials in.   8/12/87

Is the pressure of the Bears-Giants game getting to him?   I-I-I-I'm not used to being in this spot. I'm the one getting nervous. I think [the team] is OK. They've been through too many big games to let it bother them too much. My attitude is what's bothering me.   9/12/87 *Chicago Sun-Times*

Ditka described the Bears-Giants game as having global significance. After defeating the Giants, Ditka was asked to describe the next game, against Tampa Bay.   That was global. This is galaxy.   9/16/87

The difference between the old Mike Tomczak and Mike Tomczak after his best day as an NFL Quarterback against the Giants: He's much more confident. Anybody who gets a college degree has to be confident.   9/16/87

On hearing that one of the 1988 preseason games would be played in Sweden   We'll play a game, go to Sweden, and party with the Vikings for a week. It probably will be the pause that refreshes. I'm going to take lessons in Swedish.   10/29/87

After the 31–29 loss to the Broncos in Denver, Ditka was told that some of the Bears players would be singing for charity that week.   I'm surprised they don't do it at 11 a.m. Sunday and tie it in with the warmups.   11/18/87

Did the players put Ditka in their doghouse as a result of his veto concerning non-union Bears?   My dogs are in the kennel and they're not even mad at me. Take a look at this guy—how can you be mad?   10/23/87 *Chicago Sun-Times*

After the Bears victory over Kansas City   I'm in a good mood, a great mood. I guarantee you won't catch me in a bad mood again—until next time.   11/13/87 *Southtown Economist*

Taking advantage of Ditka's good mood, WBEZ-FM sportscaster Bob Greenberg, who has been blind since birth, asked if he could drive Ditka's prized antique Bentley.   I may be in a good mood, but not that good.   11/3/87 *Southtown Economist*

3

FOOTBALL PHILOSOPHY

THE NAME OF THE GAME

If you have a goal and it's important enough to you, you won't let anything deter you from the big picture. The big picture is winning and winning championships.   11/17/85

There is a tremendous amount of emphasis placed on winning, but if you're asking me if it's right, it has to be right.   12/30/86 *Chicago Sun-Times*

I really believe this: if you accept defeat, then you're going to be defeated a heckuva lot more than you're going to win. You can be gracious in defeat, but boy, I'll tell you what, you can be gracious on the outside, but you better be doing flipflops inside. If you're not churning and turning you're going to go out and get your butt whipped next time out.   11/17/85

If you lose, it's contagious. Last time out of the box we got beat pretty good [against the 49ers in the playoffs]. I think you try to dispel that as quickly as possible.   8/9/85

I'd be foolish if I stood up and told you I didn't think we're going to win the game [the Super Bowl], because I don't think that way. I always think we are going to win.   1/14/86

PLAYER COMMITMENT

The three most important things . . . are what you do in the meetings, what you do in practice, and what you do on the field in the games. The rest of it, well, I just look back to when I was a player. Discipline is important, and I'm tough on these guys, but that doesn't mean people shouldn't be people. These guys bust their tails for me, let them be themselves. The Chicago Bears aren't a reflection of my personality, they're a reflection of themselves. Maybe this league has been a little staid, a little regimented. I don't know. What the heck, if a guy is a minute late to a meeting well, then, maybe we'll go a minute longer. That's the way to do it, and if it isn't right, well, maybe I will find out in time. But football is people. It's not selling clones and images. It's selling people. Heck, I'm not exactly the image of an NFL coach. I'm not over there on the sidelines, wearing glasses, my arms folded, looking studious, am I?   12/16/85

If you're competing your confidence level should be pretty good. If it's not, be something else. Be a housepainter. I have no sympathy for people in life who quit. You can have them.   12/9/86

I don't think anything is unrealistic if you believe you can do it. I think if you're determined enough and willing to pay the price you can get it done.   9/8/85

PLAYER MOTIVATION _____

Ditka explained he wanted aces on his team

A   for attitude. Players who want to achieve and want to win.
C   for character. I don't care how much physical activity a man has, he has nothing unless he has character.
E   for enthusiasm. You have to be enthusiastic, excited about your opportunities. If you are a pessimist and think bad things, those bad things are apt to happen.   2/10/82

I believe very strongly in what I learned in 21 years in the National Football League. You have to work. You don't get to the top by dreaming. It would be unrealistic to say I have set a goal of the Chicago Bears winning the Super Bowl next year. The Cowboys set goals that were realistic. They had methods and they made plans. I have great faith in people and I have a great faith in myself. I have a commitment. 2/10/82

I think everybody in life needs discipline. People crave discipline.   1/21/82

I didn't think there was anything to clear the air about. But maybe some players took offense at being criticized. Maybe it'd have been better to go to them about it before the media, but people lose sight of the fact we can use the media as a motivator. It worked for us last year. It got us a Super Bowl. Last season would be good to remember in all this. The rewards of doing it, what it took to do. People pulling together as a team.   10/21/86

I have to get this out so they [the Bears players] can hear it. Maybe money is enough for some guys. Maybe they don't need Super Bowls, they don't mean that much to them. They mean a lot to me. But if they are willing to compromise and say, "Well, I'll just take this" and settle for less than the ultimate prize, that's what they'll get. It won't be the Super Bowl they get. Maybe it will be the Pro Bowl but who really cares about the Pro Bowl?   9/1/86

I'm gonna learn what motivates each of them. I'm gonna make them look at this [Ditka's Super Bowl ring] and ask them if that's what's important. Yes or no. Or is it the paycheck that's most important? Because if it is, I'll tell them that there are a lot of places in this world where they can get a paycheck. I want people who are going to work for the team. Team pride has to be established. If it takes pulling out the '63 championship film, I'll do it.   1/24/82

We were in a dog fight. We're gonna be in a lot of dog fights. I hope it makes us a better dog.   10/27/86

I just know in football there's a very thin line between this guy and the next guy. I learned a long time ago that nobody is indispensable.   1/5/86

There still is an element that believes we'd be better if we still had Todd Bell and Al Harris around. Well, I'm a believer that you can't do a job if you don't show up to do it. Anybody can be replaced. I told them we'd be good with what we had; we'd be competitive with the guys who were there. At first they tuned me out. Absolutely, they didn't believe what I was saying. Maybe now most of them are convinced.   12/16/85

Everybody needs a little reinforcement once in a while. Sometimes it's my fault. You get two stubborn people involved and you forget what the heck you're doing. You say, "I'm going to be as stubborn as him" or then he says the same about you and then nobody's talking. It gets stupid.   12/28/86

I don't need to pump up guys when they're not playing good. I need to tell them why they're not playing good and try to make those corrections.   10/20/86

My job is to pat on the back and kick in the butt. I'm not fooling anybody on this team. They know what my priorities are. And the only reason I'm doing it is because I love to win.   12/28/86

PLAYER ATTITUDE

You can do anything the mind wants to do. If the will is there, you do it.   9/6/82

A certain amount of confidence and cockiness is not bad. You don't want to get to the point where you roll the helmets out and think somebody is going to be scared to death of you. But I think being sure of yourself and feeling good is not a bad thing.   10/15/85

If you're the kind of guy who always looks over your shoulder, chances are you'll end up back there.   11/27/86

I tried thinking last week, "What if things don't go right on Sunday?" And I couldn't even think about it. I didn't even think it was a possibility. I'm not saying that out of conceit; I'm saying that out of confidence in this football team.   1/14/86

Our guys know what has to be done. Their heads are on straight.   1/23/86

One person didn't make us Super Bowl champions, 45 people did. 11/27/86

If you put loyalty ahead of talent you've got some problems. If we were 0–6, who'd be loyal to me?   10/16/86

THE PRICE OF SUCCESS _____

Success is about having and excellence is about being. Success is about having money and fame and endorsements. But excellence is being the very best you can be all the time. There's a beginning and end to everything. It [fame] came because we were world champions. When that ceases to be, it will end. Maybe in life you have to learn that firsthand before you take it from somebody who has been there. I've been there. I have a philosophy that for a lot of life you're part of the parade and for a lot of life you just watch the parade. I don't want to watch the parade. I want to be part of it for a few more decades.   11/5/86

I see a little selfishness out there. Too many guys are worried about "me, me, me." When you start worrying about "me, me, me" you get nowhere. We got there [to the NFC title game in '84] as a team. Too many guys are saying, "I've got to have it this way, or I'm being treated unfair." When it gets to that, it's time to start picking weeds out of the garden. That's hard to do right now because we've spent time developing these players. All of a sudden these players are what they are because of them, not because of the coaches or the organizations. That's what bothers me. The thing about success is that when it's attained individually, you know where the credit goes. When it's attained as a team, you don't always know where the credit goes. Some of the guys are giving it to themselves. We won because we played as a team. That's one of the things I said three years ago. It's not just offense, it's not just defense. It's got to be a team. All of a sudden, it's starting to split up again. "Who gets the credit? Who gets the blame?" Who cares? Evidently somebody does.   8/19/85

Sports can be a cancer because it makes a person want to achieve things only for himself. It condones an I-Me syndrome. You look at people making $300,000 a year arguing about making $400,000. It gets a little out of proportion because they're thinking too much of themselves, and I did that myself, too.   1/24/82

Every time you have success, everybody is going to say they are
instrumental in that success. And everybody is important. So if you're
successful, what do you do? Say "We're going to tear up all the contracts
and start over?" Then we win again. "Well, we'll do it again. You're
all nice guys." Can't do it. Doesn't make any sense. I don't think
anybody gets cheated in this organization, period.   10/1/85

If you are satisfied in life, you may as well pack it up. Once you're
the fat cat who says "I got it all," and you're satisfied with the money
you have, the success you have, the house you're in, it's all over.   1/2/87
Chicago Sun-Times

CONSISTENTLY WINNING

Last year was last year. Doesn't mean a thing.   9/8/85

Maybe what's happened in our organization is a fallout from what
happened six-seven years ago with some of those draft picks. There are
a lot of people who contributed to our success who aren't here now.
And there are a lot of people who've contributed to our success who
don't get the credit.   12/30/86 *Chicago Sun-Times*

You can't expect an organization to be mediocre. We all understand
that as coaches. It's not a very secure job. If we don't win, we're
gone.   12/30/86

1987

On his house next door to the Lake Forest practice field, Sports
Illustrated *writer Rick Telander painted the Super Bowl XX score,
46–10, on his roof. Ditka had a suggestion for him.*   I tried to get that
score off the roof and have him put the Washington score [eliminating
the Bears from the 1986 playoffs] up.   7/31/87

In the 1987 camp, the New Orleans Saints arrived to scrimmage against the Bears for three days. Some people expressed concern that it would be hard to restrain players from both teams from going all-out. We just have to find a good tempo where it's not all-out. There's a lot of egos involved in football. You have to be careful that somebody's ego isn't hurt. That even happens when we're practicing against one another. If somebody thinks they're getting beat, they're going to go a little harder. Then the other guy will go a little harder. We'll talk with the Saints about what we want to see out there, but I think we can control it on the field.   8/10/87

You really learn about your players in competition. Against other people [the Saints] you have a new challenge.   8/12/87 *Chicago Sun-Times*

Prior to the first exhibition game of the 1987 season, against Miami   I hope we don't embarrass ourselves Sunday night. Anytime you play, you play to win. You don't play to lose or tie. We have a losing streak of one game. We want to end that as soon as possible.   8/15/87

I think when you believe in yourself, automatically things get better for you.   8/28/87 *Chicago Sun-Times*

You can't get fooled with the idea of experience and security. It's fine, but no amount of experience ever beat talent.   9/2/87

When asked if the Bears would hire a martial arts instructor for linemen as some other NFL teams have done   I think it has merit. The Cowboys use it a tremendous amount. I've thought about using it, but I'll be honest with you, I don't think we can afford to hire anybody in that area.   11/15/87 *Chicago Sun-Times*

In baseball, if you get a hit one out of every two at bats, you're going to be all-world. In football, you do it right one out of two times and you're going to get beat. The championship level for football falls around

80 percent. You've got to do it right 8 out of 10 times. That's what my criticism is all geared at. When it embarrasses us enough, or turns our head enough, that we make a change for the good, then I've had my effect.   11/19/87

If you take the time a player is truly in motion in a game, put the clock on it, I think the total action time is somewhere around 4 minutes and 10 seconds. That's not a lot to ask for a player's utmost concentration.   11/19/87

HOW TO WIN THE GAME

You've got to use multiple formations and multiple personnel [combinations]. You have to try to get their weaker personnel on your stronger personnel, and you do that by changing formations and moving around.   1/24/88 *Chicago Sun-Times*

People remember your last time at bat, or your last game. Those kind of things. That's the way it is. Wins and losses.   3/12/88

Outside of quarterback, the defensive wing position is the most important in football. If he plays a good man-to-man defense, it opens up a lot of things you can do.   4/18/88.

4

PRESEASON PREPARATION

CAMP 1982

I told [the players] there's no difference between them and the players in Dallas or San Francisco. It's all in the head. I told them who I am, just a guy going through life who was given a job I love. If they're as proud to be associated with the Bears as I am, we'll have no problems.   4/3/82

I just told them they are going to run more than ever. They're going to be in better shape and they're going to appreciate it more than ever. They're going to be in better shape, and I hope it's the winning edge.   4/3/82

Everybody has been told they are going to run. Some say there's nowhere to run in Chicago in the winter. There's lots of places to run. They can run in the hallway here [at Halas Hall] for 30 yards. I expect some players will say I've always done it some other way. I'll say, "Yeah, what did it get you?"   4/1/82

THE BEARS REACT _____

Jim Osborne   I think he felt he had to make an impression on us to show us that he did have a plan to make us a winner.   8/8/82

Mike Singletary   Some of us haven't been this small since high school.   8/8/82

Gary Fencik   I don't think any of us knew we were going to have as physical camp as this, but we were under no delusions that it was going to be easy.   8/8/82

Doug Plank   The ship is going to be run a little differently. Before it was left up more to the individual to work out. Now it's more programmed. And Mike said we're going to be together more as a team.   4/3/82

AFTER THE FIRST CAMP _____

Anybody who doesn't come to camp is foolish. There's an old saying, "Out of sight, out of mind." You can only evaluate what you see.   7/12/85

Ditka decided that the Bear camp in suburban Lake Forest should be moved. He compared Lake Forest to the old Bears camps in Rensselaer, Indiana.   Guys I didn't socialize with or know real well I got to know much better. When you went down to the corner tap and had a couple of beers after working out for 6 hours in 90 degree heat, the camaraderie became much greater. In Lake Forest everything is very cliquish. I'd like to see us do things as a team, totally.   7/15/84

Good smart football teams get their players away for a while. I think it's wrong to come off the practice field and run into every member of your family every day.   7/15/84

If we approached it like a war, it would probably be better for us. We'd have fewer guys patting each other on the fanny all the time.   7/15/84

The Bears eventually moved their camp to Platteville, Wisconsin, a three hour drive from Chicago.   Platteville is more conducive to a training camp. Let's face it. Lake Forest has a country club atmosphere. We got good results in Platteville last year. The camaraderie is better. Everytime you walked off the field, you didn't walk into a friend from the neighborhood or your family. You ran into another player.   7/21/85

You can fool yourself about football. Basically, it is blocking and tackling. We wanted to find out some things early. Most players look forward to hitting and the ones who don't, that's what you want to find out.   7/27/82

THE DRAFT _____

Draft strategy: selecting the best athlete available   That's always worked for the Cowboys so I don't see why it wouldn't work for the Bears.   1/21/82

The draft never was my bag entirely. It never is the head coach's bag entirely. Anyone who says it is, is foolish. I have to depend upon my scouts, the general manager, the president, and Bill Tobin, our scouting director.   11/12/83

Nobody's an expert. Not the scouts and not me. You just gotta go with gut shots sometimes.   12/28/86

I think you win on defense. I don't think that ever changes. You have to keep your defense strong and you don't want to get into the position where you have to turn three or four people over in one year. I don't want to do that.   4/26/87 *Des Plaines Daily Herald*

You've got to keep a certain number of rookies every year. Good teams find a way of resupplying. If you have all the experience in the world and line up against somebody with more physical ability, you'll get beat.   8/31/83

The Bears have now got a foundation they can build on for years and if they keep drafting as well as we've been fortunate enough to draft the last couple of years and not be afraid to play people, I think they have a chance to really do good things.   7/15/84

With crowds averaging 6,000 people attending the Platteville training camp, the Bears were happy to return to Lake Forest. We can concentrate more back there, and the players will have a little more peace. That's important. I love Platteville. Unfortunately, we created an animal. You [reporters] wrote great articles, and people believe them. They came out in hordes to see us. Droves.   8/21/87

Will the Bears return to Platteville?   It's between the college and our ownership whether we come back, but if they don't consider this a good place to train, I don't know what is.   8/21/87

WIVES AT TRAINING CAMP

Commenting on Mike Ditka's rule that wives are not allowed to stay in the Platteville area during training camp, Debra McMichael explained   [Ditka] ought to be thankful I keep [Steve] under control. If he was wild, he'd probably miss practice and get drunk all the time. He ought to thank me for keeping him healthy.   12/15/87 *Chicago Sun-Times*

Ditka's response   Well, I disagree with Debra McMichael. Next year what we'll do if she wants to come to training camp is just let Steve stay [in Chicago] with her. That's why you have training camp.   12/15/87 *Chicago Sun-Times*

Steve McMichael   During the day, I'm concentrating on football, but at night I want to have somebody there to tell my problems to—and that's not some girl in a bar.   12/15/87 *Chicago Sun-Times*

NUMBER ONE, KEEP FIT

Martina Navratilova has proven in tennis that the fittest can be the best. In her case, the best was the fittest also. I think in basketball, that's going to be a factor in time. Baseball, too. A lot of guys in baseball, they don't pay the price in the offseason. There are a lot who do. A lot of them have long careers. But some of these guys, they run to first base and they're hurt. They're on the 15-day disabled list when they get bruised or bumped.   1/19/88 *Chicago Sun-Times*

If you're going to play football, you should be smart enough to know the only way you're going to be paid the kind of money we're paying is to be healthy and fit and strong.   1/19/88 *Chicago Sun-Times*

5

PHYSICAL ASPECTS
OF FOOTBALL

BEING TOUGH

Either we have the identity of being tough or we don't. We've got to find out. You have to be tough physically to beat these people [the New England Patriots]. You have to take them on. You have to have a chip on your shoulder. We just have to get more physical on the football field. We've got to be aggressive in every area. If things go wrong, they go wrong; you can't worry about it. You go after them the next play.   12/3/82

The game never changes. It's hitting.   7/20/86

We didn't win very much. Then we got smarter. I don't think we retaliated in Green Bay when they came after us. Just played hard, aggressive football. That's what we have to go back to. You're going to get some cheap shots. You take them and the next time you get a shot at a guy, you hit them good and clean. It will all even out.   8/25/86

. . . . Somewhere along the line, they're really going to have to look at protecting the quarterback again. Everybody says guys are in the air, or in movement of hitting him, but nobody ever tries to pull up. 11/26/86

INJURIES

The game is a tough game, a physical game. You don't like the injury aspect but it's part of the game.   9/25/86

When you're losing, injuries become magnified. If we were winning, a lot of [players] would be out there running around playing. I'm not blaming them. When you're losing, you get more injuries.   11/8/83

If they are not 100 percent, I'd rather keep them out of the game. I think that's a mistake that we make. Our guys are so competitive they try to go out there at less than 100 percent, and the only thing they can do is risk re-injury.   11/9/86

We've been fortunate. Maybe it's the way we do things. Maybe it's the fact that we hit more in training camp than most people that gets us ready to play. We also haven't pushed the guys who haven't been well. We let them get well before they play again.   12/20/85

In the old days, it was not only the individual but I think it was management's philosophy that if you could take a [painkilling] shot, take the shot. That's not my philosophy, and it's certainly not the upstairs philosophy at all.   9/18/84

FIGHTING

Don't count records, let everybody play for the sport of it. Then at the end of the year, give everybody miniature Super Bowl trophies. As long as there is a number one and somebody is trying to knock him off, you're going to have competition. Some things happen outside the rules once in a while. It's unfortunate. Nobody is proud of it. But it happens. 12/7/86

We don't encourage the fighting at all because it's against the rules. But I think no matter what you tell a player, what happens in the heat of the game is something that's a gut level thing.   12/23/84

On fights in the 1986 Bears-Cardinals preseason game   What they did to [tight end Pat] Dunsmore was atrocious. They should be in a gang in New York and learn what it's really like . . . Kicking a guy in his groin when he is down. That is a lot of guts. Supposedly these guys are high-paid athletes, guys who went to college.   8/25/86

I don't condone the fighting. It was a silly thing to have happen on national T.V.   8/24/86

Usually when there is an altercation, the camera will come back to you and the best thing you can do is beat the guy you're playing against and really make a fool out of him. People are going to try and instigate because we play tough and they'll try to get somebody kicked out of the game.   10/28/85

This is a winning business. If you want to win and somebody's in the way, you have to get them out of the way. You could ask them to move, I guess.   12/28/87

We have tried to emphasize not doing it [hitting] in practice because a couple of years ago it was hard to get our receivers through practice without getting maimed against our defense. We've quit that and everybody has played within the rules in practice.   12/23/84

6

FOOTBALL STRATEGY AND TACTICS

OFFENSIVE STRATEGY AND TACTICS _____

Well, the Bears don't need an overhaul. Just a few nuts and bolts. It all depends on the critical positions. Quarterback is one. Receivers are another. Tight end another. I'm not going to get too critical of the defense at this point, but I have my own thoughts on that. Placekicking's one. Punter's one. Center's another. There's the old saying that you are only as good as you are up the middle. Check the center, quarterback, middle linebacker, free safety, and you have a pretty good idea where you're going. Anyway, that'll be a start.   1/24/82

There is an old saying in baseball that your strength lies up the middle—pitcher, catcher, shortstop, and second and center field. I'm not sure that isn't true in football.   9/8/85

Being able to drive the ball consistently on short passes and run the ball is what the game is all about. The big plays will happen as often by improvisation as by design. If they happen by design, they often are set up by well-designed little plays.   9/27/83

My philosophy involves multiple offenses with different sets, the object being to keep the defense off balance.   1/21/82

You have to have time to throw.   1/4/83

You take what the defense gives you. That has been our philosophy.   8/18/82

It's important whatever team scores first. Controlling is important only if you can put points up to go with it.   12/30/84

Playing loose   What's there to be tight about? That's the worst thing that can happen. We can't do anything about it until game time anyway.   12/30/84

Our goal is to get 24 or 25 points on the board and say, "Come and get us." I don't care if the defense is the best in the world, if you can't get more than 13 points, you aren't going to win, it's all over.   9/8/85

OFFENSE 1986

We're not going to score 40 or 50 points, but if we score 17 to 24, we'll be in good shape most of the time.   12/1/86

We've got to get better on offense. I'm not going to kid you and I'm not going to kid them.   9/30/86

Our third-down efficiency is poor because we don't have time to throw the ball. We can't be effective that way.   9/30/86

Our game is to run the football.   11/16/86

We're the Rodney Dangerfields of the NFL. Nobody thinks we're very good because we don't beat people by a lot of points. We don't look devastating on offense. We have to prove we're good.   12/7/86

We got to the Super Bowl by running. How many touchdown passes did we throw in the Super Bowl? When you get past zero, tell me.   12/7/86

Our pass protection has dropped off the last three weeks. I'm not saying it dropped off drastically. It came about more by lack of concentration than being beat physically.   1/3/86

OFFENSIVE BALANCE

After losing to the 49ers in the 1984 playoffs, the Bears defeated the 49ers 26–10 in 1985.   I was not going to come out and play them the way we played last year. I was going to establish something and make them fear something and that was the pass. We were not going to run, run, run, punt.   10/14/85

We needed a spark on offense, and we needed a spark on defense. Payton will be it on offense, and Hampton and Singletary will do it for the defense. Hopefully that will mean the Bears will start playing football again.   8/25/85

You can't run it down people's throats, that was our one dimension. When you took it away from us, we didn't know what to do.   10/13/85

. . . You don't win championships because of great kicking games if you don't have anything else.   10/18/83

I'd like to put together games of 200 yards running and 200 yards passing. I don't care if we ever throw for 400 [yards]. That never impresses me. It impresses me if we win, and you win by being consistent in those two areas.   9/30/86

POSITION STRATEGY _____

They [fans] never have a chance to see the second quarterback much. They really don't know what he can do. As a result, they feel when you put the second quarterback in, you're really dealing at a tremendous disadvantage. I don't see it that way because if you keep 45 men and you don't really believe they can line up and play for you, then you've made a mistake.   11/24/85

There's no way now we'll go with any less than three quarterbacks. 8/12/86

If we have a tight end who is capable of getting clear and going deep then we will use him.   1/21/82

If the tight end is used properly, he can be very instrumental, maybe the most instrumental guy in the offense.   9/8/85

Sometimes [receivers] were the ones who got knocked down, but they went after people and that's what we try to teach.   8/18/86

DEFENSIVE STRATEGY AND TACTICS _____

On third down, you know who has to be stopped and you make sure that man is doubled regardless of what the other people do.   1/4/83

A pressure defense, you play a pressure defense you create turnovers.   1/2/87 *Chicago Sun-Times*

If we can play a base defense well, when the time comes to out-maneuver and out-trick people, we ought to be able to do a good job. 8/4/86

A lot of guys go off and do their own thing too much. If you do the things the way they're designed, you can execute them. 10/18/83

To me, defense is stopping the other guy when you have to stop him and making turnovers. Yardage doesn't mean beans. 10/3/85

With the four down linemen we have, if we don't play a four-man front, we're probably making a mistake. 7/20/86

The Bears have always played aggressive, tough defense. It was like that in the '60s, '50s, and '40s. It never changes. 1/30/86

I'm not sure we want them to play a whole lot of zone. We want them to get after people. 8/18/86

We want to play high-percentage football. We want to keep the percentages on our side. We want to keep the turnover ratio as high as it has been. And we want to be able to keep pressure on the quarterback. 2/2/86

PLAYCALLING

I called plays when I came here. I gave it up because I wanted to have more control over everything. But by having more control, I was getting too involved. I think if I just handle the offense and the plays, I'll be more calm, cool, and collected on the sidelines. 9/27/83

Two guys went into the game and each brought in a different play. I might have said both plays mumbling, but I sent in only one. 10/17/83

Does sharing the playcalling with his staff cause any problems?   We really don't have a problem. I'll ask Ed [Bears Offensive Coordinator Ed Hughes], "If we get six yards on this one, what do you think?" That's how we've done it.   11/29/83

Rethinking shared playcalling   I put too much pressure on [Ed], and I'm not going to put pressure on anybody anymore.   11/8/83

On Bears quarterbacks calling their own plays   The only thing that would be hard is if we have too many plays. The quarterback would get stuck on two or three plays and not move it around.   11/29/83

On Audiblizing   Last year [1983] it was too hard to pick up the color system. They were missing a lot, so we changed to a more foolproof way of doing it. The main thing is we'll be audibling the first day of camp. Sometimes you wait until you get into the season to put audibles in.   7/10/84

I'll be calling the plays. I'm not going to put that burden on anybody else because I have a feeling for what I want to see. The character of this football team has to reflect me, and if I want to do certain things, I can't just wish that they're going to happen out there or wish that my offensive coordinator makes the call. I've got to do it.   7/10/84

When offensive coordinator Ed Hughes was asked if he saw a problem in the Bears playcalling, he said,   What are you trying to do, get me in some trouble with the boss? Mike Ditka is the guy calling those plays. I signal them into the game is all. I think Mike has done well.   11/28/86

STICKNEY-FOREST VIEW LIBRARY

TRICK PLAYS _____

You're not going to win football games tricking people. The more new plays you try, the more you are only fooling yourself.   9/16/85

Referring to the Bears victory 20–7 over the New England Patriots   Every trick play we called got stuffed.   9/16/85

More on the 20–7 victory   We emptied the bag. It's all over. From now on, it's straight handoff right, straight handoff left. That should get the fans back on my side.   9/17/85

[Trick plays are] not Bears football. Some trick plays are essential. We had become so staid in what we've done, we did it to give other teams something to think about.   9/16/85

FOOTBALL STRATEGY AND TACTICS 1987 _____

Our back-up people have got to be people we can put on the field if someone gets hurt.   9/1/87 *Chicago Sun-Times*

During the Bears' 31–28 victory over Kansas City, Jim McMahon ran several plays early in the fourth quarter (when the Bears were losing by two touchdowns) without a huddle. Would Ditka consider using more of the no-huddle offense?   We could open the game with it. I have no problem with it.   11/3/87 *Chicago Sun-Times*

Teams that run 40 times win. When you start not doing that, you start winning games the way we're winning them, with heroics.   11/15/87

After losing to the Denver Broncos, Ditka expressed concern that the Bears defense gave up 31 points.   You win with defense. You keep replacing defensive players. Defensive guys wear out quicker. When you look at all the great teams that have gone downhill—the Dolphins, the old Chiefs, the old Vikings—when the defense went, they went.   11/18/87

7

BEARS FOOTBALL

WHAT IS BEARS FOOTBALL?

We play a brand of football that threatens people at times. We're not going to intimidate everybody; but we're going to intimidate some people with the way we play.   9/8/85

He [Halas] always had a term he called "Bear Football." I think that's important . . . It's a type of football played on more than talent. It's played on heart and pride.   1/25/86

We give no quarter and ask none.   1/26/86

[We] want to be the best of all time. When you talk about the best of all time, that's something special. That's what we're shooting for. Anytime we deviate from it, we've got to get back on track.   10/13/86

Dan Hampton, after the Bears beat the Giants 34–19 Last year everybody talked about the Giants' great physical strength and how they could physically overwhelm people. I didn't see that. I think it was the other way around. Coach Ditka calls it Bears football. Call it whatever you want to. It leaves welts.   9/16/87 *Chicago Sun-Times*

BEAR DYNASTY?

I don't believe in the word dynasty. I believe you take one year at a time. You don't judge a team on one game or playoff series or one year. The great teams, the Packers under Vince Lombardi and the Steelers with Chuck Noll, made their mark over a period of time.   1/28/86

Great football teams win a number of Super Bowls. You talk about the 60's you talk about Green Bay, the 70's Pittsburgh. When you talk about the 80's, who are you going to talk about? We'll find out.   1/2/87 *Chicago Sun-Times*

We're appreciated in Brooklyn, Pittsburgh, Scranton, Wilkes-Barre, Birmingham, good work areas where people know what it's all about. We wouldn't fit too well in Beverly Hills, Miami, places like that. 1/26/86

THE HALAS-DITKA RAPPORT

Jim Dooley, Director of Research and Quality Control for the Bears, commented on Ditka's coaching style during a Tampa Bay/Bears game I saw a man with fist raised jumping out on the field, and I jumped back as if it was an apparition. What I saw in Ditka doing these things was the Halas spirit, Halas was there. It's eerie, Halas had bad hips. Mike has bad hips. But I always say to Mike that Halas would have still outrun him if they were the same age and they had their bad hips together. I don't know. Maybe not. Neither one could accept losing. Violent men, good men.   11/16/86

I took this job not because it's head coaching. I took it because it's the Bears. Tough. Like George Halas. I didn't understand what he was all about when I was a young punk playing for him. But I do now. This is the best job in the world.   12/4/84

What you do in life by yourself doesn't mean as much as what you accomplish with a group of people. It's because of Mr. Halas that I'm here. I'm just trying to pay some dues.   1/27/86

HALAS' SPIRIT IS STILL ALIVE _____

On Halas' play—the quarterback sneak   I'll still call it and I'll call it again and I'll call it again. If I don't, Mr. Halas will roll over in his grave.   10/6/86

After winning the Central Division title in 1984   I think it's important that this game goes to the man that deserves it the most, and that is Mr. Halas. I gave a game ball to Ed and Virginia McCaskey [George Halas' son-in-law and daughter].   11/26/84

After beating the Rams in the 1985 playoffs to reach the Super Bowl   He [Halas] sent the sunshine, the snow, the touchdowns, everything.   1/13/86

Look, if George Halas was coaching this team you know what he would do with the Super Bowl Shuffle? He'd take a copy of it, call a team meeting, then put it on the floor and jump all over it.   1/12/86

Everything we do is dedicated to him [Halas] as long as I'm here. When I'm not here, they can dedicate to anybody they want to, but it's dedicated to him as long as I'm here.   1/6/85

Johnny Morris, Chicago sportscaster and former Bears player, was asked when he last saw Ditka cry prior to Vanisi's firing. Morris answered Probably when Halas died.   1/16/87 *Des Plaines Daily Herald*

Why Ditka's excitement at winning the job as Bears head coach? Because of him [Halas] saying he wanted me to have the job.   11/2/83

The gratifying thing about this [success] is when people ask me what it means, it means one thing: I've repaid a confidence [to Halas].   11/17/85

THE DEATH OF GEORGE HALAS _____

I feel very bad about it. But the sport of football and the city of Chicago should feel bad because of what he has meant to the city, and what he has meant to the sport. Whether you always agreed with Mr. Halas or not, he is the reason the league is what it is today. The contributions he has made to this city are unbelievable also.   11/1/83

Enthusiastic to the end I hadn't talked to him in a couple of weeks. Before that, I had talked to him quite regularly. As a matter of fact, I had seen him quite regularly before that. The improvement he had made since March or April, when he had the bad time, was phenomenal. He was very enthused about everything. Very up on everything. He wanted to talk about players, the team, and was still very much involved mentally in everything.   11/1/83

. . . this is a different era. If I walk into a lounge the night before a game and a player's in there having a beer, what am I gonna do? Fine him? So he goes to his room and has a beer. Heck, we have beer at our team meal on Saturday nights. We didn't have any beer in 1963. You make up all sorts of rules, and it just creates rebellion. You have to be flexible. You can't legislate the way you used to. This team is loosey-goosey, yeah. But when it comes time to play on Sunday, they're ready. I don't worry about all the other stuff.   1/12/86

LOOKING BACK ─────────────────────────────

On contract sessions with Halas   I never expected to win, to get what I asked for, but it was a great experience.   11/2/83

What's the difference between Halas and Ditka?   The difference is that when he [Halas] said something to the officials, they listened. When I say something, they don't listen.   11/2/83

8

THE BEARS
ORGANIZATION

DITKA ON McCASKEY

*Mike McCaskey, grandson of George Halas, was named new Bears
president in 1983. Ditka was positive about the selection.* Mike is a
bright, sharp young guy. His thoughts on winning are the same as mine
and Jerry's [General Manager Jerry Vainisi]. Mike will make progressive
changes, not changes for the sake of change. 11/12/83

*When Jerry Vainisi was fired in January of 1987, Ditka was hurt and
visibly upset. Ten days later he seemed resigned to the fact that Vainisi
was gone.* . . . I learned as a kid the guy who owns the ball and bat
can call the game any time he wants to. So I accept that. 1/21/87
Des Plaines Daily Herald

What does Ditka think of Mike McCaskey? He's a fine man, and he's
my boss. 6/15/87

McCASKEY ON DITKA

But just because we're perceived as opposites doesn't mean we can't operate well as a team. On the contrary, the meetings we've had with all our people have been extremely good. Jerry Vainisi, Bill Tobin, Mike, and I have a strong relationship.   12/4/84

I found out that we both share a respect for what a lot of people call old-fashioned values. That work, effort, character, and heart mean as much as anything else. Everybody knew he was a motivator. The question was always raised about his football smarts. This is a savvy and clever football coach, who will do the smart thing.   11/17/85

The head coach is in charge of the offense and defense. It's up to him to set up the dynamics. He has complete charge and control. I won't interfere.   11/12/83

It's absolutely critical that the head coach be one who will bring tough, aggressive, and smart football, and by the way, the Bears have played this year and in prior years; the job Mike Ditka and his coaching staff have done has shown that's the kind of team we are going to have.   1/3/85

The important thing is how well Mike and I work together.   1/3/85

I hope he [Ditka] respects me as much as I respect him. It's not necessary for the president and head coach to be real close. I happen to be very close to the general manager [Vainisi].   9/2/84

McCASKEY FIRES VAINISI

On January 10, 1987 Bears President Mike McCaskey stunned Chicago by firing Jerry Vainisi, Bears General Manager and Mike Ditka's best friend. A few days later, McCaskey was asked if Mike Ditka would leave the Bears at the end of the 1987 season. McCaskey replied I don't think so. I told Mike all season and I'll tell you publicly, that he's done a fine job as head coach of the Chicago Bears. I hope and expect he'll have a long career as head coach of the Chicago Bears. 1/16/87

I have to really want him [Ditka] to be head coach too. There's too much at stake to do it differently than I'm doing it. Ditka wanting to be head coach is what's important about the way the decision gets made. 2/1/87

Can Ditka put the Vainisi situation behind him? McCaskey's view I don't know. Time will tell. I don't consider Mike and me to have a problem. I don't see any reason why he won't continue to coach the Bears for years to come. 2/1/87

Things have their own time and part of [relieving Vainisi of his job] was so things could settle down from Mike's emotional reaction. I knew he would react that way and I don't want a decision based on emotion. 2/1/87

The Chicago media asked if any other teams had expressed interest. McCaskey confessed No team has ever asked my permission to talk to Ditka. 2/1/87

Shortly before the NFL draft conducted April 28, 1987, there were rumors that the Bears would draft a quarterback whom Ditka didn't support. Mike McCaskey responded I think Mike Ditka has had a great deal of say in personnel matters. You just cannot force people on a head coach and the Bears have never done that. So preparing for the draft and on draft day and on those rare occasions when a trade comes up, Mike's always been a very important part of the discussion and he'll continue to be. 4/5/87 *Chicago Sun-Times*

McCASKEY SUMS IT UP

First of all, I think Mike Ditka has done an outstanding job being the head coach of the Chicago Bears and I look forward to his being the head coach for a lot of years to come. I think everything's going to work out just fine. I think he does want to be the head coach here. I think he has Chicago Bears blood running through his veins. I think he's excited about what the future holds as far as our being able to make a real strong run at several Super Bowls, and I think he wants to be a part of it.   4/5/87 *Chicago Sun-Times*

VAINISI ON DITKA

From the very start, Mike Ditka has been unbelievable. In camp I would brief him on the status of Bell and Harris. He never complained at not having them. He said, "Don't compromise, we'll go with what we have."   1/8/86

He [Ditka] was very confident last year. I think he's gained even more confidence in himself, his program, and the club. I think he believes stronger than ever that it's a team sport and we don't rely on any one individual. He's got to try to convince everybody that the quarterback is another guy out there.   1/3/87 *Des Plaines Daily Herald*

He's just more a complete coach. I think this was his greatest coaching challenge this year—having the injuries we had coupled with the changes that occurred in the off-season and having to coach a defending championship team.   1/3/87 *Des Plaines Daily Herald*

DITKA ON VAINISI

On the early Bears years   I didn't have anybody in my corner except Jerry Vainisi. Everybody else had the magnifying glass out and they were looking really hard.   11/17/85

On Vainisi's firing   Fellas, I really thought that I wasn't going to say anything but I don't know that that would be totally fair to anybody concerned. But I'm going to just say a very brief statement, and uh, because I think it's a situation which I am not really entitled totally to comment on. Let me just say that I was totally taken by surprise, totally. And I was very, very hurt. Jerry Vainisi is respected in our business as one of the best. And he deserves that because he's earned that. He was called upon to take this job by Coach Halas, as I was. And I think that's probably the reason we're so close. I deeply respect that. It was his [Halas'] last wish that Jerry Vainisi be the general manager and that I be the coach or it would have been changed. We've worked together the best we can. We've tried to do things intelligently to put a football team on the field that the people in the city of Chicago could be proud of. And I think we've done that. What hurts me the most is that he [Vainisi] is my best friend. And I and the players on the Chicago Bears are gonna miss him very, very much. I wish him the best that you could wish for losing a best friend. And he'll land on his feet, believe me, because he's good at what he does. I feel very, very sorry for his wonderful family, his children, Doris [Vainisi's wife], his parents, who have really lived and died with him with the Chicago Bears because it has become a major part of his life. You just don't cut off an appendage from your body and then go on and live normally. As I say, Jerry Vainisi's a class person and he'll end up in good shape. I really don't have anything to say.   1/10/87 *Chicago Sun-Times*

Five months later, Ditka still felt the firing of Vainisi was a mistake.   I wouldn't have gotten rid of Jerry [Vainisi], I know that.   6/15/87

It was a shock when he left, but when you analyze it, Jerry came out in good shape. We thought we would make it work and have fun doing it in Chicago for a lot of years, but it didn't work out.   3/19/87

DITKA ON THE ASSISTANT COACHES _____

On Vince Tobin, Defensive Coordinator   I've always admired what Vince has done. Some people get more credit than other people for what's done in life. He's not a guy who stands up and takes all the bows.   2/2/86

It's nice to see the defensive staff working together. It's no longer a one-man show.   5/11/86

I feel good for Vince and the other assistant coaches. I knew we would be compared, analyzed, criticized. I got letters that said, "Forget your ego and ill feelings and play the '46 defense." They said, "You won't play a defense because you don't like someone." That's a bunch of bull. We play the defense and we play it the way it's supposed to be played.   1/2/87

On Dick Stanfel, Offensive Line Coach . . . the best offensive line coach in football.   9/7/86

On Bill Tobin, Vice President, Player Personnel Bill Tobin and his department deserve tremendous credit. They've taken some criticism. They might as well get the credit. What Bill Tobin and Jim Finks drafted was outstanding.   11/10/85

Sometimes our players may not relate to me, but they sure relate to our assistants.   12/30/86 *Chicago Sun-Times*

THE BEARS ORGANIZATION ON DITKA _____

Dick Stanfel, Offensive Line Coach I think he tried to control himself more [in 1986]—his personality on the field. I think he realizes that sometimes he gets excited and pulls somebody who's not at fault and shouldn't be pulled. I think he's adjusted to that by apologizing to them and telling them. He's not afraid to tell them he's wrong. Every year I think you mature more and more in your job. He's done an excellent job in what he's doing—by his motivation and by his coaching. I think he's one of the top guys in that.   1/3/87 *Des Plaines Daily Herald*

Bill Tobin, Vice President, Player Personnel   He's a joy to work with, he's not afraid to listen.   11/17/85

Steve Kazor, Special Teams Coach   He's kind of a person as a head coach who depicts what a guy is supposed to be. He knows how to positively reinforce people and negatively reinforce people, and gets the most of them.   1/3/87 *Des Plaines Daily Herald*

Ed Hughes, Offensive Coordinator   In the back of Mike's mind, he has a lot of Landry in him. Tom worried that the defense would get a scheme on you. He always wanted to keep them from having that perfect defensive scheme.   9/27/86

Dick Stanfel   Mike Ditka is the rod, and I'm the smoother-over. He gets on the [offensive] line. I don't blame him. It's his team. I'm the one who has to smooth it over and say, "It takes time for people to get timing and coordination."   8/13/87

When you have a backup who will come in and take over, you are a solid football team. That's really what Mike Ditka is looking for. 8/13/87

Vince Tobin, when asked if it bothered him when Ditka yells at him on the sidelines   I try not to, but I don't know if you ever get used to it. The big thing is, you've got to continue to go ahead and call the defenses. The plays go on.   12/8/87

Mike McCaskey   I like Mike. I admire him as a man. It's a good working relationship. Both of us know the other has an enormous pride in the Bears being the best. The fact we're different personalities is good in that respect, not bad. People think you need personalities that are alike to be successful. I disagree. The strongest team, management or football, has a diverse set of characters.   9/15/87

Greg Landry, Bears Quarterback Coach   I think one thing [Ditka's] looking for by maybe allowing one of the offensive coaches to call the plays is that now he can keep involved with both sides and we as an offensive coaching group can discuss it with the players. Why didn't the play work? Maybe someone didn't execute his assignment. Or maybe we should get off it because it's not good against their defense. We just need to communicate better on the sidelines and find out what's going on. We've got experienced players. They have a good understanding of what's going on. We need to use that knowledge in game situations. 1/24/88 *Chicago Sun-Times*

Vince Tobin, on television coverage of Ditka yelling at him on the sidelines   I think when it happens that it undermines your authority as a coach when the players see it. We have talked about it. Mike's working not to let it happen again. Really, the main time it happened was in the second Green Bay game. He tries. But you're not going to change him. Mike's emotional and very, very competitive. He has a quick temper. What he wants is for every team to be shut out and not make a yard. That's how he is, and he is not going to change. I have a very good relationship with Mike, and I think he has total confidence in me.   1/8/88

Bill Tobin   We lost 21–17 this year to Washington in the playoffs for a combination of reasons. But not because we were outcoached or outmanned. A dropped ball here, a poor pass here, a wrong route, a missed blocking assignment . . . little things. All it requires is some fine tune-ups. No overhauls. Just continue to add some new blood. That's my responsibility: to convince Mike Ditka and Mike McCaskey what players would be best for us and why they'd be best. We've done a good job in the past at it, and we plan to do a good job again.   2/5/88

JERRY VAINISI LOOKS BACK _____

Vainisi on Flutie   I still think getting Flutie was the right decision, even though McCaskey and Tobin didn't agree. But McCaskey made the trade, not me. He asked me to find out what the Rams wanted for Doug, and that's all I did.

Maybe it's true that the Bears would have beaten Washington [in the playoffs] if Mike Tomczak or Steve Fuller had started instead of Flutie. But getting Flutie was right because we didn't know if Jim McMahon would play again with his injury. Tomczak was having an off year, and Ditka had lost confidence in Fuller. Fuller had probably the worst year of his career. We had an excellent team, needed stability at quarterback, and I still don't think the decision to get Flutie was that outrageous.   11/20/87

Vainisi on his friendship with Ditka   It sometimes paired us off against McCaskey and Bill Tobin. I'm sure that had an influence on McCaskey's decision.   11/20/87

Vainisi on Perry   In the 1985 draft, McCaskey and I were anti William Perry. We wanted Jessie Hester, the wide receiver who went to the Raiders on the pick after we took Perry. Tobin and Ditka wanted Perry and talked McCaskey and me into the decision. The Raiders would have taken Perry if we chose Hester.   11/20/87

Vainisi on the 1985 season   We had a midpoint swoon in 1985, the year we won the Super Bowl. It's natural. It's hard for any coach to keep his team motivated every week. No one is pressing the Bears in the Central Division, and they're relaxing a little bit. Come December 1, Ditka will have them refocused and built up. I don't think this Bears team has as much depth as we had in 1985, but they're still the best team in the league.   11/20/87

DITKA ON THE BEARS FACILITIES _____

Could the Bears still use an indoor facility?   I don't think about that anymore.   8/29/87 *Chicago Sun-Times*

On switching from artificial turf to grass in Soldier Field in 1988   What a marvelous decision. Hip hip hooray! Hip hip hooray! This is wonderful. I'm serious. That's a major step forward.   9/4/87 *Chicago Sun-Times*

On the Halas Hall Ground Crew   We've got the greatest people in the world. These guys are the greatest people I've ever seen. These people know the idea of work. We've got great leadership in this organization to get these things done.   12/28/87 *Chicago Sun-Times*

9

BUDDY RYAN AND MIKE DITKA

Buddy Ryan was the Defensive Coordinator for the Bears for eight years, from 1978 to 1986, when he resigned from the Bears to become the Head Coach of the Philadelphia Eagles. Ryan was known as the architect of the famous Bears "46 defense," which led the league in defense in 1985 was well as helped the Bears to an 18–1 record and the Super Bowl Championship. Prior to Ryan's departure there had been rumors of a personality conflict between him and Ditka. Until the drafting of William Perry, however, this conflict did not surface publicly.

FEUDING

To Buddy Ryan's criticism of picking William Perry in the draft, Ditka responded   Kinda makes me look like an idiot because I'm the guy that picked him.   8/8/85

A reporter commented that Buddy Ryan made the statement about Perry to motivate him. Ditka replied   I'm not sure I believe in reverse psychology, but everyone has his own way of doing things. I learned if you can't say good things about people don't say a whole lot about them.   8/8/85

Buddy Ryan's view   Ditka and I get along just fine. We might have a difference of opinion, just like you [the reporter] and I might have a difference of opinion. I always get tickled when I read Ditka and Ryan are fighting. I don't see it that way and neither does he [Ditka]. But I guess it sells a lot of papers.   8/12/85

A few months after the William Perry draft pick, it was reported that Ditka and Ryan exchanged heated words at half-time during the Bears loss to Miami. Ditka reportedly was furious with Buddy Ryan's defensive alignments against Miami's speedy receivers. Said Ditka   I was upset with some of the things that happened [against the defense] because I thought we weren't making adjustments to them. But my goodness we had the right [defensive] plays called. We had individual breakdowns.   12/4/85

Ryan's response   That was not a one-way deal. I was chewing him out, too. In the paper it said Ditka was hollering at me. It didn't say I was hollering back. Where I come from we chew each other out.   12/4/85

As the Bears moved into the 1985 playoffs, they shut out the New York Giants 21–0 in the first playoff game. Next they shut out the Los Angeles Rams 23–0. This was the first time a team had back-to-back shut out playoff games. The Bears then defeated the Patriots 45–10 in the Super Bowl. Ditka commented   Our players had a mission, the defense, you gotta love them. The job Buddy did was just great.   1/26/86

Shortly after the Super Bowl, Buddy Ryan accepted the head coaching job with the Philadelphia Eagles. Ditka's response   I bet a lot of people thought I'd be looking for the highest building to jump off of this morning. The challenge will be tremendous for us to come back. There will be a new dimension of Bears football. I think everyone will like it.   1/30/86

Will the defense be affected?   We will overcome it. I have to make the players believe that it's not what you can't do, it's what you can do, if you want to do it. It's going to be a tremendous adjustment and challenge for me and the players. The guys who can't face the challenge will move on.   1/30/86

THE BEARS REACT TO RYAN'S DEPARTURE _____

Otis Wilson   Well, it's no secret they didn't get along. It was in the papers all year. They're two pretty stubborn guys who say what they think. I just hope Ditka doesn't hire a yes-man now. I hope he doesn't want that. Buddy wasn't like that at all. And look how we wound up. On top.   1/30/86

Mike Singletary   I lost two teeth at the dentist, my best friend and defensive coordinator . . . Just makes you appreciate the good times that much more, I guess.   1/30/86

Dan Hampton   Everybody was close, with a common goal. Mike Ditka handled the offense, Buddy the defense, and we went all the way. I didn't really see any problems. We had the two best coaches in the NFL. Mike and Buddy. Now we've lost one. It'll be hard without him. Real hard.   1/30/86

Steve McMichael   Buddy was here for how long? Eight years? And we had the No. 1 defense the last two? Well, he's a real genius, wasn't he? What about the first six?   9/14/86

RYAN AND DITKA REACT _____

Buddy Ryan   [Ditka] wished me well and I'm sure he was sincere.

Mike's a good man, regardless of all the stuff you read. Usually people would ask, "Buddy, what do you think about this?" Then they'd ask Mike, "What do you think?" He doesn't give the same answer I do, so they say, "Oh, there's a disagreement."   1/30/86

Ditka didn't know what was going on on defense and we cussed each other out, but we would do that every three or four weeks.   2/7/86

Ditka   [Ryan] took a lot of bows and I let him take them; but he didn't let any of his assistants take any bows. Why doesn't [offensive line coach] Dick Stanfel get more credit? We led the league in rushing three years in a row.   2/7/86

For five months the Ditka-Ryan feud subsided. However, Mike Singletary's book, Calling the Shots, *opened old wounds in quoting Buddy Ryan on Ditka*   Will I miss Mike Ditka? Yes, I guess I will. Sure we had our fair share of arguments, mostly when he tried to make defensive suggestions. But he never really told me what to do; I never let him. I said who played, how much, and when. Every now and again, when things weren't going well on the field, Mike would come by and make some suggestions. I'd just tell him to go blank himself, and he'd turn around and walk off. But honestly, I never felt a rift. Maybe Mike did. Maybe he was upset at all the publicity the defense generated, but the way I see it, anything I ever got was the result of how my players played. Ditka and I never had a confrontation; in fact we hardly ever spoke. I'd just put the game play on his secretary's desk when I finished it, and she'd put it on his. Not that he understood much of it.   7/22/86 Quoted by permission.

BEFORE THE BEARS–EAGLES GAME _____

Ironically, the Bears were scheduled to play the new Ryan-led Eagles early in the 1986 season. On a Philadelphia radio show with a telephone link to Chicago, Ditka was asked by the Philadelphia media if he was feuding with Ryan. Ditka replied   I have no feud with anybody. This is a concern between ballplayers. It has nothing to do with myself or anybody else. If you play football games, they're played on the field, with the teams. I've tried to explain that to people over the years. Some people think coaches play and win games. Players win them. I've never said anything about anybody. You guys [the media] want to talk about football? Because if you don't I'll hang up. You'll get no story from me on that other stuff. You've got enough stories in Philadelphia. You ain't got enough paper to write what [Ryan] says.   9/11/86

BEARS 13-EAGLES 10

Although the Bears won, it was obvious to all concerned that this wasn't just another game. Bears players noticed that Ditka wanted very badly to beat Ryan's Eagles. Commented Walter Payton   One time on the field, I told our guys, "Come on, let's play our type of game. Let's not get uptight like Mike is. Let's do what we do best and not let him affect us."   9/15/86

Ditka tried during the pregame interviews to downplay the personal aspect of the game. After the victory he explained   I made it too much of a personal thing. You can try to do individual things and that's wrong. We're in a team sport and when I have to start thinking I have to rely on being a genius to win football games, I've got a lot of problems. 9/15/86

He [Ryan] has talked about the Super Bowl in three years, he'll be lucky to have a job in three years.   9/16/86

After losing to the Bears in 1986, Buddy Ryan and his Eagles were scheduled to play in Philadelphia in 1987. The game lost significance since it was to be played with replacement players. Reportedly, Buddy Ryan had a hard time getting emotionally involved in the game. However, he told his son   Maybe if I see Ditka, I'll get fired-up.   11/8/87 *Chicago Sun-Times*

After the Eagles lost to the Bears, Ryan admitted   There's no question about it that we got soundly outcoached in every phase of the game.   10/5/87 *Chicago Sun-Times*

10

JIM McMAHON

JIM McMAHON, ROOKIE QUARTERBACK

In McMahon's case, he is unusual. He's read defenses, he's hit outlet passes. When you throw 50 times a game [in college], you've got to do those things. It should be no problem for him.   5/2/82

Never entered my mind to take him out after the interceptions. Jim is never going to lose confidence in himself. He'd have to get hit by a truck.   11/22/82

Jim McMahon is the best quarterback. He's the quarterback of the future. He's the starting quarterback and will not come out unless he is injured. If the Bears are going to win, Jim McMahon will be the catalyst.   11/8/83

I've been around some veteran quarterbacks who don't handle themselves much better than Jim does. Sure he'll improve, but I'm saying he's doing the job as far as understanding and reading and moving out of the pocket. When he comes out of that pocket, he comes out with design. He doesn't come out in panic. He's looking for something downfield or looking to make something work. He knows what he wants to do. And when he runs, there is no indecision. He runs to make a first down or get as much as he can.   12/10/82

McMAHON SPEAKS UP

I think I proved some things last year [1982] that I can play in this league. I proved it the first couple of games this year. In the Denver game he [Ditka] got real upset when I threw a couple of bad balls. It was not like I was just trying to give 'em back the football . . . I try to forget what has happened because everyone knows how Mike is. He's temperamental. We're the people who have to accept that. When he says something that could make you upset, he's saying it out of frustration. We've just got to understand.   11/1/83

We're still all playing fairly tense. We're not just loosening up and going out having fun. We're all just too worried about our jobs instead of playing with reckless abandon . . . We're worried about being replaced and we can't worry about it.   11/1/83

DITKA'S RESPONSE

They ought to be afraid to make mistakes. That's their job. I'm afraid to make mistakes too. If you make enough of them, you're not going to have a job.   11/1/83

JIM McMAHON, TOUGH GUY

[McMahon] was losing his color he was in so much pain. I didn't expect him to run like that. He ran like he had no fear at all.   9/18/84

On telling McMahon to run out of bounds occasionally to avoid getting hurt   Because of his competitive instinct, he's going to chafe about that. It runs contrary to everything he believes in.   8/11/85

Every play can't always be a great play. McMahon has had to learn this, just like Joe Montana had to learn it, and Joe Theismann, and Roger Staubach. A quarterback has to live again to fight another day.   7/14/85

You won't intimidate him. It will just make him work harder if you get to him or frustrate or pressure him. He's a scrapper. He's not going to give up or quit on you.   1/1/86

He put his butt on the line out there. The things he does nobody else does. The hits he took, the running, the scrambling. He's trying to make things happen, trying to do things for the football team, trying to get a first down by diving and sliding and jumping. Other guys just aren't going to do that. He plays it different.   10/27/86

He's some kind of gutty guy.   10/27/86

THE SUPER BOWL _____

In an effort to relieve the pain on Jim McMahon's bruised hip, McMahon arranged to have an acupuncturist treat him in New Orleans. Ditka was supportive   I think it's a great idea if it helps. It's all mental anyway. Some of it is physical. If it helps, it helps. Heck, 30 years ago they didn't use x-rays. Now they use it to cure cancer.   1/21/86

McMahon's view   McCaskey doesn't have to worry about controlling the club. And I don't care about who pays for the doctor. Main thing, he's here. Mike Ditka was all for it. So was Jerry Vainisi. I don't know why McCaskey got all uptight. Heck, we got so many people running around here worried about my butt, they're gonna be so nervous, they'll need a few needles before this thing is over.   1/23/86

Jim McMahon put pressure on himself by drawing media attention to his antics in New Orleans. Ditka's response   Pressure is not a bad thing if you can handle it. People who don't handle pressure don't last very long as coaches or players. If Jim knows he's created pressure, then he has to deal with it accordingly and I think he can handle it.   1/25/86

He's fun and he's going to create excitement. He'll put you people [the media] on a little bit and have a few laughs. But he's a pretty good person. I'll say he's a very good person. He has a lot of qualities that are important to have, the way he treats his family and his kids and what's important to him. Maybe this thing is not quite as important to him as a lot of people think it should be.   1/25/86

He's a guy that thrives on pressure. You beat him up pretty good in the media and maybe he deserved a little bit of it. But I love Jim and have a lot of respect for him. He doesn't regard his body as anything important in a football game. Very few can play quarterback the way he does. He plays the game hard . . . he has a lot of courage and you just don't coach that.   1/28/86

INJURIES

Injuries have been a recurring problem throughout McMahon's career because he is an intense competitor with little regard for his body. Ditka expressed his concern   He has to be on the field before he's really of value to us. I'm sure he hears me say that, and if he would stop and think about the pain and anguish he had last season, he would hear me very well. But I'm sure right now that's way in the past, like it never happened. He thinks he has to do what he has to do.   9/8/85

Early arm trouble, 1985   I heard so many conflicting stories I'm not sure what I've heard. You would think it's no major thing, but it evidently bothered him. His passes floated again. He couldn't get anything on it.   9/17/85

I'm concerned. If it's a bruise, it should have healed by now. There's a possibility it could be more than a bruise. We'll just have to wait and see.   11/15/85

Jim and I talked last week. I really like Jim. I don't care what people think. It's important that's understood. But I like him healthy. I want him to be the best Jim McMahon can possibly be for himself and for the Bears. And the only way he can be like that is healthy.   12/10/85

Jim McMahon missed the 1986 preseason because of his arm injury. Ditka was concerned McMahon would not be available for the season opener against Cleveland   We'll try to have the other two guys ready if Jim can't go. We've won games when Jim wasn't in there before, and we can win them again. But that's not the object. Jim's our quarterback, and he's proven he's an excellent quarterback when healthy. The object is to get him back on the field.   8/18/86

LOSING McMAHON AGAIN

It's a bad break for Jim and a bad break for us. But it's silly to sit back and mope about it. We lost one of our best football players. Now we have to have everyone pitch in and pull and get the job done.   9/9/86

I think he's going to make it through the season, but I'm an optimist. I couldn't look at it the other way. I don't like that scenario. We've proven we can win with somebody else, but I don't think we play nearly as well. It's not nearly as smooth.   10/7/86

A month and a half later a gloomy Ditka announced   I doubt very much we're going to have his [McMahon's] services very much for the rest of the year.   11/25/86

The way it looks, there's something in there that causes a catch in his arm when it comes up to a certain point and it looks like that is going to have to be at least shaved down. If he has surgery now, his year is definitely wiped out.   11/25/86

SURGERY _____

Jim McMahon decided to have surgery to repair his arm problem. Ditka's comment   It's what he does after surgery that is important. He needs to have a conditioning program that is second to none and have the discipline necessary to carry it through. If he doesn't, the arm may never get better. But I think he wants to play really badly. Anyone can do anything, as long as they want to do it.   11/27/86

Ditka, just before McMahon's surgery   Will you be back for the Dallas game?
McMahon   I'll try.
Ditka   Good luck to you, kid.   12/8/86

While still medicated after surgery, McMahon wise-cracked   Now I know how Ditka must have felt when they picked him up [for driving under the influence].   12/14/86

Ditka, 1987   I think Jimmy's going to be okay. He's approaching it in his way. I'm not worried about his arm. I do worry about him getting the strength back he had in 1985 and being able to take the hits.   4/24/87

FEUDING THE McMAHON–DITKA WAY _____

When asked by a T.V. talk show host how he would describe Mike
Ditka via word association, McMahon said   Intense.   9/10/86

Johnny Carson   Is McMahon crazy?
Mike Ditka   He doesn't like me because I happen to be the coach and
there's a certain amount of authority there.   1/21/87   *Chicago Sun-Times*

Jerry Vainisi on McMahon   We just want Jim to realize that he has
to do things Ditka's way. By that, I don't mean we want Jim to change
one bit as a character, as being Jim. Ditka, when he was a player, lived
on the edge a bit himself. So he understands. He doesn't care whether
Jim wears a Boston College jersey to practice or any of that other stuff
that makes Jim unique. Mike is very good that way, and I don't know
of another coach in the NFL who allows his players to be individuals
as much as Mike does.
  Mike puts up with a lot, but there's a point where he might say,
enough. I don't think that's going to happen with Jim. We'll learn if
he's sincere about what he says this spring, when it's time to get ready
for next season. But Jim's a winner, and I think he's upset with the
way this season has gone. I think you'll see the same McMahon in
training camp, only without the belly.   12/11/86

Jimbo Covert   They're not two different personalities [Ditka and
McMahon]. I think they're almost the same personality. On old teams,
they'd say if you fight with teammates or the coach, there'd be
dissension. It seems like stuff like that brings us closer together. It's
kind of weird, but it's the Chicago Bears, I guess.   8/19/86

ON McMAHON'S CASE _____

[McMahon's] got to spend that (preseason) time studying defenses,
studying film to be able to make the proper reads. You earn the right
to call plays. We earned that right as coaches.   7/10/84

I don't think Jim is the greatest practice player in the world. Maybe the problem is his throwing too many spirals. Last year his ball might wobble and then be right on the button.   9/2/83

On reports they were not speaking   [McMahon's] full of it. If the whole thing is to pout anytime you disagree with somebody, forget it.   8/12/86

I don't think you get better by watching. The only thing I said that probably burned him up was I'm tired of watching the guy sit on his helmet for three days of practice. If he's hurt, fine, get treatment.   8/18/86

Jim came to camp in great shape last year, and could do all the things he tries to do. He couldn't do those things this year since he was not in great shape coming to camp.   8/12/86

McMAHON BITES BACK

He keeps ripping me for not coming to camp in shape. Well I did more running this year than I did the last four years. And I'm down to 195 pounds. But I'm hurt and what's the use of playing hurt now? Why not get ready for the regular season? Is that so hard to understand? And nobody knows this body of mine, what it can do and when, better than me, right? Do I have to prove I can take pain all over again? Look at me. This ol' body is going straight to the Smithsonian when it's done with me. The leadership stuff, that's fine. But I don't think I've been all that bad as a leader. I've done everything I can to help us win. I've played with broken bones, a lacerated kidney, played whenever I could. I can't see why Ditka would start thinking I'm lazy now. I hope my teammates know I'd go through a brick wall for them and I know I'd go through a brick wall for them. Is that being lazy? Not caring? I mean there were other guys getting treatment Thursday. But did they get fined? Why me?   8/18/86

Everybody says I haven't been practicing. That's a bunch of B.S. I'm out there at practice. I go through all the drills. It's just that I don't do any throwing after I get out there at first and warm up. I throw about 30 balls and try to get my arm loose. By that time, we go into calisthenics and some different drills and I don't throw for like half an hour and the arm stiffens up. So I just don't throw during the team period and everybody's been saying I haven't been practicing. That's crazy. I've been out there at practice. The doctor told me to limit my throws to about 50 a week, so I don't know what to do. It's not that I'm not practicing at all. I'm out there; it's just that I'm not throwing during team drills and it's kind of upsetting to read in the paper every day that I don't practice.   10/22/86

I throw hard in practice, it takes another day or two to get [the arm] back to where it was before I threw. If they want me to go out there and throw hard in practice, and then not be able to play Sunday, what kind of logic is that?   10/22/86

IMPASSE

Ditka   We're going to have a meeting. I'd like to sit down and talk. I'm not mad at anybody.   8/18/86

McMahon   A meeting? What happens if we have it and one of us doesn't come out of there?   8/18/86

THE ACQUISITION OF DOUG FLUTIE

McMahon   I doubt if [Ditka] will chew [Flutie's] butt out the way he's chewed out Mike [Tomczak] or Steve [Fuller] or me.   10/16/86

Ditka   Jim's the quarterback and he knows it. He has to carry us. But he hasn't been healthy. He's played in four of our seven games. At that rate, he'll play in nine of our sixteen. That leaves seven unanswered and we need insurance.   10/22/86

Experience doesn't mean a thing. If the coaches have experience and the other players have experience, then the quarterback doesn't matter. There were a lot of people who probably doubted [McMahon's] ability going into the Super Bowl.   12/28/86 *Southtown Economist*

Commenting on McMahon's criticism when Ditka decided to go with Flutie in the playoffs   [it was like] a hot coal down the back of my shirt. It really made me mad. I thought it was unfair to the kid. 6/19/87

McMahon on Flutie in the playoffs   The way things turned out, [Ditka] came out smelling like a rose. But at the time, I didn't think it was necessary.   12/28/86 *Southtown Economist*

MORE FRICTION

Ditka   You are going to find I don't talk to him about anything.   12/28/86 *Southtown Economist*

We went through that one little week where there was some misunderstanding because we had more than one guy trying to be the head coach.   1/3/87 *Des Plaines Daily Herald*

[McMahon] plays the game like a lineman. It doesn't work because he's only 195 pounds.   1/21/87 *Chicago Sun-Times*

Ditka and Jim McMahon   . . . probably would be good friends if I wasn't the coach. We talk once every leap year. Jim doesn't respect authority. When I played, I spoke my piece and I didn't always agree, but I respected authority. I'm an authority figure. That's my opinion. He might say something else. I'm sure he would.   3/19/87

McMahon   We don't always agree on everything but I think [Ditka's] fair. He'll let you know if you screw up, and that's the way it should be. There's no wishy-washy person in Mike and that's the kind of guy I like to play for. I don't like guys who tell you one thing and then go and tell somebody else another thing. He's not like that. He'll tell you to your face you screwed up or you didn't. It's the way it should be.   1/1/86

SYBILIZING

McMahon   Well, I don't think our problems are as bad as they are made out to be. I just don't understand him all of the time. We had that talk recently and I figured everything was okay. Then, after that, he tells me at practice one day he doesn't believe I'm hurting as bad as I say I'm hurting. He says they are going to put me on the injured reserve list. I say go ahead, if that's what they want to do, but I didn't think I needed that much time. As it turns out, the shoulder separation didn't. It's healed. It's the other thing I hope Mike understands now. He's been Sybilizing a lot lately with a lot of guys, not just me . . . . You know, going through all different personality changes—like Sybil, the girl in the movie. I don't know why he or anybody else would think that all of a sudden, I don't want to throw a football.   11/23/87

McMahon   Remember the Oakland A's in the 70's? They argued and kicked and screamed all the way to three World Series titles in a row. We could be just like them. I know we can argue right up there with anybody, and I'm confident we can win a few Super Bowls, too. That's all that matters. Winning. Then we can all Sybilize together and be happy again.   11/13/86

Mike tells me I'm more mature. I don't know what the heck that means. My wife asked me why these hairs are growing on my chest. I tell her it's because I'm more mature.   9/2/84

CAN McMAHON COME BACK? _____

I think Jimmy's going to be okay. He's approaching it in his way. I'm not worried about his arm. I do worry about him getting the strength back he had in 1985 and being able to take the hits.   4/24/87

His conditioning, other than the shoulder, is very, very good—bordering on excellent.   5/13/87 *Des Plaines Daily Herald*

The whole package is [in better shape this year]. No question about it. He's done a lot of other exercises for other parts of his body. I was with him a week ago. I know.   7/21/87 *Des Plaines Daily Herald*

He's done isolated shoulder exercises and a lot of tumbling exercises to learn how to fall. He has done a lot of things to get other parts of his body in shape. I don't think the physical thing will be nearly as great as the psychological, though. We won't really know if he's all right until game pressure and someone misses a block and the linebacker catches him flush with a tackle and you say "uh, oh" and see how fast he gets up. Any of us could pretty much go out there and throw it good in practice.   7/21/87

My gut feeling is he'll play, and he will be healthy. He's stronger to a degree from all the exercises he's done. I feel that the biggest thing that hurt him last year—and he doesn't agree, of course, with this— was being overweight. He didn't move as well, and that's where a muscle pull came from, I believe, early in training camp last year.   7/21/87

I'd bet on him. He wants to prove a lot of things to a lot of people, especially me.   6/15/87

THE FUTURE

We have no intention of trading Jim McMahon.   11/11/86

[McMahon is] very much in the future of the Bears and is going to stay that way.   11/13/86

THE 1987 SEASON

Ditka   There's no question he's in better shape over all.   8/2/87
Chicago Sun-Times

McMahon   I'd like to be ready to play the last couple of preseason games. Mike makes those decisions, but it just depends.   8/3/87

Ditka   Jim's arm is a little sore but it has nothing to do with the shoulder. It's muscle soreness. We're letting him throw at his own pace. By the end of the week, I hope he's throwing better and we can get a lot of work out of him.   8/5/87

Jim can't throw and he knows he can't and it's bothering him. He'd have to tell me he was ready to play. But I'm not blind. I can see when there's zip on the ball and when there's not.   8/9/87 *Chicago Sun-Times*

McMahon   Coach Ditka and the other coaches think I'm making the right reads and throwing pretty well. They know I've got to get stronger. I'm glad they're being patient with me. I don't know how long it's going to take to build this up.   8/11/87

Ditka   He threw it but not the way he has to throw to play in the NFL. He knows that and I know it. Anybody out watching knew it. It's not a secret. He threw decently at times, but when it came time to really put the soup on it to get it there, he couldn't do it. A lot might be the [wet] footballs and the conditions, but as of right now, we would have to go with the kids we have.   8/26/87

Could the team adjust to not having Jim McMahon as quarterback? Ask them. I've adjusted to it because I've gone through it for a couple of years. You can't expect miracles. If the guy's not healthy, he's not healthy. You can't wish it. We stood around last year and wished he was healthy.   8/26/87

Jim's name is not on the injury list. It's going to be a day-to-day thing, a guarded thing, and, like I said, he has to tell me he's well and I have to see it. Him telling me he's well and me not being able to see him throw, well, technically it wouldn't work. I'd feel like I was betrayed. I don't want that to happen. Whatever it takes to get him better, I'm willing to do. There's no hurry right now.   8/10/87

He's not ready to play, but let's take one step at a time. If he's going to throw one day and take four off, then he won't be ready. If every pass hurts, then we have a problem. If he progresses, he'll be the starter, no question. If not, right now I'm leaning toward Mike [Tomczak], but we have to wait and see what happens. McMahon has got to do it every day now. I think that's what it boils down to. 8/19/87

WHERE'S JIM?

Jim McMahon missed the last day of training camp. When reporters asked Ditka about Jim McMahon, he responded Jim who? Jim didn't come out. He must have had a bad night, but he'll be fined accordingly. He wasn't excused from practice. He just didn't come out.   8/21/87

When asked if he personally checked McMahon's room, Ditka's snapped back There's no excuses this time. I didn't check his room, the bathroom, the closet, I didn't check any of that. And I don't intend to. I checked the field and he wasn't there.   8/21/87 *Chicago Sun-Times*

Jim McMahon   I was in getting treatment with a bunch of other guys. If he wants to fine us all, he can go ahead.   8/21/87

READY OR NOT? _____

Would McMahon be ready for the 1987 opening game against the New York Giants?   A lot has to do with Jim's practice this week, and whether he's going to play next Monday [against St. Louis]. I think he is. He threw the ball well the last couple of days, and he threw it well before the game on Saturday. Not as well as he can, but it's getting better. He's getting strength in the arm and more confidence. I'm not going to rush him at all.   8/24/87

McMahon   Mike was talking about me starting the Miami game, but that was after the first day I threw. I'm not going out there till I'm ready and I doubt I'll be ready by this weekend. Because once I get in a game, I forget everything [about taking it easy] and go on instinct. I don't know how long it's going to take to build the muscles up in the back. But the ones [where he was cut] haven't had any pain since a month or two after the surgery. I don't have the velocity now. It doesn't do any good for me to throw in the teams and not put anything on it and get guys hung up. Coach Ditka and the other coaches think I'm making the right reads. They know [the arm] is going to get stronger. I'm glad they are being patient with me.   8/11/87 *Southtown Economist*

McMahon on why he did not attend morning workouts   I told Mike a couple of days ago that I'm not getting anything accomplished in the first part of the morning when the quarterbacks are working on their footwork and handing the balls off to the running backs. I'm just standing around there gaining weight. I have to do something constructive [doing weight work].   8/11/87 *Southtown Economist*

I don't know how to play protectively. To play protectively is to sit on the bench. A couple of years ago, Coach [Ditka] and [Minnesota quarterback Tommy] Kramer were just standing there and got blasted on the sidelines.   8/11/87 *Southtown Economist*

Last year, I tried to convey my thoughts when I was hurt through other people, and I guess it didn't get to him. Now I go straight to [Ditka]. There's no problem.   8/11/87

Ditka's view   I think it's evident right now that if we played the Giants tomorrow, Mike [Tomczak] would start. Unless he [McMahon] took a complete flip-flop in the next two weeks, I couldn't see any way he wouldn't start.   8/28/87 *Chicago Sun-Times*

We do have to start thinking about IR [injured reserve]. We have to find a way to get him well.   8/28/87 *Chicago Sun-Times*

Joe Theismann [former Redskins quarterback] on Jim McMahon   My feeling is the Bears should put McMahon on IR for four weeks or so and give him a chance to rehabilitate. If it's [his shoulder] not ready to take a major hit, I'm not thinking about Jim McMahon for the 1987 season. I'm thinking about the 1988, 1989, and 1990 seasons.   8/28/87 *Chicago Sun-Times*

Ditka   Maybe he came back too quick. I don't know. You hope and wish things would work out, and if they don't you have to be practical about it and say, hey maybe it is too soon.   8/28/87 *Chicago Sun-Times*

Maybe Dr. Jobe will have a recommendation. I don't know that it will help. Jim's tried everything. He wants to throw it.   8/28/87

You've got to stay on the offensive when you're on offense. You can't get defensive. That's what's good about Jim.   9/13/87 *Chicago Sun-Times*

The best thing we can do is win as many games as possible without him. And when he comes back, if he's ready and fit, we win as many games as we can with him.   9/13/87 *Chicago Sun-Times*

McMahon threw it outstanding last night at practice. As good as I've ever seen him. I want to sit down and talk to Jim, because I want to know where he is in his mind. He has to be willing to say, "Hey, I'm ready," before I make a decision.   10/17/87

READY

From watching him throw the football, I'd say he's ready. But I don't know if he could throw it every day or what he'd do if he threw it 60 times in a row. Don't forget Mike has played well. But McMahon is the guy who has been under the gun here for a lot of years. If he's ready to play, there's a very big chance he'll be playing. I don't want to run and jump into something before we look at everything. There's a final exam that has to be made by a doctor. I'm just evaluating him eyeball-wise. Yesterday, eyeball-wise, he was maybe 200 percent better than the best he ever threw it this whole year. That's quite an improvement, because he did throw it well at times this year. He threw during the whole practice last night, threw at least 70 times warming up and all.   10/17/87

He looks different. He's throwing the ball much better.   9/8/87 *Chicago Sun-Times*

On the first game that the Bears regulars would play   I would think it's not the best thing in the world to start him this week. But it's not out of the question.   10/20/87

After flying to California to check with Dr. Frank Jobe, Jim McMahon was cleared for regular duty.   Jim McMahon had a great report. He feels pretty good.   10/21/87 *Chicago Sun-Times*

He threw the ball very well in the mud and slop out there.   10/21/87
Chicago Sun-Times

*When asked about Mike Tomczak's role as starter now that his shoulder
was fully recovered from surgery, McMahon replied*   I feel the job is
mine.   10/22/87

Could his shoulder survive a NFL-type hit?   I'm not worried about
taking a hit. I took a good one during the strike from Fridge playing
basketball. I went up for a lay-up and all of his weight hit my arm
and knocked it back. I don't think I'll get hit any harder than
that.   10/22/87

That was really the motion the doctor was worried about, to have the
arm back and someone take it and yank it back farther. It hurt like
hell for a second, but it went right away.   10/22/87

Ditka   I tried to tell you how well he was throwing in practice. I was
shocked. He throws well on anticipation, as well as anybody I've ever
seen.   10/26/87

Jim is our starting quarterback. He will be our starting quarterback
until there'll be an injury. That question should never be brought up
again.   10/26/87

CALLING THE PLAYS _____

Jim McMahon   I told Mike I was going to call the plays. I told him,
"Put in the players you want because they're not going to come
out."   10/26/87 *Chicago Sun-Times*

Ditka   We should not have won [the Tampa game]. We had no right
to win. Maybe that's what champions are made of, I don't know. But

I'm not surprised at anything Jim McMahon does in life.   12/26/87
Chicago Sun-Times

The play he called on the 6 yard line, Coach Ditka couldn't have called.
Impossible to call.   10/27/87

On McMahon's Tampa Bay performance   For him and for all the
people who doubt his talents or couldn't remember how good he played,
it's easier he did it this way. They believe again. At least they believe
this week.   10/27/87

It makes me feel good to see him healthy. I just hope he stays healthy
and starts performing. I'd like to see him be on the field and be
productive for us and himself and get his career where he wants to get
it.   10/27/87 *Chicago Sun-Times*

SAME OLD JIM

Nothing's changed. He ran the ball [against Tampa Bay] and dove head-
first instead of sliding. He's not going to do it the way you tell him;
he's going to do it his way, because the only thing he's trying to do
is make a good play happen. The only thing I worry about is he got
ripped, really nailed by Ron Holmes on one play. I didn't know if he
would get back up or not. Those things bother me.   10/29/87

*Did McMahon experience any pain or soreness in the shoulder after
the Tampa Bay game? Ditka's response*   Unbelievable. Let it go right
off the bat. Threw it as good as he threw it Sunday.   10/29/87

Try to keep [McMahon] out of the Hall of Fame this week. Just let
him get through this one, and then we'll induct him automatically.
Give him a break.   10/29/87

He's got a confidence in himself that permeates not only to the players but to the coaching staff.   11/1/87

Our goal is to keep him healthy. It's hard to be recognized as one of the best in the league when you're injured so much. He can take his spot with the very best in the league.   11/1/87

He has no regard for doing anything pretty [because he plays so hard].   11/1/87

After another spectacular comeback performance, rallying the Bears from two touchdowns back late in the game against Kansas City, Ditka commented   Jim called the great majority of the plays in the second half.   11/2/87

Jim McMahon   I was surprised he let me do it. I was happy. You could see I started throwing the ball right away.   11/2/87

McMahon, asked if Ditka said anything to the Bears at half-time while losing 21–14 to the Chiefs   I was in the training room getting iced down, but I heard yelling and screaming. Pretty normal stuff.   11/2/87

In the Kansas City game, McMahon chose to operate without a huddle. Ditka explained   It gets people out of position. As long as we know what we're doing, the offense has the advantage.   11/2/87 *Chicago Sun-Times*

You're never out of any football game that Jim McMahon's in, ever. He's good. Let's face it, he thrives on that stuff [come from behind wins]. He thrives on throwing the ball and running a no-huddle offense. That excites him.   11/3/87 *Southtown Economist*

JIM TAKES OVER _____

Prior to the Green Bay game Ditka was asked if he would be calling the plays.   What we'll do is we'll just go out and call a few plays, and if they don't work, then probably Jim will take over and do whatever he wants to do out there anyway.   11/8/87

McMahon the leader   When I go in, I take control. I either call plays or change plays, and they feel something good is going to happen. I try to make plays on my own and they respond to that. They understand me, that I don't like to lose, and that I'll do whatever it takes to win.   11/5/87

Ditka explains   It's like he was an outsider looking in at the strike anyway, and he's so excited to be playing again that he's not worrying about things the other guys are worrying about. I just hope he doesn't change. He can't start going out on the practice field screwing around.   11/17/87

Would Ditka trade McMahon for Elway?   Dan [Reeves, Denver Head Coach] would probably have gray hair if he had Jim.   11/16/87 *Chicago Sun-Times*

He's still rebellious about some things, but I haven't seen much of that this year. He's been a joy to be around, and his teammates can see the same thing in him. He's been ideal. I think you're seeing the maturing process. He doesn't spend as much time putting people on anymore.   11/17/87 *Chicago Sun-Times*

When asked if calling his own plays upset Mike Ditka, McMahon replied   . . . I'm out there to win. If it hurts people's feelings, I'm sorry. Like he always says, life goes on.   12/15/87 *Chicago Sun-Times*

Give him [McMahon] credit. He's got talent. Some players are more physically talented. But he has a way of seeing, understanding, and making things happen. He can take control of a football game.   1/10/88

Realistically, there's no question Jim McMahon will be the starting quarterback. I hope it ends that he gets hurt, but it hasn't ended. That would provide an opportunity for somebody else, whether it's Jim Harbaugh or Mike Tomczak.   1/12/88

11

WILLIAM PERRY

WEIGHTY MATTERS

On William Perry The other guys in our division are sitting there wondering, "How are we going to control this guy?" I feel sorry for the centers, and for ours in practice. 5/1/85

Responding to criticism that William Perry might be too heavy to play in the NFL, Ditka explained The stuff about his weight is the biggest fallacy around. The important thing is his strength and stamina. Can we get him in shape? It's foolish to speculate on his weight. 7/14/85

There are a lot of guys who weigh 255 pounds and have the same body fat as Perry. 7/14/85

I'm not adverse to having him at 350 pounds, if he can play at that weight. If he's better at 300 pounds, then we'll play him there. 7/14/85

Why should I be worried about him? The opposition should be worried. His weight's not that bad. He'll be down to where we want him to be. I know he'll be ready by the second game of the season.   7/17/86

WELCOME TO THE NFL ⎯⎯⎯⎯⎯⎯⎯⎯⎯⎯⎯⎯

After Perry had to leave practice as a result of exhaustion, Ditka commented   I don't think there will be any problem with the way he works. Tuesday was a killer. It just got to him. It maybe was the first day he's really worked hard in three or four years.   8/8/85

He's got to learn to go on every play.   8/11/85

I played against a lot of players who have come into this league. Some are in the Hall of Fame and some will be. A lot of them in their first year and first games weren't very spectacular. He's showed enough that when he's going, he's going to be tough. That's all we can ask. We're taking three years of bad habits and trying to break them.   9/1/85

On noticing that William Perry was not being used by Defensive Coach Buddy Ryan in practice   I thought he was fitting in pretty good last week until I looked at practice today and I didn't see him fitting in quite so much; so I'll have to check that out. I didn't plan for Perry to watch, period. He wasn't drafted to watch. He played well last week. He adds another dimension to our football team.   10/3/85

THE BIGGEST BACK IN HISTORY ⎯⎯⎯⎯⎯⎯⎯⎯

Bill Tobin   From the first, Mike Ditka and I thought, "Can you imagine tackling that guy?" When I saw Mike the week of the San Francisco game, I told him this might be the week. He smiled. When I had dinner with him the night before the San Francisco game, he told me he put [Perry] in.   10/30/85

Why did Ditka put William Perry in the backfield?   I just wanted to see if he could run with it.   10/14/85

Was giving the ball to Perry in the Bears 26–10 victory a payback to the 49ers for putting a lineman in the backfield during the game the Bears lost to the 49ers the previous year?   You think I'd do that? I'm not that kind of guy. I wouldn't try to get one-up on people. I just don't forget very easily.   10/14/85

William Perry   I was looking for the end zone. When the 49ers saw I was the ball carrier, their eyes got real big.   10/14/85

Ditka   Gives you a little food for thought on the goal line, doesn't he? I mean, it's really something you've got to think about realistically. There's a chance that could happen.   10/15/85

I think we'll use him again. At least until they put somebody bigger than him in there to plug up the hole.   10/22/85

The hilarious thing about this Perry thing is it's kind of busted the staid image in the NFL that all running backs are slender, 6 ft. tall, between 185 and 215, and built. This has made a farce out of that. Every underdog in society relates to Perry.   11/17/85

William Perry told a disbelieving media   Coach Ditka said he has some pass plays in mind.   10/22/85

Ditka   He can throw the football.   11/5/85

Here's the play: H-44, I want you to score, big guy.   1/27/86

SUPER BOWL HERO _____

William Perry   I want to thank Coach Ditka for letting me score. He told me later, "I made you a hero in the Super Bowl." I said, "Thank you, I appreciate it." It's the end of my whole life. What I dreamed of as a boy was to play in the Super Bowl. To score a touchdown in the 20th Super Bowl—I'm overwhelmed by it.   1/27/86

Maybe we can make him President, too.   1/27/86

We'll keep using him and teams will keep saying, "We can stop him," and they won't.   8/4/86

THE 1986 SEASON _____

He's a little overweight, and when he gets down to normal weight and gets his quickness back, we may stick him back in the backfield. I don't care what he weighs. I really don't care. He's overweight.   10/14/86

He says he feels weak at 315 pounds.   8/12/86

He's established himself as one of the best in the league. He's been our most dominant lineman.   9/3/86

He played well but he's still too heavy.   11/7/86

Other than the knee, I haven't seen a difference in Perry this year from last year. He's a better player. He hasn't moved quite as well because he's heavier, but you also have to consider the knee.   11/29/86

WEIGHING IN AT 350 _____

It's not astronomical. Sometimes you can't keep those things under control. That's up to the individual, and the individual's wife, also. She cooks, doesn't she?" 12/27/86 *Des Plaines Daily Herald*

I just see a very, very, very short career if he doesn't change it. I worry about him five or six years down the line. 12/28/86 *Southtown Economist*

If he doesn't take [the weight] off, he'll be in jeopardy of not being here, period. And I think I speak for the whole organization when I say that. I'm saying it'll be a different color jersey next year. 12/31/86 *Chicago Sun-Times*

If what I think doesn't matter, then it doesn't matter. We'll take that up after the season and we'll make a decision on where he's gonna be. 12/31/86 *Chicago Sun-Times*

Either the dog wags the tail or the tail no longer is a part of it, that's all. 12/31/86 *Chicago Sun-Times*

William Perry Coach Ditka's gonna speak. He's the head man and he runs the show. So you just sit back and listen. 12/31/86 *Chicago Sun-Times*

Ditka He knows what he did. He'll be okay. He'll take it off. If he gets down to what he said he would, it will be unbelievable. 1/6/87

He'll report to minicamp at 315 pounds or he won't report at all. But 10 pounds is nothing for him. He can pass up two meals and lose 15 pounds. 4/24/87

I think the kid will play at 305 or 310 and that's where he belongs. For us to use him the way we want on offense, he has to be in that area. If you look at film and realize how much they double team him, you realize how valuable he is to our football team.   5/13/87

THE 1987 SEASON

At the mini-camp in May, it was reported that Ditka personally weighed Perry in at 317 lbs. Ditka responded   Book it. Take it to the bank.   5/13/87 *Des Plaines Daily Herald*

Because of publicity surrounding his weight, Perry adopted a strategy.   I'm keeping a low profile. I'm not letting everyone follow me around. I'm fine.   5/13/87 *Des Plaines Daily Herald*

Ditka was angry about rumors that Perry's weight was over 325 lbs.   If his weight is not under 325 lbs., he will not be at Platteville. He can go back to South Carolina and do whatever the hell he wants to do. We'll go on without him.   7/21/87 *Des Plaines Daily Herald*

. . . I'm not going to mess around with Perry anymore. It's up to him. I played around with him enough. If he wants to get his weight down, fine. If he doesn't, fine.   7/21/87 *Des Plaines Daily Herald*

If his weight is under 325, he'll be the best defensive tackle in football. That will irritate some other people, too, but it's the way I feel. I think Perry can go down to 305 and play effectively if he'll work at it and discipline himself.

I want him to be the best he can be. Right now I don't know if he wants to be the best he can be. He has to make his mind up about it. If he ever maximizes his talent, no one will touch him.

But you know what the old saying is: To be No. 1, you have to reach deep down in the gutsack and make it hurt. His rear should drag off the field daily. And anyone who gets in his way at training camp, he

ought to knock them down. He needs a little of [former Bear] Doug
Atkins' temperament. A little of Steve McMichael's temperament.
7/21/87

THE BIG BACK IS BACK

He was 318 the other day after a workout. The only reason he isn't
[310] is because he didn't work at it.   8/12/87 *Southtown Economist*

*When he was told he'd be carrying the ball in 1987 after being grounded
in 1986 because of weight problems, Perry, in Ditka's words, was*   Like
a big kid in a candy store.   8/6/87

During an intrasquad game, Perry carried the ball.   Someone tried
to cut Perry [tackle him low] and he still went four or five
yards.   8/6/87

Why does Perry's weight hover between 315 and 325? Ditka's view   He
probably drinks too much beer. Either that or he eats too much. He's
living a country club life.   8/10/87

It's just silly. I don't want to go through all the fines, but if that's the
only thing he understands, that's what I have to do. He told me by
the end of camp he would be down to—cough, cough—about 315. He
got lazy on his diet. He's working hard on the field. He's got to discipline
himself.   8/19/87

When asked about Ditka's order to shed pounds, Perry responded   I'm
not talking about it. You just ask him about it.   8/20/87 *Chicago
Sun-Times*

*Perry was seen practicing punt returns after punt returner Lew Barnes
broke his leg. When reporters questioned Ditka, he responded*   He'd

be the only guy to run 10 yards . . . then hope somebody would catch him—and they would catch him, believe me. 8/28/87 *Chicago Sun-Times*

SAME OLD TUNE

Once again William Perry's weight was reported to be over 320. Ditka confirmed that Perry was now up to 333. Ditka had had enough. For the first week, Perry would be fined $25 a pound. After that, the fines would double. $400, $800, $1,600, $3,200, $6,400, $13,200 a pound. When it gets to that and he's not down to weight, you'll know he's silly. If he gets up to $5,000 a pound, he'll understand. 9/2/87 *Chicago Sun-Times*

Maybe someone will ask him why his wife doesn't understand the importance of getting down. Let me get right to the heart of it. I think somebody has to help him. I think she would be the most logical person to help him. I'm not evading the issue anymore. It's time to get down to what is important in his life. And I think that [his weight] is more important than a new gold chain. 9/2/87 *Chicago Sun-Times*

Has he talked to Perry's wife about the Fridge's weight?   Very hard. I don't get much of a reception anymore. I'm not a welcome guy. 9/2/87 *Chicago Sun-Times*

William Perry   I don't have any reaction to what Coach Ditka has to say. The only thing I'd like to say is just keep my wife out of it. It's between him and me. 9/3/87 *Chicago Sun-Times*

He doesn't eat here [with the team]. He eats there [at home]. Or else between here and there. 9/2/87

William Perry   We had an agreement I'd weigh 320 by the first game and that's what I'll be. Everybody goes up and down.   9/3/87 *Chicago Sun-Times*

The Bears office staff received so many angry calls defending Perry's wife that Ditka commented   We have women up there [answering calls in the office] wearing earplugs. I came in today and we had three people with swimming hats.   9/4/87 *Chicago Sun-Times*

I have the best interests of William Perry at heart. I just want to clarify that for all the people that think I'm exceptionally cruel.   9/4/87 *Chicago Sun-Times*

THE FRIDGE MAKES WEIGHT

On September 12, just two days before the Bears opening game, Perry reportedly weighed 315 pounds. A happy Ditka told reporters   Bill has responded great.   9/12/87

The lowest I can recall him being is 308 around the Super Bowl, and he was excellent. I think maybe he can work at 305 and not be hurt at all. He's done his part. If I want to bring him down lower, I better make sure I'm not hurting him.   9/12/87

It shows what people can do if they really want to do it. Unfortunately, I have to be the heavy. Maybe my methods were a little wrong, but he's done a good job.   9/12/87

With two injured centers, Ditka experimented with Perry as the special teams center.   We've looked at everybody. We even looked at the Refrigerator, but we closed the door on that right away. He didn't do bad, really. That's my project for 1991.   9/12/87 *Chicago Sun-Times*

He can be 315 one day, 325 the next. I'm sure it's liquid weight.
9/18/87 *Chicago Sun-Times*

DITKA'S MESSAGE _____

I'll tell you something: William Perry is the furthest thing from my
mind. I don't care if William Perry ever comes back. William Perry
means nothing to me. We don't need William Perry that much. And
if he comes back out of shape, he won't start.   10/6/87

You people think my life depends on William Perry. You guys are all
wrong, man. His career depends on Mike Ditka a hell of a lot more
than my career depends on him. You can book that.   10/6/87 *Chicago
Sun-Times*

*After the strike, rumors were that the Fridge had gained weight.
William Perry* I'm not saying what I am.   10/10/87 *Chicago
Sun-Times*

When told of Ditka's criticism of him, the Fridge was philosophical.
You can't let anyone bother you. If I was the coach and I just got me
a brand new contract and everything and I thought I could be back
to the Super Bowl, I'd be talking out [of] my head, too. That's his
job.   10/10/87 *Chicago Sun-Times*

He's not going to be 315. We want to get him back on the schedule
to get his weight where he can move at his best. I thought the guy was
playing pretty good at 315. I imagine if he's over 315 now, we have
to give him time to get down. We can't just cut his leg off and say now
you're 315. He didn't really look any different to me.   10/17/87

The target goal is 315. Ideally, it's 305 with a lean body weight
somewhere around 16 percent, which he'll never make because he
doesn't do anything about it.   12/29/87

William Perry   As far as getting back on offense, Coach Ditka runs the show. I have to go by what he says. He's the coach, I'm the player.   11/3/87

After two wins in close games against Tampa Bay and Kansas City in which blocked extra points and field goals were crucial, Ditka explained   Perry is keying the push-through, making the penetration. He took the guard last week and put him on his back every time. That's essential, because it leaves a gap for those guys to push through.   11/8/87

He's doing a lot of good things. I thought he showed a lot of hustle against Denver. He stayed after John Elway well. I wish he was in a little better shape. But he wishes he were in a little better shape. He'll get in a little better shape. We're going to run more from here on out, and hopefully that will help him. But, as far as his playing, he plays pretty well.   11/19/87

THE TRUCE

After years of fighting William Perry's weight, Ditka accepted the fact that Perry would always be heavier than Ditka would like.   I look at the grades and the films, and as long as I and the defensive coaches are happy, I have no problem with it.   11/27/87 *Chicago Sun-Times*

It doesn't do much good to rant and rave about it. It's too hard on me mentally and physically. I beat a dead horse to death before. · 12/19/87 *Chicago Sun-Times*

William Perry   As far as playing the run, I can do that with my eyes closed. That's why Coach Ditka drafted me.   11/27/87 *Chicago Sun-Times*

William Perry, analyzing his 1987 style of play   I'm not just going out there and bull-rushing, I'm trying to make some moves. The name of the game is to improve each and every day.   11/27/87 *Chicago Sun-Times*

PERRY'S WEIGHT IN '88 _____

Back to Perry's weight-loss program   It has to be structured. I think he will listen and I think he'll go on to be a good player. Maybe I'm thinking and wishing on the same hand, but . . .   1/12/88

I would hope that William will do the things he has to do to become the player I think he can be. I think that's the message.   3/12/88

His mother just passed away and I haven't been able to get ahold of him. I'm not crazy; I'm not optimistic about his weight. I suspect it is about what it was at the end of the year, about 350. William is a nice kid. He tries. When I have him around me, I can control him pretty well. But when he is in South Carolina and we're in Chicago, we have no control.   3/12/88

I think all his best football is ahead of him and he hasn't gotten the credit he deserves.   4/6/88 *Chicago Sun-Times*

If he has to play tackle to be on the field, he'll play tackle. If he has to play end, he'll play end. He's a pretty good football player, we can't kid ourselves about that. When we take him off the field we just make it easier on the opposition. All you have to do is take the films out and look through them. Unless he's double-teamed on the running plays, he's usually to the ball.   4/6/88 *Chicago Sun-Times*

The only mistake I made was putting him on the bench. If I had it to do over again, I wouldn't. He's too good.   4/6/88

On his return from South Carolina, Perry began working out at the Bears' Lake Forest facilities. Ditka commented   The Fridge is a mere large shadow of the man he used to be.   4/6/88

He's not down to 325, I know that.   4/6/88

Sherry Perry, William Perry's wife   The only thing I have to say is, we don't put football first. Whatever Mike Ditka does is his right, but we put the Lord first and that's the way it's always been. We don't drill on football because football is just a game that comes and goes. We put our family and we put the Lord first. If you put football first in your life and then you're pulled off the field, you hurt. It doesn't affect either of us, because we know it's a game. We just need each other and our Bible, that's all.   12/30/87

DITKA HAS THE LAST WORD

Folk heroes come and go. Just think about Davy Crockett. I haven't heard his name mentioned all week. You're only a hero when you're a part of it. If you're not in the parade, you watch the parade—that's life.   12/29/87 *Chicago Sun-Times*

12

WALTER PAYTON

THE BEST FOOTBALL PLAYER EVER

I can't say enough about Walter Payton. Walter owes me nothing and he owes football nothing. He's given it all he has.   12/27/82

It's hard to compare. They're all unique. But Walter is the best because he's the most complete. He's the whole package. He may not do some things as well as someone else has done, but he does **everything** better than anyone else ever has.   9/2/84

Nobody would have done what he did, nobody I know. Nobody ever. We'd get some people, if they had that injury [a dislocated toe] in training camp, they still wouldn't be back from it. Walter, I talked to him, and once he said he was okay, that was it. There's only one of him.   11/10/86

I've not seen anyone approach him as a football player and he's probably the best athlete I've ever seen.   11/11/86

The very best football player I've ever seen, period. At any position. 11/5/85

CONTROVERSY: THE SUPER BOWL

More than anybody else's, though, this was Walter Payton's day. He deserves more credit for what happened than anybody else on the team.   1/27/86

Bears fans attending the Super Bowl game in New Orleans were chanting "Walter, Walter!," hoping that Walter Payton would get an opportunity to score in the 46–10 defeat of the Patriots. Walter never did. Ditka commented It's unfortunate Walter didn't get a touchdown, but Walter's contribution . . . nobody has to talk about it. The Patriots keyed their whole defense on him.   1/28/86

I wanted to get Walter into the end zone. But our plays are designed to score and I didn't know who had the ball.   1/27/86

Walter Payton I was upset, a little hurt. Was. Not now. I got over it right away. You know how it is. You work all these years, you want to do well in the big game, and then, something like that takes away from the moment. Maybe Mike Ditka got caught up in the game and didn't notice it.   1/30/86

In July Walter Payton was late in reporting to camp, prompting Ditka to remark I understand some feelings were hurt in January. Well, my feelings were hurt when not everybody showed up here . . . I'm sure I'll get over it.   7/17/86

BELIEVING IN EACH OTHER _____

People just believe in him. They know we have more than one way to get it done, and it's not necessarily the guy who takes the snap from the center. We rely on a lot of people in our offense, but nobody more than him. 1/2/87 *Chicago Sun-Times*

Walter Payton [Ditka] knows what it takes. He's been in this situation before. What he tries to instill in us is that we can only count on the team members. We can't believe things we read in the papers or what we hear on television. It's what you believe in your heart and what's on the team that counts. 10/21/85

WALTER PAYTON AND THE FUTURE _____

I want to use him intelligently and use him to highlight our offense, yet I want to take him out in certain situations and put someone else in and not get him beat up. 9/4/86

We design plays and ask him to do them. But I'm going to put him into situations probably differently than a year ago when I would have used him as a lead blocker. I don't think that's what I want him doing. 9/4/86

When asked about the possible retirement of Walter Payton, Ditka replied He's the only person who can answer that. A guy has to feel how his body feels and his mind feels. 9/4/86

I know Walter will come to training camp in better shape than anyone. 2/1/87

After meeting with Pete Rozelle on buying a new football franchise, Payton commented If I get a team, Mike Ditka will be the coach.   5/13/87 *Des Plaines Daily Herald*

Ditka We'll run a lot of two-halfback offense, and once in a while we'll use him as a fullback.   6/15/87

Walter played as well as ever [1986 season], but you can't play forever and he knows it. We'll use more formations with two halfbacks. Walter is still the best all-around player we have. Nobody admits, and Walter doesn't admit it, when an athlete is getting one step slower. I think he can be just as effective and be on the field less.   3/19/87

WALTER PAYTON: 1987 SEASON

I guarantee you Payton's production will not drop. It will be as good as or better than last year.   8/2/87

When you get older as a player, you can say, "Well, I don't have to work as hard." Or you can say, "I have to work twice as hard." And that's the way Dan [Hampton] and Walter look at it. I think Walter is working harder, but he's always worked hard. When you've accomplished what he has and then people in the media have the audacity to say we should do other things with other people . . . I just think he's going to shove that down people's throats.   8/7/87

We have the best football player in the league and a kid [Anderson] who is going to be one of the best. I'm happy with them. I love everything about it.   11/4/87

Responding to people who want to see Walter Payton used sparingly It's really interesting to see how soon people forget. I really think it's a great lesson to everybody in sports. Fame is fleeting. A lot of people are very unappreciative about what it's all about. I'm not one of them.   10/30/87 *Chicago Sun-Times*

In the Bears 31–28 victory over Kansas City   Walter was outstanding as a blocker. I'm elated with the job he's doing.   11/3/87 *Chicago Sun-Times*

There are exceptions you make in life, whether it's what you want to do or not. There are exceptions in life and Walter Payton is an exception. A lot of people told me I'm wrong already. I'll have to live with that. Twelve years take a lot out of a person and when you lose a little bit, you've got to remember the defenses are always gaining. So many things offset a guy who has played 12 years like Walter. He's lost a step and he'll be the first to admit it. It's hard to admit, though, because you realize the end of something great is coming.   11/17/87 *Chicago Sun-Times*

When asked if he felt Walter Payton should have retired at the end of the 1986 season, former Bears player Gayle Sayers responded   No question. Mike [Ditka] is being so kind to Walter. Starting him, letting him play . . . Water looks good, says he feels great. Still, it comes that time when you have to go out . . . He has nothing to be ashamed of. He has all the records you could want. He should say: "Lord, thank you very much. I enjoyed it. Good-bye."   12/3/87 *Chicago Sun-Times*

Ditka reacts to Sayers' criticism of Walter Payton   It's kind of ironic that Gale Sayers and Jim Brown would keep down-playing [Payton's] achievement. Regardless of how good runners they were, not either one of them could have carried his jock as a complete football player. Sayers was probably the most exciting runner ever to play the game. Brown was a great, great runner. But they didn't have the longevity. They didn't have the conditioning. They didn't have the heart. They didn't have the desire. They didn't have the records. They didn't have the blocking of Walter Payton. They didn't fake as good and they didn't catch as good. So it's kind of boring to keep letting those guys on television to take shots at Walter. It's unfortunate they do that. They don't have to do that. Their place is assured. They're in the Hall of Fame. Payton will be there right next to them. I don't think it's something Payton would do, either. I don't think he'd criticize the next running back for Chicago. I think he'll compliment him.   12/3/87 *Chicago Sun-Times*

When asked if he went out of his way to make Walter Payton a hero in the Bears last regularly scheduled game of the season   You don't have to go out of your way to make Walter Payton a hero. That's unfair. Walter Payton looks good regardless of what he does.   12/21/87 *Chicago Sun-Times*

I believe I was fortunate enough to deal with the best football player this league has ever seen, and he didn't bend rules. He abided by them. He was a great leader for them. Some of the other guys couldn't carry his jock strap and never will. They want to be catered to. They want to be individuals. They want to get away with not practicing. Here's the best who ever played the game, and if he's not a good example for them, they must be blind.   2/8/88

13

DOUG FLUTIE

THE ACQUISITION OF DOUG FLUTIE

If things were right, we'd probably be a lot more interested. We'll explore it softly for the time being.   10/3/86

There have been a lot of good football players at that position who weren't real tall. If a guy can do other things, you find a way to make sure he can throw the football. I just think he's a talent. I wouldn't have an interest in him at any other position besides quarterback. 10/3/86

The Bears signed Doug Flutie on October 15, 1986. When reporters challenged the logic for acquiring him, Ditka explained It goes back to what he accomplished in college. He did all that with players who are not household names in the NFL, so it must have been him. 10/15/86

It's not like we broke the bank to get him. I like our position.   10/15/86

The acquisition of Doug Flutie brought accusations of disloyalty to the back-up quarterbacks Fuller and Tomczak, particularly from Jim McMahon. Ditka shot back   I haven't given up on anybody. I didn't bring him in to threaten anybody. We're going to take a look and see what happens.   10/16/86

Doug Flutie on Ditka   Ditka thinks I'm a winner. He has a lot of faith in me. I'm happy to have a chance to develop at my own pace. Look at John Elway. He had a terrible year as a rookie and this year he's been fantastic. But everyone knew he had great potential. If Doug Flutie had that kind of year as a rookie, all you would have heard is the "I-told-you-sos. He's too short."   10/15/86

DOUG FLUTIE, BEARS QUARTERBACK _____

Will he play in 1986?   I think he could play, but that would be unfair to him. That's all we'd have to do is put him out there and things not go right for him.   10/31/86

Doug Flutie got his chance to play in the Bears 13–10 victory over the Atlanta Falcons. Flutie narrowly missed connecting for a touchdown pass on the only pass he threw, prompting Ditka to say   I get excited when I see Doug Flutie missing a pass and then getting mad because he didn't get it. It meant something to him.   11/16/86

Ditka promised that Doug Flutie would see action in the Bear–Tampa Bay game even if the Bears were losing. He couldn't resist teasing the media by adding   I may have him hand off the ball five times. That is really what I want to do because it'll drive you guys nuts, make you berserk.   12/4/86

In Flutie's first game he was 2 of 7, throwing a touchdown pass to Walter Payton and running for another touchdown. Ditka couldn't resist commenting   There may be a few sad people [because of Flutie's success]. They'll just have to live with that.   12/8/86

When President Kennedy won, they said he had charisma. This kid has character, charisma, and personality. And he works at it. I've been here five years and he's the only quarterback I've seen who is here early in the morning studying films and who comes back on Wednesday for the game plans early. It'll pay dividends. I see Doug being an excellent, excellent quarterback in the NFL, period.   12/9/86

Flutie was named as the starter for the Bear–Cowboy game. Ditka explained Flutie's role   We ask him not to turn the ball over and to throw the ball downfield when we need that. If you ask me if he can do that, I would say he can do that better than a lot of people playing in this league right now. He just needs a little time.   12/18/86

Flutie quarterbacked the Bears to a 24–10 victory over the Cowboys. A happy Ditka commented   He's a winner. He's got great leadership quality.   12/22/86

The little guy is pretty special. I've thought that for a long time, and the more he plays, the more I know he's pretty special.   12/22/86

It's just like hollering at Bambi. I get letters from schoolteachers all over America telling me I'm not allowed to do that. So I probably won't do that anymore.   12/30/86

Doug Flutie   You like to have a coach have confidence in you. At the same time, it comes with a little responsibility. I feel I let him down. He put me in, and there were some bright spots. He believed in me, but we didn't get the job done. People were jumping all over him for starting me in the play-offs, but I still believe it was the right thing.   5/13/87

Ditka   I did not misjudge Flutie. Maybe other people think I have, within and without the organization. I did not misjudge Doug Flutie. I stand on that and back that and we'll see what the competition is.   4/29/87

Flutie has to work on not overthrowing the ball. And we have to be sure and not put him on the field in compromising positions.   7/21/87

We've had him on a stretching machine for three months, and he's 6'7". A little thin, but he's 6'7". I have elevator shoes in my office that will make him 6'8".   3/19/87

DOUG FLUTIE: 1987 SEASON

Doug Flutie   I sat down with Coach Ditka after the [1986] season and he told me there were times I had an opportunity to run, and I kept my eyes upfield. I think he's right. Because of the situation last year, I wasn't always looking to run, and I didn't react as well as I can. I think the quarterback always has the green light to run.   8/3/87

Doug Flutie   It didn't shock me that they drafted Harbaugh, because Coach Ditka mentioned to me the week before the draft they might. My attitude about it is, either I'm good enough to make it or I'm not, and it doesn't matter how many quarterbacks are here. I'm encouraged by the way I'm throwing the ball now. If I let my athletic ability take over in game situations, and as long as I stand in there and throw the ball well in practice and start to do it consistently, there's not much to worry about.   8/3/87

Ditka   He's trying. But sometimes the ball isn't as accurate as he'd like it to be.   8/5/87

I think Doug's doing OK. He's not knocking the roof out, but the last couple of days he's thrown the ball very well. 8/15/87 *Chicago Sun-Times*

When asked why he hasn't gotten to know Doug Flutie well, Jim McMahon responded Because Doug chooses not to relax with us. 8/20/87 *Chicago Sun-Times*

Does Doug Flutie get the same support from the team that other quarterbacks get? Ditka's response That's the same question people asked me for years about Steve Fuller. It almost appears that way. But everybody is trying the same when he's in the game. 8/20/87

After the Pittsburgh preseason game I thought Doug played pretty good when I looked at the film. He made a couple of mistakes. The ball Keith Ortego dropped, he should have hit him on the money. There was no one in his face. He threw it low, but Keith should still catch the ball. 8/24/87

After the Raider preseason game I thought [Flutie's performance] was good and bad. The name of the game in life is consistency. You've got to be consistent, especially in that position. 9/6/87

TRADED

On October 14, 1987, the Chicago Bears announced that Doug Flutie had been traded to New England for a future draft choice. Flutie decided to cross the picket lines and play for the non-union New England Patriots. I firmly believe in the union and the things they are fighting for, but I saw this as a chance to get to New England and an opportunity that probably wouldn't have happened down the road. 10/14/87 *Chicago Sun-Times*

Flutie on Chicago   I saw the situation in Chicago as not a healthy situation for Doug Flutie to play.   10/14/87 *Chicago Sun-Times*

Responding to reports that some Bears criticized Doug Flutie for crossing the picket lines to play for the Patriots, Ditka commented   I've heard a lot of things. If the people who said them had half as much class as Doug they wouldn't have said those things. He's a classy young man. He'll do fine in life. I have great respect for him as a person. That's much more important than anything he'll ever do in football. I would have done nothing differently with Doug last year. It was a coach's decision, and I've always accepted that responsibility. I'm only disappointed he didn't lead the Bears to victory in the Super Bowl. I probably made a mistake going into camp this year. I kind of put Doug behind the 8-ball by not making him the starting quarterback when camp opened. I don't know why I did that. But you don't tarnish quality. The trade wasn't even our idea. New England wanted him.   10/15/87

Trading Doug Flutie to New England seemed like an admission that acquiring him had been a mistake. Ditka responded   Who says it didn't work out? It doesn't take a Phi Beta Kappa to understand it was the best thing for Doug. And it's probably going to be a good thing for the New England Patriots. It remains to be seen how good a decision it is for the Bears. Contrary to what you experts [the media] think, I haven't eaten crow or backed off one bit. I love Doug Flutie. I love what he stands for and how he plays. Hopefully, in his new situation, people will accept him the way he should be accepted. We made a decision based on what we felt was best for Doug and his situation. He wanted to play football. It didn't look like it was going to happen here.   10/15/87

Joan Flutie, Doug's mom   I'm glad he's home and I knew he'd do well. All he needed was a chance. The Bears seemed to think he had his chance last year. As far as I was concerned, they didn't give him much of a chance. They're McMahon's gang, and I guess they never wanted Doug. All I knew is he was miserable there. He didn't fit in with anybody. It's kind of difficult to go about your daily life when you don't have friends. Doug has never had that problem before in his life. He's never been treated like that before. He just resigned himself to play there if he wanted to play football. Emotionally, he suffered, and we suffered with him long-distance. He needs a lot of praise and self-confidence, and he just got nothing there. Not even from the coaches, not even when he threw a good pass. He may never get to play again [for New England]. They say he's going to be fourth-string. I don't care what happens from now on. He came back home, period. No matter what he does, the people here love him.   10/20/87

Flutie   I had a feeling Jim McMahon would come back. No matter how well I played, it looked like being the Bears No. 3 quarterback was as far as I could go in Chicago.   10/28/87

Flutie   People have a right to their opinions. Some of them have to take the opposite point of view. Whatever the coach wants, they want something else. I never talked about this in Chicago, but when Ditka saw the way I ran his system in practice, he decided to start me in the play-offs. We had the lead until the Redskins threw a couple of touchdown passes and the game turned around. I still believe I could have done the job for the Bears. It's kind of ironic, but adjusting to the system so quickly got me into a win-or-else situation against Washington. When the fans reacted strongly to the loss, I could see there was a lot of pressure on the Bears to make changes for this season.   10/28/87

I have no bitterness toward the Bears or their fans. The time in Chicago was a good experience for me.   10/28/87

14

BEARS CURRENT OFFENSIVE PLAYERS

NEAL ANDERSON

I don't know that we'll ever have a replacement for Walter Payton. I don't think we will. But in such a great year for running backs, we would have been foolish to pass up one as good as Neal Anderson. 4/30/85

He doesn't run around people a whole lot; he runs through them. He can make them miss, but when it's time for impact, he's going to make the most of it.   4/30/85

I told Neal when we talked that we're not looking to replace Payton now. Told him we need him on special teams, which I'm sure he is not overjoyed doing. But I also told him we would fit him in our plans piece by piece.   12/5/86

We haven't even seen him full speed yet. I think the thing is, too, that he runs with such abandon you've got to be sure and hit him when you try and tackle him or else you are going to have a problem bringing him down. He's a slasher.   12/24/86

It's been a hard year for Neal. His recognition has come through how he has played on special teams. If he had started for us, there's no question in my mind he'd have been NFL Rookie of the Year.   12/24/86

I don't think we can ask him to do that again. He's just too good and will be too valuable on offense to make him do those things.   3/19/87

Neal Anderson was asked how he would react to Ditka using intimidation as a motivator. He replied   That won't work with me.   8/17/86

On Anderson as a Fullback   His blocking has got to get a little better, but it will. In one week you can't turn him around and make him a devastating blocker . . . Neal is a bit of a long strider and really doesn't have the quick steps you need at fullback . . . We've got a way to go right now with Neal at fullback. I know he can do it, but right now it's a little foreign to him. I still think it's too early to judge.   8/18/87 *Chicago Sun-Times*

He gives us a dimension at fullback that nobody else in the league has, and that dimension is speed outside.   9/2/87 *Chicago Sun-Times*

When asked who was the better dresser, Anderson replied   It's a toss-up between myself and Mike Ditka. We both have good taste. 10/30/87

Ditka felt that Neal Anderson's injuries would probably keep him out of the first two play-off games of the 1987 season.   After that, I don't know. I have a lot of experts who advocate we go back to the regular two-back offense anyway. They didn't like Neal generating half our offense every week. Got tired of it. Then there was the sympathetic group who said he was too small and was going to get hurt. Of course, they were the people who were right. He did get hurt.   12/29/87

CALVIN THOMAS

Thomas was banned from practice because he was overweight. Ditka explained   We want to make sure he can stay alive. I don't care if his feelings are hurt. What he told me he was going to do in the off-season and what he's done are a lot different. All I've seen him do is eat so far.   5/13/87

[Thomas] told me at the end of last season in a one-on-one conversation that this would be his hardest off-season and that he would report to camp in excellent shape, weighing 235 pounds. That [weighing in at 254 pounds] shows me a guy who really doesn't have his heart into what he's doing. He's a message [to the other players], and it's not a good one.   8/1/87 *Chicago Sun-Times*

Thomas' reply   By the way Ditka tells you guys, I was just waddling around the field . . . If my heart wasn't in it, I wouldn't have made this long trip up here. I can still do the things I've always done. I'm just naturally heavy. But if it means staying on the team, I'll lose weight.   8/2/87 *Southtown Economist*

Ditka's hard line   If he plays well enough, he might have a spot; if not, he's gone. His situation is similar to [defensive lineman Mike] Charles in Miami, who was a very undisciplined person.   8/5/87

I don't know if he'll fit into our plans. That's a guy who shows me he doesn't have his heart into what he's doing. You've got to wonder where his head is. His comfort zone is threatened so much it doesn't even exist.   8/12/87 *Southtown Economist*

Thomas isn't worried   Mike's been known to be like that. He has gotten on other guys when they came to camp, and when they respond to his criticism positively, he backs off.   8/20/87 *Chicago Sun-Times*

Ditka sums up   I like what I see. He's heavy, he's big, but if he can keep fluid off those knees and keep those knees from hurting, he can contribute tremendously to us this year.   8/20/87 *Chicago Sun-Times*

Calvin Thomas is 235 lbs., and that was a darn near impossibility when camp opened. I had a long talk with Calvin and he understood my position.   9/12/87 *Chicago Sun-Times*

With the 1987 season approaching, both Thomas and William Perry reached their assigned weights. Ditka was happy but puzzled.   I really don't know why they did it now, but they did it. If the [fines] scared them, I doubt that. I just think at the time they realized it's the best thing to approach this season the best they can be with their weight down.   9/12/87 *Chicago Sun-Times*

THOMAS SANDERS

Everything I see of him I like. He's a tough kid. He's working all the time. He's going to provide some good competition.   7/26/85

Sanders has played so well, it's unbelievable. He didn't catch the ball last year. He's blocking well now too.   8/17/86

DENNIS GENTRY

Gentry is too valuable. I don't know how we can keep him off the field.   8/14/86

He's explosive. He makes things happen.   8/8/86

Sometimes when they try to kick away from Gentry, they wind up kicking short and we get good field position.   11/15/86

I'd love to have him out there more; he's very valuable. But who do you suggest I take off the field? The coach? Dennis isn't dropping the ball when it's thrown to him. He's looked quick running. It's great now to see all of the things happening for him. He's been so important to us the last five years, it's amazing. Worn a lot of hats and worn them well.   12/11/87

MATT SUHEY

He really complements Walter [Payton] well, and he's a great pass receiver for us. He's also probably as good a blocker as there is in the league. He's an excellent all-around player. The kind we need on this team.   9/8/85

After losing to the Lions for 3 quarters as a result of an ineffective passing game, the Bears switched to a running game, which defeated the Lions 16–13. Ditka's comment   The first statement after the game was when Suhey said, "If it ain't broke, don't fix it." We went ahead and fixed something that isn't broke. We tried to throw instead of run the ball.   12/16/86

SUHEY ON DITKA

If he gets his point over stronger by yelling, that's fine. Mike Ditka is Mike Ditka. If were were winning and he was yelling, everything would be okay. People are searching for things. We've had great game plans. We've had every opportunity to win every game. I can't believe he is keeping us from winning. I think the yelling provides some intensity.   10/16/83

He wants a standard and we have to live up to it. But if you go up and down the line, there's no doubt the players respect Mike Ditka the man.   1/7/86

If you violate things that hurt the progress of the team, there's no question you won't stay in a Bears uniform long. He means what he says. It's not a mind game. He wants a dynasty attitude on the Bears. He wants it to be an attitude that's good for a number of years.   11/12/86

Coach Ditka has a great imagination. It puts a tremendous amount of pressure on a defense when they don't know what formation we are going to run out of.   12/21/86

Should the Bears have run the traditional halfback-fullback offense instead of having Payton and Anderson in the same backfield in 1987? *Suhey's view*   You're asking me to contradict [Ditka's] feelings. I can't do that. We have been productive. I would never contradict that to the press or public. Richard Nixon once said, "You don't go to the bathroom in your living room." You do some things in private.   12/27/87 *Chicago Sun-Times*

MIKE TOMCZAK _____

I have all the confidence in him that I had a year ago. He was forcing the ball to try and look impressive early in camp. He's stopped doing that.   8/17/86

I don't care if he doesn't like me much. The only way someone is going to learn at the position is to be told. Somewhere along the line, coaches quit criticizing quarterbacks, figuring they shouldn't ruffle their feathers or else the coaches might be to blame.   9/2/86

No one said he was gonna do everything perfect. I still think he's got moxie, a lot of talent, and I think he's still going to be a helluva quarterback.   9/15/86

TOMCZAK ON DITKA

He's a nice guy. He warned me Saturday night that if he goes off the deep end and goes schizo on the sidelines, just ignore it.   9/17/86

When told Mike Tomczak was disappointed that the Bears acquired Doug Flutie, Ditka responded   I frankly don't give a damn. Wasn't that a line in a movie?   10/16/86

DITKA ON TOMCZAK, 1987

Mike's hungry.   5/24/87

Tomczak has improved in the off-season.   7/21/87

I think he's more determined this year. He understands what the stakes are. And the stakes are high.   8/5/87

Mike found out there are more important things in the world than women. Mike is a cute kid. If you're a nice-looking guy and you've some talent, you should be able to have some fun in your life. The thing I saw with Mike is that he worked on his mind. His take-charge ability's much better. I feel good with Mike in there.   8/23/87

He seems so much more in control. He feels better about being in the huddle, and the club has responded to him better.   8/16/87

TOMCZAK ON DITKA _____

This year I have to play football. But I'm not the head coach. Sometimes he's not going to be happy and sometimes I'm not. I'm not saying if I'd been in there we would have won the Washington game. Maybe it was some motivation to work harder. Because if that situation arises again, he won't have to second-guess himself or even think about putting someone else in.   8/16/87

If my stock goes up day to day, that's one more feather in my cap. But I can't get complacent about what Coach Ditka says. Sometimes you do get a little lackadaisical and you fall off a notch.   8/3/87

We're communicating a lot better this year. He tells me when he sees a few things in the secondary that I might not get a chance to see. Last year, he chewed my [rear end] out instead of talking to me. We're back on the same page.   8/13/87 *Southtown Economist*

DITKA ON TOMCZAK _____

Mike played awfully well [in the exhibition game against Miami]. He controlled our football team and he was having fun, too.   8/19/87 *Chicago Sun-Times*

After the Pittsburgh preseason game   Mike threw the ball well and put it in tight spots. He's played exceptionally well. Good lord, I don't know how you play any better than that.   8/24/87

I'm more comfortable with him, because I believe the team is more comfortable. Nobody is sitting back and saying, "Well, we're not going to do this, we're not going to do that."   8/24/87

Anybody with two eyes would have to see we would go with Mike [Tomczak]. Those who have eyes, let them see. The kid would have to do a complete flip-flop and go completely backwards not to be the starting quarterback if McMahon wasn't healthy.   8/26/87

After Tomczak completed 8 of 9 for 134 yards in the exhibition game against Pittsburgh   What more could the guy do? Unless he throws it, runs with it, and catches it. I don't care what your name is—you can go [Dan] Fouts, [Vinny] Testaverde, [Phil] Simms, they couldn't have done it any better.   8/28/87 *Chicago Sun-Times*

Tomczak on Ditka   You never know what's going to happen around here. Sometimes you get the starting nod and Jim comes out of the woodwork and says "I'm ready to play." I don't know if Coach Ditka will let that happen. He'll make his decision for the best of the team and I'll respect it either way. I'm not saying it's always fair, but he's been coaching a lot longer than I've been playing.   8/29/87 *Chicago Sun-Times*

Analyzing Tomczak's performance in the Bears loss against St. Louis, Ditka said   He played well. The ball club should have had 23 points when Mike was in there.   9/2/87 *Chicago Sun-Times*

I think Mike's feeling some pressure, but I'm happy with his progress. If he didn't feel any pressure, he wouldn't be human. Here's a kid who basically was a rookie last year. This is a big thing now. He knows from the go that he's going against the best defensive team [the Giants] in football. It's going to be no easy task for him. I don't think he's going to be intimidated by anything that happens, but we have to protect him from taking some shots that might rattle him.   9/12/87 *Chicago Sun-Times*

Last year, Mike really keyed into the receiver a lot without being able to find a second receiver, a third receiver, and outlet man. I don't think he does that now. He's come a long way.   9/13/87 *Chicago Sun-Times*

He's trying to prove something. I don't blame him. I'd try to prove something too.   9/13/87 *Chicago Sun-Times*

Tomczak threw an excellent touchdown pass to Tim Wrightman during the Pittsburgh exhibition game. Ditka was impressed.   He picked the hardest target but he made it. I remember No. 9 [Jim McMahon] doing that a lot, picking the hardest throw and making it.   9/13/87

We have to play football as a team. Mike's the quarterback. Let's give him the best we can and he'll give us the best he's got, and we'll get it done.   9/13/87

The area he improved in the most was mentally, in his self-belief.   9/13/87

I think the great limitations in life we put on ourselves. There's a lot of starting quarterbacks in this league that I'd much rather have Tomczak over. He'll never be an Elway. But no one else will be an Elway, either. He'll never be a Marino. But he's going to be something good in his own right. He's a guy who can develop himself to become a leader and quarterback along the lines of a Roger Staubach. That's not bad.   9/16/87 *Chicago Sun-Times*

TOMCZAK ON DITKA

In Ditka's restaurant during the strike, Mike Tomczak saw Mike Ditka, his wife, and another young man seated at a table. Tomczak to Ditka   I haven't seen your face in a long time, Coach. I miss you.   10/14/87

Ditka   I'd like to introduce you to the quarterback [strike quarterback Mike Hohensee] for the Chicago Bears.   10/14/87

Tomczak to Ditka   Always a pleasure to see you, Mike.   10/14/87

Mike Ditka has said a lot of things to me over the years and he's hurt me, but it's all behind me now. I've seen the worst of him and hopefully, from now on, I'll see the best of him.   10/14/87

Nothing the Bears organization does shocks me. I thought Mike Ditka might like Doug Flutie as a player, but maybe I've erased those thoughts from Coach Ditka's mind. Maybe this paves the way for Hohensee. 10/14/87

DITKA SUMS UP

Will putting McMahon in the second half of the Tampa Bay game affect Tomczak's confidence?   Mike understands; his confidence will be great. Jim Harbaugh will be fine. Steve Fuller will be fine. Doug Flutie is doing fine in New England. Everybody is fine.   10/27/87

He knows that we've got confidence in him as a team and as coaches. He knows that if he makes a mistake, all he's going to be called is a name.   12/10/87 *Chicago Sun-Times*

JIM HARBAUGH

[Drafting Harbaugh] was a sound decision. Down the road he's going to be a very good player.   4/29/87 *Des Plaines Daily Herald*

On Harbaugh at mini-camp   He looked doggone good—everybody looked good. Anyone who says he doesn't have a major-league arm is almost funny.   5/13/87 *Des Plaines Daily Herald*

Jim Harbaugh's dad, Jack, on Ditka   I look at Michigan coach Bo Schembechler and I see Mike Ditka. Both are winners who demand a lot of respect and who respect players who give the work ethic they give. Jim will do that.   4/29/87

HARBAUGH: THE 1987 SEASON _____

I get the feeling Jimmy wants to know everything. He wants to understand everything. That can be a drawback too, but he's a very thorough guy. When he does something out there, he wants to know exactly what happened. How the defense was playing. If he read it right or read it wrong, he wants to know why. That's the only way you're going to learn.   8/9/87

Harbaugh on Ditka   Looking into Coach Ditka's eyes is just like looking into Bo's [Michigan coach Bo Schembechler's] eyes. I see fire and competitiveness. It's real comfortable for me.   8/4/87

In an intra-squad game words were exchanged between Harbaugh and Hampton and Dent. Harbaugh pushed Dent in the face mask. Ditka was happy.   I like that in life. I'm not knocking anybody. I'm saying we're all on the same team for the same reasons, and if that guy can get us to the Super Bowl, I'd sure be on his side. I wouldn't be taking pot shots at him. Harbaugh doesn't pick up the papers every day and read how good these guys are. He's just trying to make a football team and be the best he can be. He forgot to read their press clippings. The Redskins [who beat the Bears in the 1986 play-offs] didn't read our press clippings, either . . . He has a dimension that's going to be tough to defense, because he's willing to run with it and he's smart. He didn't get out of Michigan because he's good-looking. He knows what he's doing.   8/10/87

It's still a little bit of a maze out there to him. But once the maze clears up, he's going to be very capable of putting points up on the board.   8/20/87

Harbaugh's Harbaugh. Even when he does the wrong things, you're going to like him because he can make things happen out there. 8/20/87

Could Harbaugh handle starting in the 1987 opener against the Giants? He could probably handle the football. But he couldn't take me. He's a good young man, and whatever my method is with him, he'll understand it and it'll make him better.   9/2/87

In his first NFL play, Harbaugh was sacked for a 15-yard loss. Harbaugh's view Coach was mad at Mike [Tomczak] about something and he just said get in there. Actually, I spun out and tried to make a big play instead of just stepping up to pass.   11/23/87

Comparing Ditka to Bo Schembechler, Harbaugh commented When it comes to going after officials, Ditka is worse than Bo, except maybe when Bo was younger. He uses every word you can think of. At Denver last week, Ditka went after this one official and spit gum right in his ear.   11/23/87

DITKA ON STEVE FULLER

Supposedly we had no chance to win in Washington with Steve last year, and we got it done. It's not just one man. As long as the supporting cast helps him, he'll do fine.   11/17/85

In the 1984 play-offs, the Bears knocked out the Washington Redskins 23–19. Ditka commented Steve Fuller was super. He's the same as No. 9 [Jim McMahon], a winner. They just do it in different ways. 12/31/84

He's not a dominant guy. He doesn't make a lot of noise. He's all business. He's got a quiet confidence around him.   8/2/85

In the Packer game, Ditka replaced Mike Tomczak with Steve Fuller, who led the Bears to a 25–12 victory. Ditka observed Steve is like a forgotten man. Everybody writes him off. The kid can play football. He stuck some tough passes in there when it counted.   9/23/86

Fuller responded   I haven't felt forgotten. The Bears have always been fair.   9/23/86

When Ditka acquired Doug Flutie during the 1986 season and then drafted Jim Harbaugh, Steve Fuller felt that the coach had lost confidence in him. He remarked   Mike is the one I have to convince, not the players. I think they have the confidence in me.   1/3/87 *Des Plaines Daily Herald*

Ditka's view   With Steve it wasn't so much his technique last year. He had a poor choice of decisions in a couple of instances. But in 1985, in tight game conditions, Steve was outstanding. So you weigh that, too.   7/21/87

Steve Fuller reinjured his shoulder in the 1987 camp.   When I talked to Coach Ditka tonight, his concern was that if I didn't have the surgery now, if I waited four weeks for a chance to play and then was injured again two weeks later, I'd be in the same situation. He left it up to me. At this point, I really don't know what I'll do. [Steve Fuller was placed on the disabled list.]   8/8/87

WILLIE GAULT

We think Willie can have the same impact on the Bears as Bob Hayes had on the Cowboys and James Lofton had on the Packers. We're looking to become a fast football team.   4/27/83

Now I have no excuse for not winning this year, none at all.   8/28/83

I love his attitude. Nobody's perfect, but he's worked every practice. He's going every play.   8/4/85

When you run Willie across the field, it's really tough to cover him man-to-man.   9/29/86

We have to get the ball to Willie. If we get 200 yards passing, I'd be the happiest guy in the world. If we can run for 175 or 200 and pass for the same, we'd be a good team.   11/10/86

I like him because he's worked hard in practice and I like what he's done in the game as a blocker. He catches the ball better.   1/3/87

He has impressed me since Platteville. He has worked tremendously hard to dispel the image of being a trackman and not a football player. He proved to us in two play-off games and the Super Bowl that he was the reason we were able to throw the football.   1/28/86

Gault on Ditka   Jim [McMahon] has boosted my confidence. So did some other teammates and Coach Ditka. They've stuck by me. I feel comfortable here.   10/1/85

GAULT: THE 1987 SEASON

Watching films, I've never seen Willie work harder. He works hard in practice, too. The thing that's encouraging, that people don't see, is Willie is blocking as well now as any receiver in football. Good things are happening for him, and it's good to see because he's worked very hard. He has a gift of speed, but he has other gifts, too. They're starting to surface.   11/19/87

How does Willie Gault compare with premier receivers Anthony Carter and Jerry Rice?   Except for number of catches, he's as good as anybody in football. He's a better blocker than [Rice and Carter] will ever be on their best day. If [Rice and Carter] put real big pads on, [Gault's] a better blocker by accident.   12/8/87 *Chicago Sun-Times*

DENNIS McKINNON

He gives you everything he's got. It may not be enough sometimes, but he gives it his all. A coach's delight, period.   1/5/85

There are players and coach's players and other players. He's a fan's player and a coach's player. He goes across the middle and knows he's going to get hit, so he figures, he might just as well catch the ball.   9/18/85

He's one of our best football players.   1/5/85

He's the most unselfish player we have.   9/18/85

McKinnon on Ditka   Mike hates it when you do everything right and get yourself wide open and then you drop the ball. He hates that more than anything.   9/18/85

Dennis McKinnon sat out the 1986 season with a knee injury.   People ask, "How are you going to get your job back?" I say, "Be real." Mike Ditka will welcome me back with open arms. I want to play with reckless abandon.   10/25/86

Mike Ditka was optimistic about McKinnon's chances of coming back.   He hasn't started running yet. When he starts running, we'll find out more about him. I think Dennis McKinnon will be back. I think he'll play. I think he'll play very well.   1/5/87 *Des Plaines Daily Herald*

McKINNON: THE 1987 SEASON

On Dennis McKinnon's recovery from knee surgery: He's got to be able to do this every day, run full speed. If he can run like that, it's fine.   8/6/87 *Chicago Sun-Times*

After the Miami preseason game   Dennis did well Sunday, except for the dropped ball. He ran well and blocked well. I thought he should have caught the ball. But it's all new to him. He's been away a year. That's the first contact he's had since the Super Bowl in game conditions, and that's tough. You can understand [the dropped ball] when the first pass thrown to him is in traffic, slanting in, and he doesn't hold on to it. But that's no excuse either.   8/19/87

After a dramatic 94-yard punt return against the Giants, the longest in Bears history   It's the best return I've ever seen. Ever. And I've seen a lot of them. He cut through everybody; should have been tackled twice, and after he came up from being on one hand. I didn't think he could outrun that other guy. He's not supposed to catch it on the 6 [yard line] like that.   9/16/87

Before the Bears' division championship victory over the Vikings, Dennis McKinnon criticized the Viking team. After the game, Ditka was full of praise.   I have to admire McKinnon. He backed everything he said up. He played well. Just ask the guys who got in his way. He got knocked down a few times but he also knocked them down. And he caught the ball in clutch situations. I'm happy for him.   12/8/87

RON MORRIS

Great ability to catch the ball. Runs good routes and is able to escape the bump and run and has good speed.   8/15/87

Morris on Ditka   Right now things are looking real good for me. The coaches like what they see in me. Coach Ditka and Coach [Greg] Landry tell me good things all the time.   8/19/87

On Morris after the Pittsburgh preseason game   We only threw him the ball once. But he hustled out there on his blocks and went after people.   8/24/87

Commenting on the limited number of passes thrown to Ron Morris   They [the quarterbacks] are just not throwing to him as much, evidently. We don't design the routes to throw the ball to Ron Morris or Willie Gault or anybody else. We design it for them to run the pattern and for the quarterback to read the defense.   11/28/87 *Chicago Sun-Times*

MORRIS & McKINNON

I feel we have two starters at that position [flanker]. We just named Ron because Ron was the healthier of the two throughout camp and worked more.   9/12/87 *Chicago Sun-Times*

THE BEAR WIDE RECEIVERS

We have three capable receivers [Gault, Morris, McKinnon] who can really burn people. With Dennis Gentry coming on, that position will help us. 9/6/87

CAP BOSO

The Bears cut Riley Walton and then picked up Cap Boso from the Cardinals after he was waived. Ditka explained   He blocked some of our better guys off their feet [in the Bear-Cardinal exhibition game]. He'll be fine. We needed somebody who was a better blocker than we had. As far as catching the ball, he'll catch the little shake patterns and things we do.   9/10/87

On Boso's strained tendon   They shot him up before the game and again after the game, with cortisone. But he's hurting. We're lean at that position, but Emery Moorehead did a good job in the game.   9/17/87

Boso made a couple of key catches in the Tampa Bay game. Ditka commented   He's not the swiftest guy in the world. But he moves. Emery's still our starter. But Cap's got a chance to play a lot more football and I'm gonna alternate him in there some.   10/27/87 *Chicago Sun-Times*

After four catches in the Kansas City game, one for his first NFL touchdown, reporters were apparently more excited about Boso's performance than Ditka.   What do you want me to do, give him balloons? I've got no balloons. He's tough, he's going to be a good football player. He's still learning. He made some mistakes, but he knows how to catch it and have some fun out there.   11/2/87 *Chicago Sun-Times*

MOOREHEAD AND BOSO

After the Lions game   They are complementing each other well. I was happy to see Emery make a couple catches. Our tight ends could be more high-profile receivers, but we have such good outside receivers we use them mostly for blocking. But I'm happy the way they are coming along.   11/24/87

TIM WRIGHTMAN ON DITKA

. . . [Ditka's] not going to die of having a lot of stress built up inside. 11/17/85

Jim Dooley was here when Mike Ditka was a player, and he says Ditka used to complain if he didn't get the ball thrown to him at least five, six times a game. Maybe Mike is waiting for Emery Moorehead or me to come to him and start yelling about it like he did.   9/13/87

I worked hard in the off-season to improve some things Mike Ditka wants to see out of the tight end. He really wants someone who can block, and when he makes a point of saying it over and over, you're smart to work on it. I think I'm finally coming of age.   9/1/87 *Chicago Sun-Times*

DITKA ON KEITH ORTEGO _____

We don't have anybody who catches inside like that kid does. It takes a little courage to go in there.   10/6/86

I think Keith will have to have surgery on his shoulder. I think he's got a bad shoulder like Jim [McMahon] had, and I think he'll have to have that done.   1/5/87 *Des Plaines Daily Herald*

Elaborating on his reasons for selecting Keith Ortego over Glenn Kozlowski for the last receiver spot on the 1987 Bears roster   I'd think back to last year's Minnesota game, or Green Bay, and realize how important Keith was. I haven't seen Koz do that. Not that he wouldn't. He's a tough kid and to get as far back as he did from his knee injury is remarkable.   9/9/87

TOM THAYER ON DITKA _____

I think he was putting a lot of undue pressure on himself for things that couldn't be helped and putting pressure on people that just couldn't be helped in critical situations. The more we played and the more success we were having, the more he relaxed. And the more he realized that people were really trying.   1/3/87 *Des Plaines Daily Herald*

TIM WRIGHTMAN ON DITKA _____

I didn't know who Ditka was when the Bears drafted me, beyond being head coach. So he wasn't someone I tried to emulate. I always wanted to play like Dave Casper [former Raider tight end]. But it doesn't hurt me, in trying to make the team, for the media to say I'm a Ditka kind of player.   8/28/86

DITKA ON THAYER

After a 1987 intrasquad game   He made some bad decisions. My goodness, if he would have played a whole game he probably would have had six [penalties]. That's poor. I'm sure everybody's going to be offended when I say something to these guys, but we don't teach it, we don't condone it. If he doesn't play better we'll put somebody else in there, it's that simple.   8/9/87 *Chicago Sun-Times*

JAY HILGENBERG ON DITKA

The coaches and the organization have been behind me. They instilled the confidence in me. Ditka said opportunity doesn't come very often, so you've got to take it when you've got the chance. That's what we try to do.   1/13/86

Ditka's the greatest motivator in the world. He puts that fear of your job out there all the time, and that's the motivating factor.   7/3/87 *Chicago Sun-Times*

The most stressful time is the Monday morning meeting with Mike Ditka. Against Denver, we gain 500 yards and he's all over us the next day. We give up eight sacks against Detroit and we have a nice, quiet meeting Monday with no problems. He had us all wondering as we were walking out the door.   11/25/87

JIMBO COVERT ON DITKA

Coach Ditka comes from Aliquippa, right across the river from me in

Conway [Pennsylvania]. They always said he was the greatest player
to ever come out of Beaver County, and that includes Tony Dorsett
and Joe Namath.   4/27/83

He tells us, "Hey, you're no different than teams that win the Super
Bowl or go to the play-offs every year. You've got the same personnel,
the same talent. You're just the same as them. All you have to do is
go out and beat 'em." He makes you believe because he's been there
before. He's a winner.   1/6/85

DITKA ON COVERT

*During the 1987 Lions game, Jimbo Covert's shoulder popped out of
the socket three times. Ditka commented*   Covert's having a lot of
problems. It's hard for him to pass block, and that's the thing that Jim
does.   11/23/87 *Chicago Sun-Times*

DITKA ON KURT BECKER

There's a certain kind of people who play hard for me. I was very
pleased with Kurt Becker's attitude out there. He plays hard. He doesn't
take any crap off anybody. We've got to have people like that.
12/28/87 *Chicago Sun-Times*

DITKA ON PAUL BLAIR

His improvement from last year to this year is unbelievable. It's like
night and day. Paul can be a stabilizing factor for us on the offensive
line.   8/21/87

*With an injury to Bears all-pro tackle Jimbo Covert, Paul Blair started
against the Vikings in Minnesota, facing star Viking defensive end Chris
Doleman. Ditka commented*   I'll tell you, he went downtown and

fought him. You've got to love him for that. [Offensive line coach] Dick Stanfel told him during the week, "This is when you find out whether you can play in this league." He blocked him, he can play.   12/8/87 *Chicago Sun-Times*

KEITH VAN HORNE ON DITKA

Told that Mike Ditka had said he could play better, Van Horne explained   You just got to let that kind of stuff role off your back and do what you've always done. Sure, it has some effect, but you can't let it bother you. You just have to go out and play as hard as you can, and I plan on starting.   5/13/87

DITKA ON VAN HORNE

Keith's been in the league five or six years now and he should emerge as a top tackle in this league. He can play better with his size and strength. This is the year he has to do it or we are going to get better at that position some other way.   5/17/87 *Des Plaines Daily Herald*

DITKA ON LEW BARNES

Lew played college ball for Oregon. When his first year with the Bears started badly, Ditka joked   Lew must be longing for Oregon.   8/7/87

Lew Barnes on Ditka   At first I didn't understand what Coach Ditka meant [referring to longing for Oregon]. Getting used to Coach Ditka takes a while. His comments did motivate me, but it was scary. You don't know what to expect. You don't know if you're going to be sent home after the next game or not. This game is supposed to be fun, but we're responsible for putting food on a lot of families' tables. You can't risk having someone out there who is inconsistent.   8/7/87 *Southtown Economist*

Ditka on Barnes   Last year [1986] Lew was good. The only thing wrong was, Lew got into a slump and forgot to catch the ball. He was open—look at the key plays at Detroit and Houston. He had plays last year, game-breakers, where he didn't hold onto balls that Jim McMahon threw well. Now Lew is holding onto the ball. And as for his explosion coming off the ball and catching it, I see no problem with that. I see him being a much bigger threat as a return man this year.   8/7/87

Lew Barnes broke his leg in a collision with Maurice Douglass. Ditka philosophized   A freak accident. It happens to every team. You just go on.   8/26/87

MAURY BUFORD

If any kicker can keep his confidence and keep taking a whack at it, that is all you can ask, because Soldier Field's a tough place to punt, with the wind and all.   11/21/86

During 1987's first two preseason games, Ditka was unhappy with the Bears punting   Is Ray Guy [former Raider punter] retired? Maybe I could get him out of retirement.   8/25/87

After trading reserve guard Stefan Humphries to the Denver Broncos for punter Bryan Wagner, Ditka explained   [The trade was made] to give Stefan an opportunity to play. He wasn't going to play regular here. We didn't do it to bring a punter to challenge anybody. We're not mad at Maury.   8/26/87

After the Bears–St. Louis exhibition game   I was very impressed with Wagner. He took the ball against the wind 46 yards. The next ball he had against the wind was good, too. Excellent hang time, over 4.5 seconds. The ball Buford kicked traveled 37 yards, bounced back 6, and was in the air 3.4 seconds. With the wind. So what can I tell you? Wagner's stock went up tremendously.   9/2/87

After being cut, Maury Buford offered his own explanation   I was trying a little bit too hard. Coach Ditka stresses consistency.   9/8/87

Ditka's view   I don't know what the future holds. There might be a day when he's back here.   9/8/87

BRYAN WAGNER

Ditka expressed dissatisfaction with Bryan Wagner's punting during the 1987 Denver game.   We've got Maury [Buford] in the back of our minds. We're going to stay with Bryan. His average was fine the other night, but the ball only went 30 yards in the air. He's got to kick it better. Of all the punters we've seen, Bryan has the best hang time, but it's not happening in the game. I have confidence in Bryan. I want him to know you have a job when you earn a job, and if you don't earn it anymore, then somebody else is going to get a look.   11/20/87

Wagner has not done a good job. I'm not very happy with him right now. Not happy with his punting or kickoffs. He finally punted one at the end of the game Sunday when we needed it. But he's not punting well overall. He could be the best kickoff man in the league. But it seems like under pressure the ball goes everywhere but where it's supposed to go.   12/8/87

TOMMY BARNHARDT

The Bears' third punter of the 1987 season was Tommy Barnhardt. After the Raiders game, Ditka commented   He hit most of them with his knee. The object is to hit them with your foot. He was a little high on most of them, but he'll be okay.   12/29/87

KEVIN BUTLER

I told you about Kevin Butler. He has the ability to be in the top one

or two in the league. You gotta love him. Nothing bothers him.
10/14/85

He gets paid to kick the football, and if he doesn't kick it well enough,
we have to find somebody else to kick it.   12/1/86

. . . I have all the confidence in the world in Kevin. He made his last
kick and that's the only one I'm going to remember, and it's the only
one you should remember too.   9/15/86

*What did Ditka tell him after his mistake in the Cleveland game? Said
Butler*   You can't print what he had to say.   9/15/86

15

BEARS CURRENT DEFENSIVE PLAYERS

MIKE SINGLETARY

He's a great example of what a football player should be. He works harder than anyone we have on the team. He's a joy to be around.   1/1/86

Mike got up and was telling the defense what they had to do to stop the Rams. By the time they were done, they had turned over tables and chairs.   1/14/86

Mike Singletary told me early last week there was no question in his mind we were going to shut out the 49ers. Pretty big statement to make, and yet they [the defense] held them to three points.   10/15/85

Singletary on Ditka   We know what Mike wants. We know what every man on this team wants.   10/13/86

In the NFL you've got to wear so many hats as a head coach. It's so hard to come out there and have one set mind. I often wondered how I would coach a guy who, if you look at him, might moon you, and another guy who, if you look at him, might say "Good morning." Mike's not perfect, but I guarantee you, none of us is. He really does a great job. He's one of the greatest motivators I've ever met. He fits the moment.   11/12/86

Ditka on Singletary   I've always said the most successful people are the proudest people. I think Mike has a great amount of pride. He wants to be the best. He pushes himself to be the best. From a coach's standpoint, that's an ideal situation.   9/13/87 *Chicago Sun-Times*

Kudos for Mike Singletary after the 1987 Lions game   When the other people around him aren't playing well, it's hard to see sometimes because he's a product of a team defense. Mike has played really well. He does a lot of good things for us out there.   11/24/87 *Chicago Sun-Times*

GARY FENCIK ON DITKA

. . . as far as I and a lot of veterans feel, we have a lot of faith in Mike Ditka.   10/16/83

Ditka provides the transition to the Bears' past.   11/26/84

Mike Ditka provided the bridge between what the Bears represented in their glory years and what they are today. A lot of players had really lost a sense of what the tradition of the Bears was. I actually wrote a letter to George Halas saying that. He [Halas] had not visited us in the seven years I had been with the Bears. Mike did us a great service in telling us how the Bears [once] were.   1/6/85

We had a great guy before in Neil Armstrong [Ditka's predecessor]. I don't think he received the support from the organization he should have. But Mike has really kicked around some people and demanded a lot of us. I think professional players tend to get a little bit lazy when they don't have someone making certain they're doing their best.   1/6/85

He's always said that if we won the Super Bowl, he'd wear that ring forever. We don't have to hear about 1963 anymore. Now people can talk about this year.   1/28/86

He came in here and kicked some butts. He let us know that you don't have to like your head coach, but as long as he gets you to the Super Bowl, that's what he's supposed to do.   1/6/85

Mike Ditka and I probably are very similar in that we both make comments and don't realize the impact it has on the person we're directing the comments to. It's probably our ethnic background.   1/6/87

DITKA ON FENCIK

Gary Fencik talks too much. He's got a big mouth. If he doesn't like it, he ought to come and see me and turn in his uniform.   12/17/86

Gary says things at times that irritate me. I'm sure I say things that irritate him.   1/5/87 *Des Plaines Daily Herald*

I read all the things people say—that he's getting older and his speed isn't there. I watch the films. I don't see that. I see him playing very, very good. He's been excellent.   1/5/87 *Des Plaines Daily Herald*

FENCIK, 1987

Fencik responds to his demotion from starting safety position   I had some very candid talks with Vince Tobin and Mike Ditka after the [1986 season]. I recognize what I have to do to keep my job, and I worked harder this off-season. I feel the best I've felt in the last three or four years. It's always painful to be demoted. It was hard emotionally to accept, but intellectually I knew it was probably the right decision. I look back at how many good things have happened and how many years I've been in the lineup for every down, and I didn't think it was worth making a big fuss over.   8/6/87 *Chicago Sun-Times*

Ditka on Fencik's new role as a back-up   I truthfully have a very high regard for him, but you have to be realistic. If people don't start for us, they back up, and back-up people must be full-time special teams players. We've got to get better help for special teams and it's got to be the back-up people whether they're young or old or whatever. 8/26/87 *Chicago Sun-Times*

Fencik's view   I worked very hard in the off-season. If I had thought that after last year there would be the changes I see now, I'm sure my thinking might have been different. I would have retired six months ago.   8/26/87 *Chicago Sun-Times*

DITKA'S LAST WORD

Fencik's absence is not the problem. If we feel he should be in there, he'll be in there.   11/20/87

Will Ditka cut Gary Fencik and activate Shaun Gayle?   It would be something I don't want to do. But sometimes you do things you don't want to do. Right now I don't see that as the decision. They both can contribute.   10/30/87 *Chicago Sun-Times*

OTIS WILSON

After a Bears–Raiders game   Otis is the guy who has the fire. I don't know anybody who played any harder than Otis.   12/23/84

WILSON VS DITKA, 1987

Ditka and Wilson exchanged words at half-time during the Bears come-from-behind victory over the Chiefs. Wilson's view   Mike said a few things that I didn't like and I said a few things he didn't like. He told me to go home and I said, "I'll go home."   11/5/87 *Chicago Sun-Times*

Did Ditka mean he was finished forever?   That's what he told me when I walked out the door. He said I'll never play anywhere else.   12/31/87

DITKA'S RESPONSE

He's a liar.   12/31/87

It's something that I think has blossomed into a misunderstanding. Hopefully we can get it straightened out tomorrow, because he is a very important part of our football team.   12/31/87 *Chicago Sun-Times*

It starts out as a very calm conversation. All of a sudden, it gets heated up. One guy hollers, and another guy hollers, and one thing leads to another.   1/1/88

Sometimes we don't take the time to communicate. I take the blame for those things. I don't ever put that on the players. It's all worked out, in the family.   1/1/88

Otis Wilson sums it up   Merely a case of two misunderstandings.
1/1/88

AL HARRIS _____

He's too big right now. He couldn't get in this room. He'll squeeze the
other players off the field.   4/24/87

*Ditka wanted to select a first-round defensive end in the 1987 draft,
but the Bears selected quarterback Jim Harbaugh instead. Said Ditka*   I
was pretty strong [in insisting on a defensive end]. But the only thing
that made me ease that a little is that we think Al Harris can play hard
and put some competition up for our other guys. We want to find out
how good he can play, and he wants to find out. I think he can be
a good one.   4/29/87 *Chicago Sun-Times*

On switching Al Harris from linebacker to defensive end in 1987   His
pass rush is getting better. Al is doing pretty good. He's a big guy now;
he weighs 278. His quickness is 278. What's that on a scale to 10? A
five.   8/16/87 *Chicago Sun-Times*

After the 23–10 Bears/Green Bay win in Soldier Field   Al Harris played
awfully well. Al just plugs along doesn't say much and gets the job done.
You've got to like that.   11/30/87 *Chicago Sun-Times*

Al Harris   Coach Ditka and I have talked, and there's more of a need
for a defensive end than a linebacker. The main thing is, I want to
get on the field and make a contribution.   5/17/87 *Des Plaines Daily
Herald*

DAN HAMPTON _____

Hampton explained dumping water on Ditka when the Bears clinched the Central Division championship in 1984   Somebody had to show him the players were happy and joyous. I hope he took it as it was intended. We'll find out later.   11/26/88

Ditka's response   The boys had their fun, they're entitled to it. 11/26/84

Dan Hampton   Like Coach Ditka says, everyone has a perception of us. We're 9–0. We're the bad guys. We're the Monsters of the Midway or we're the Mouths of the Midway. It doesn't matter. They have to do their talking on the football field. Up until now, no one can stop us because we're playing good, sound football. We don't do a lot of cheap tactics or a lot of crazy things.   11/5/85

DITKA ON DAN HAMPTON
AND STEVE McMICHAEL _____

They busted their butts, and in that heat it wasn't easy. They didn't take any plays off and it really is encouraging when you see an all-out effort like they made. You've got to take your hats off to them.   9/30/86

More on Hampton   It doesn't matter where he plays. We're that much better when Dan is on the field.   1/8/86

I think it's his best year [1987] I've ever seen in the last five that I've been here.   1/2/87 *Chicago Sun-Times*

Dan Hampton is a man's man.   12/6/82

Hampton was charged with a 15-yard penalty for tossing his football helmet off the field as a reaction to bad officiating during the Tampa Bay game. Ditka temporarily benched him. Said Hampton   I wasn't embarrassed by it. I'd been frustrated all day by the lack of officiating. The [the Buccaneer offensive linemen] were getting away with murder. I'd been held, my face mask grabbed, and on that play [a Reggie Phillips interception] I was tackled. Ditka told me what I did was selfish. In a way it was, and Ditka's the coach and he can do what he wants. But I didn't know it was a penalty to throw your helmet. Maybe that's a penalty and being tackled by an offensive lineman isn't. I guess I have to learn the rules.   9/21/87

RICHARD DENT

You can go back the 20 years I've been around and be hard-pressed to find a defensive end play any better in a big game [the Bears–Giants play-off game] than Richard Dent played.   1/7/86

Dent on Ditka   I don't think we have a problem. It's the same as ever with us. We speak, and we say some good things and bad things to each other. I know what I can do and what I can't.   10/18/86

Is Dent in Mike Ditka's doghouse?   I'm not a dog and I have my own house.   11/1/86

DITKA VS DENT, 1987

Robert has a little boo-boo. He didn't get enough respect as Richard Dent, so he's Robert now. He gets those little nicks, and he gears it way down to a walk.   8/15/87

Dent told reporters he was offended by some of Ditka's comments during the strike but didn't remember what upset him.   It goes in one ear and out the other.   10/27/87 *Chicago Sun-Times*

Ditka called some players prima donnas during the strike. Dent's view There were some guys who didn't feel good about it. I didn't feel good about it. But it's over, said and done with. We go on to other things. Words don't hurt anybody.   10/27/87

I don't think I'm undisciplined. I've probably never been offside [in the Denver game] that many times since I've been playing. We were getting terrible breaks. On a crucial play with 40 seconds left, the Broncos jump offside and they [the officials] won't attempt to reach in their back pockets.   11/19/87

Always, when things don't go well, the finger's pointed at me. I guess I'm the finger guy.   11/19/87

Ditka, after Dent was offsides several times during the Denver game He hurt us more than he helped us.   11/19/87

Dent When we lose, I'm the target. When we win, nothing is said about what I did.   11/19/87

Ditka Reputations come and go. People remember the last time at bat. Successful people who relax become mill-of-the-run.   11/19/87

Dent I think I've been playing well. I don't think I'm playing poor. The year's not over, so I can't evaluate it.   11/19/87

It would be different if I wasn't getting close. I know I'm in the thick of things. I don't feel like my game's off. Words and names don't bother me at all.   11/19/87

MORE DITKA VS DENT _____

After the Detroit game   Where's Robert? I've got a game ball for him.   11/23/87

He played like Richard Dent can play. Well, I guess he showed me.   11/23/87

Dent   The Coach's comments, they don't make me play any harder. Do I feel like I get the proper respect? If my mother wanted me to be Robert, then I wouldn't be Richard.   11/23/87

I felt very embarrassed by being called out of my name. It was something negative on my mind. I don't care who I work for, I like to be respected. I know I'm a classy ballplayer and I like to be treated like one. Mike has to be able to get closer to his players. He has to find a better way of motivating his players, especially me. That's the only way to get the best out of everybody.   4/1/88 *Chicago Sun-Times*

Richard Dent was awarded a game ball for his defensive play in the Lions game. Said Ditka   Richard played like Richard Dent is capable of playing. He knows where I'm coming from.   11/23/87 *Chicago Sun-Times*

Did Ditka's criticism inspire him to play better in the Lions game? Dent replied   He changes his opinion every week. What I did today is nothing new at all.   11/23/87 *Chicago Sun-Times*

Why does Ditka single him out for criticism? Said Dent   It's always me . . . been that way as long as I've been here. Is he messing with my mind? Nobody messes with my mind. I'm just out there to do my best. I did last week. I did this week. This week, no doubt about it, we had to have this game.   11/23/87

The history you have to live up to is a big test, and having a guy like Coach Ditka around makes it tough.   11/23/87 *Chicago Sun-Times*

Ditka's frustration   We expect production. We pay our players pretty well, not as well as Seattle pays some of its players. I don't know if you can motivate a guy like that [Dent]. The greatest motivator is personal pride.   12/19/87 *Chicago Sun-Times*

DAVE DUERSON

When a Detroit kicker appeared to be showing up the Bears, Ditka gave Duerson a surprising order. Said Duerson   He told me, "Go get him." So I got him. I never had that assignment before. Yeah, I was baffled.   10/17/83

Ditka's view   I told Duerson to go out there and take out the kicker. That's part of football.   10/17/83

More on "Go get him"   What actually was the matter with it? There was not a thing the matter with it. It's a football play that's been done from day one. The man wears pads and he's coming downfield. Duerson did not hit him first off; he hardly touched him. The kid put on an act that could have won an Academy Award.   10/18/83

On Dave Duerson   He has the best nose for the ball on our defense.   9/8/85

I think he'd like to prove to some people with other teams that he's the great football player we know he is and some people never thought he was or would be.   9/15/86

. . . the best strong safety in football.   5/17/87 *Des Plaines Daily Herald*

TODD BELL _____

After the Bears Super Bowl victory, Ditka had a message for Todd Bell, who sat out the season in a contract dispute. Ditka said   I hope Todd Bell was watching today and will come back. He is one of the greatest players I ever saw. We love him and I wish he had been with us on this great day.   1/27/86

Todd had a disappointing year in my opinion. He came in late because of his contract and never really became a part of this football team. I think he'll need to approach the game a little bit differently in terms of attitude and asserting himself physically and mentally and conforming to what we're trying to do.   5/17/87 *Des Plaines Daily Herald*

After the 1987 Denver game   Todd has not played as well as we hope he would play. He hasn't played badly, but you expect certain people to play at a championship level.   11/18/87

Before the Packers game in Soldier Field, Ditka and Todd Bell met to discuss how he was playing. Said Todd   There was concern about my All-Pro play on Ditka's part. He went to [defensive coordinator] Vince Tobin, and Tobin came to me Thursday. He told me Ditka was saying he was concerned over my play, my emotions. I wanted to talk to Ditka about this. He seemed like he thought I wasn't playing like I did in 1984, my All-Pro year. So I went right from Tobin's office to Ditka's. Ditka said to me, "Regardless of how you do it, I want you to do it full-tilt, all the way." And I agree with him. It wasn't one of those meetings where he was chewing me out, or I was trying to get my point across. It was just coming together and trying to get an understanding for what was going on. It just made me more convinced to go ahead and lay the chips on the table, to let things go.

I dedicated myself this week to getting that old form back. I put my ears back, so to speak, and went all-out today. I was able to make some plays, but there were a couple of plays I could have done better on. But I'm on track right now. I'm going in the right direction.   11/30/87

Ditka on Bell's role in the Bears victory over the Packers in Soldier Field We didn't put as much coverage responsibility on him, and I think that's important with Todd. Sometimes you take a guy's natural aggressiveness away when you give him too many things to do. Sunday he was able to use his talent a little more and be more aggressive. 12/4/87 *Chicago Sun-Times*

STEVE McMICHAEL

Steve is the kind of guy who will play on one leg if he has to.   12/29/85

. . . I'll tell you who's playing good. Steve McMichael. He just lines up and goes. He brings a lunch bucket and goes to work. Starts at noon, and he doesn't stop until the whistle goes. That's what it's all about.   10/1/85

He has fun with it. He likes coming every day and getting it on. He aggravates a lot of our people in practice since he does all week what he does Sunday. He has a good appreciation about who he is and what he's doing. I had Steve on my TV show the other day and wasn't even sure what he said. But the people laughed.   10/8/86

Does McMichael have the ideal make-up for a football player? All depends what era you mean. Nineteen twenty-five and he'd be right in there. He's a good ol' boy.   10/8/86

McMICHAEL ON DITKA

Ditka is our constant. He keeps us together. People seem surprised by how he acts sometimes and I don't know why they are. I know how he'll react every time. Mellow coach means mellow players. I hope he keeps getting on our butts the same as always. He expects the best. I do, too.   10/8/86

You know, when I came here, we had some players who felt they didn't have to give it that extra effort. We had that kind of attitude in abundance. But Mike Ditka got rid of all of them. You can take all the geniuses with computers and chalk talks and films and stick it. You got to have people who want to play hard. It's Mike's team. It's Mike's baby.   10/14/85

If I became a coach, chances are I'd be the same way [Ditka is]. 10/28/87 *Chicago Sun-Times*

I think I'm him reincarnated. Everything I stand for is his attitude. I am the same kind of football player he was. I love the guy.   10/28/87 *Chicago Sun-Times*

Mike is a great motivator. He plays mind games and they work. Every business in America is founded on that principle—the boss motivating his workers to do their job.   10/28/87 *Chicago Sun-Times*

Have some players lost confidence in Ditka?   He should get rid of them. It's his team. But losing confidence in the head coach is a bunch of crap. When you're out there, you're playing for yourself first. You do your job to the best of your ability and get the most out of it.   2/4/88

He's the boss of this team and everybody should realize that. His philosophy and emotions about football all are sound.   2/4/88 *Chicago Sun-Times*

Mike Ditka always said, "If you guys are playing for the money, you're stupid."   2/7/88

DITKA ON McMICHAEL _____

McMichael played an outstanding game in the division championship against the Vikings, leading the defensive line in stopping the Vikings four times from the 1 yard line late in the game. Ditka praised McMichael's point total for the game.   I never heard of anyone scoring 39 points. He made two of the four plays on the goal-line stand at the 1. He was the reason they ran away from the middle on fourth down.   12/8/87

DITKA ON HAMPTON AND McMICHAEL _____

Reportedly, in 1986 Dan Hampton and Steve McMichael were feuding over a commercial with William Perry. Ditka had some advice.   They shouldn't let things like that bother them. That's like letting wives come between friendships. That's stupid, too, and I've seen that happen. Friends are hard to find; you can find a wife anywhere.   11/22/87 *Chicago Sun-Times*

MAURICE DOUGLASS _____

I like Mo. I like the way he dresses.   11/27/86

Ditka was told that Maurice Douglass was employed as a male stripper in the off-season.   I thought he was a dancer, I didn't know he was . . . you know . . . Some's got it, some don't.   8/5/87 *Chicago Sun-Times*

On starting Maurice Douglass in the Lion game   I see good things in Maurice Douglass. I want to see if he can make them work in a game like he can make them work in practice.   11/21/87 *Chicago Sun-Times*

He's more than a pretty face, gang.   11/23/87 *Chicago Sun-Times*

Douglass' reply   I hope he means I've got a little bit of talent.   10/23/87 *Chicago Sun-Times*

Mo Douglass is a football player. He played good man-to-man coverage, he banged people around. He's a tough little booger.   11/23/87 *Chicago Sun-Times*

After the Lions game   I really enjoyed watching Maurice Douglass. He responded to a challenge, and that's what you've got to do in life.   11/24/87 *Chicago Sun-Times*

What does Ditka think of Douglass' part-time career as a stripper? Whatever you do in life, do what you do the very best you can do it. Martin Luther King said it, if a street sweeper were to sweep streets like Michelangelo painted, then that's what he should do.   11/24/87 *Chicago Sun-Times*

Douglass played well in his first start against the Lions. Ditka said   I really, really enjoyed watching Douglass. He's like a man who said "I have a job to do, here's the guy I cover." He got in their face and bumped him. You might have caught the ball a little on Mo, but it would have had to be a perfect throw. He was on them. He responded to a challenge.   11/24/87

Ditka was further impressed by Douglass' play against the Raiders.   We had the best bumps on receivers that we've had all year. That No. 37, he dresses funny, but he's a football player.   12/28/87 *Chicago Sun-Times*

MIKE RICHARDSON _____

I doubt that he'll be with us. We've seen neither hide or hair of him since that last football game. That's an indication that I don't think he'll be around. It will be a very long shot for us to sign him.   8/2/87 *Southtown Economist*

Mike missed a lot of time and we have two young men [Reggie Phillips and Vestee Jackson] playing the corner position we're very happy with.   9/1/87 *Chicago Sun-Times*

Mike Richardson did sign with the Bears. Ditka commented   He thinks he's ready. I don't think he's ready. We'll see how he does.   9/4/87 *Chicago Sun-Times*

RICHARDSON VS DITKA _____

I really don't know my status on the team. I had a long talk with Ditka and didn't really get good vibes from the conversation.   9/4/87 *Chicago Sun-Times*

He thinks he's ready. I don't think he's ready. He hasn't worked [practiced]. He has to work.   9/5/87 *Chicago Sun-Times*

Richardson speculated that he was not starting in 1987 as punishment for being a holdout earlier in the season.   That's the only thing it is, I think. When I have talked to Ditka, it's been a lot of negative talk. It's something I don't think is true and I don't want to hear. Not positive at all. If Ditka doesn't want me to get out of his doghouse, maybe he should send me somewhere else. I prefer to stay here and play, but I don't know how long this is going to go on. I don't know how long I can sit and be quiet.   11/2/87

Ditka responds   If you're a competitor, sometimes you get to where you're airing your gripes and you just say what you say. Mike missed a lot of time [as a holdout] but he's made it up. He's not in my doghouse. Nobody's in my doghouse. There is no doghouse.   11/3/87 *Chicago Sun-Times*

Ditka expanded Mike Richardson's playing time to two full quarters in the Green Bay game. Richardson commented   I guess maybe I'm off punishment now.   11/5/87 *Chicago Sun-Times*

Ditka   It's not like he was being punished and this is a reward. It's doing what's best for the team.   11/5/87 *Chicago Sun-Times*

Ditka   Mike's been practicing well lately, and if he can come out there and get some turnovers for us, it would really help.   11/8/87

THE 1987 SEASON

Ditka on Wilber Marshall   He takes it as a personal affront when he's blocked, and that's the way you have to.   12/4/87 *Chicago Sun-Times*

Sean Smith on Ditka   I'm really not into watching sports on TV. If I can't be there to see it, or be the one playing, it's not as exciting. The Bears were about the only team I'd watch because they had Coach Ditka. I'd heard about how wild he was as a human being and then how calm and relaxed he was as a coach.   8/25/87

Ditka on Reggie Phillips   He's intense, feisty. Sometimes I get on his butt too much, but I want him to be as good as he can be.   8/29/87 *Chicago Sun-Times*

Ditka on Ron Rivera   He's not as fast as Otis [Wilson], but he is a very heady player.   11/11/87

Maybe he's not as glamorous as some people around the league, but he makes things happen. He is a pretty good blitzer. That was his forte in college.   11/12/87 *Chicago Sun-Times*

Ditka on Mike Hartenstine   Mike works to be in shape, spends time with the weights as he should, and has a commitment and discipline that's impressive.   9/30/86

On Cutting Hartenstine   Here was a guy who has given a lot to the Bears. We could have given him another year, but where does that leave us in the development of somebody?   9/8/87

Mike Hartenstine is a guy who has given a lot to the Bears and has been instrumental in the growth of this football team. But the one constant in life is change. As silly as it sounds, that's constant.   9/8/87 *Chicago Sun-Times*

Hartenstine was signed by the Minnesota Vikings. Can Hartenstine still play?   The Vikings think so, Mike thinks so, and I probably think so. This might be a great opportunity for him. He's something special and I'm happy the opportunity came up. What he's contributed to the Bears in 12 years is more than most people who ever played for the Bears.   10/30/87 *Chicago Sun-Times*

Ditka on Vestee Jackson   I like Vestee Jackson a lot. I like the way he challenged people. He didn't back off anyone, and if they're going to keep picking on him, I guarantee he'll get his share of interceptions.   1/2/87 *Chicago Sun-Times*

16

CHICAGO AND THE GRABOWSKIS

WINNING AND LOSING IN CHICAGO

On defeating the Washington Redskins 23–19 in the Bears 1984 play-off game It's time for Chicago to take a bow.   12/31/84

The next week the Bears were shut out in the N.F.C. title game by the San Francisco 49ers, 23–0.   We have no excuses. We were beaten soundly by a good football team. I am disappointed for the players and for the fans in Chicago. I apologize to the fans and the team.   1/7/85

Responding to statements that the Bears had replaced the Dallas Cowboys as America's team All we have to be is Chicago's team.   11/17/85

Before the 1985 NFC championship game, Ditka reflected on the Chicago jinx.   I realize people here had high expectations for the Sox and Cubs and were disappointed. But I don't think you can compare different teams and different sports. If you can't get excited about the things in life that excite you, then something's wrong. Then do something else. If you're worried about hitting the ball in the water on the fifth hole, then don't play the fifth hole.   1/12/86

After the Super Bowl XX victory, Ditka scoffed at those who said Chicago teams choked during big games.   Now they can't say that about us anymore, or about any Chicago team. Chicago has a winner. This victory today was a credit to the city of Chicago, and I hope the fans are loving it. We're supposed to be the city of big shoulders. Well, this is a team of big shoulders, a team that works together and gets a lot of things done.   1/27/86

This is great for Chicago fans. They have been shellshocked for a number of years.   1/27/86

I love to win. I love what it means to the city of Chicago and this organization. If anybody can't pay the price for that, we're in the wrong game. We ought to be delivering mail.   12/28/86 *Southtown Economist*

GRABOWSKIS

I don't think we come in favor with some people. There are teams that are fair-haired and some that aren't fair-haired. There are teams named Smith and some named Grabowski. We're Grabowskis. The Rams are a Smith team.   1/7/86

This [the NFC title game vs the Rams] is the Smiths against the Grabowskis. Chicago's been knocked too much. It's a great city, but it's been knocked too much. I'm happy we've meant something to the people here. I get letters, letters from wives. Wives thanking the Bears for making this winter so much fun. "My husband's never been in a better mood," one lady writes, "because of your football team." People in Chicago, they've got passion.   1/12/86

John J. Kulczycki, history professor, University of Illinois at Chicago [Grabowskis] don't wait for something to fall into [their] lap. This means a sustained pushing of the rock up the hill.   1/19/86

Jan Novak, Chicago novelist   The Smiths are kind of reserved . . . We [Grabowskis] are the kind of people who yell and get angry and break our hands on lockers when we lose.   1/19/86

Ditka   Let me tell you about these guys. We're down there [in Georgia prior to the Super Bowl] three days. We eat together, practice together, meet together, eat again together, then go to bed, and we wake up and look at each other again. I don't know if that makes you ornery or what, but these guys are ready. Not excited. Anxious maybe. They feel this is just part of the mission, this game here Sunday, no matter who we're playing or matter what the weather is . . . in other words, I like my Grabowskis.   1/12/86

AFTER WINNING THE SUPER BOWL

. . . my interpretation of Grabowski is, he's the Crown Prince of Poland, he always dressed well. When we lose a couple, I'm sure you guys [the media] will have a ball with it. I can't remember a coach, when you look back at the 1960s, that didn't wear a coat and tie.   9/19/86

When asked if the Bears were still keeping the Grabowski image, Ditka said yes.   But the bowling shirts are going more toward Givenchy. 12/28/86

Being a Grabowski   It reflects the work ethic, the great attitude, and that's what it is all about, it was the way I was raised. We said it was the attitude of the Bears, but it's the attitude of the city and of people who aren't afraid to work, who really live the American dream, who are trying to get ahead.   7/16/87 *Chicago Sun-Times*

Reflecting upon signing his new contract and making money outside of football in Chicago   It's such a great city. It's provided me with opportunities kids don't even dream about.   8/30/87 *Des Plaines Daily Herald*

When told that the "Grabowski Shuffle" video had sold 50,000 copies and qualified for a platinum award, Ditka replied   It's an early Christmas present. I'm excited for the Grabowskis and the fans, but I'll still be looking in my stocking for a Super Bowl ring.   12/3/87 *Chicago Sun-Times*

17

THE HATED PACKERS

RIVALRY

Jerry Vainisi on Ditka and the Packers/Bears rivalry   I thought the rivalry had changed because the younger players on both teams don't remember the glory days. Maybe it picked up since Ditka has been coach. Since then, the spirit has been rekindled. Our players and [Packers coach] Forrest Gregg's players have picked up on that. 9/22/86

Ex-Packer Larry Rubens   They get you jacked up in Green Bay to play the Bears.   9/17/86

Ditka on Packers Spies   In those days [the 1960s] there were spies around. We had people looking at the rooftops. Doug Atkins was always pointing to the pigeons.   10/21/85

A Packers Mistake—Firing Bart Starr, 1983   The mistake was in anticipating they would automatically be in the play-offs. In the topsy-turvy world of football, anything can happen and did. It's unfortunate. I don't feel they'll get a man who will fill his shoes that will bring to the organization the same class and character.   12/20/83

They [Green Bay] are going to try to muscle you where they can, and we're just not a team that can be muscled very easily. We respond back to what they do, and they respond back to what we do.   9/18/84

The players would never mention the words "Green Bay" the week before a Packers Game. We were afraid the coaches might get all choked up.   10/21/85

Keith Van Horne, Bears Lineman   Both teams have a chip on their shoulders, and they don't want to take anything from anybody. 9/18/84

[Ditka] told us to bring our baseball bats up there. What do I do? I gave up baseball a long time ago, I don't have a bat.   9/16/86

Ditka   When we play the Packers, you notice their players don't pick anybody off the ground and ours don't pick any of theirs up.   1/26/86

DITKA DECLARES WAR

It'll be a war.   9/16/86

It's not going to be like last year. We're not going to be the hittees. We're going to be the hitters. That's fact.   9/18/86

They need to back off some because we'll need all our energy to play Green Bay.   9/17/86

It will not be for the faint of heart. We'll play whatever has to be played to win the game.   9/22/86

Mossy Cade, Packers player   I think Mike Ditka's game plan was to try and embarrass us.   11/24/86

It wouldn't have been as nice if we had blown them out . . . They (the Packers) just knew they were going to win the game. I think it hurts more when you squeak it by.   11/25/86

A PACKERS–BEARS EXCHANGE

Forrest Gregg, Head Coach, Green Bay Packers   I resent the statement by Mike Ditka that our football team is nothing but a bunch of thugs and has no character. That is a reflection on me as a person and a football coach. I totally disagree with his assumption about our team.   11/26/86

Mike Ditka responds   I don't rescind what I said. I said the character of some of the players for the most part was questionable.   11/26/86

THE PACKERS: 1987 SEASON

Charles Martin, Ex-Packers Lineman   Coach Ditka called us a bunch of thugs. But we're just like his players. We're only human. Sometimes, we get a little physical, but it's a physical game. If you can't take it, it's not your game.   8/24/87

Forrest Gregg   I know our games with the Bears the last couple of years have been pretty intense. That's just the way both of our teams play football. That's the way I played the game, and that's the way Mike Ditka played it. I like Mike, regardless of what some people may think. We just compete. When we're at the league meetings, we converse. Believe it or not, we don't arm wrestle or hiss at each other. 9/13/87

Mike Ditka   I think our guys are really looking forward to this game. REALLY looking forward to it. You can take that anyway you want.   11/3/87 *Chicago Sun-Times*

Alphonso Carreker, Packers Defensive End   You're going to see some big plays and some big hits. I don't think the Packers have been dirty or committed any unsportsmanlike fouls in the Bears games. Well maybe one or two. But other than that, it's usually the Bears. If they cheap shot someone, then it's OK. If another team does it to the Bears, it's looked at as a cheap shot.   11/3/87 *Chicago Sun-Times*

Rich Moran, Packers Left Guard   From the first time I stepped onto the field against the Bears, it's been different than any other game. The intensity level, the way the coaching staff reacts to the Bears—it's just different.   11/3/87 *Chicago Sun-Times*

MORE FUEL FOR THE FIRE

The Bears were looking forward to playing against Charles Martin, who body-slammed Jim McMahon in the 1986 Packers–Bears game. Unfortunately, or fortunately, for Charles Martin, he was playing for the Houston Oilers in 1987. Ditka engaged in a little wishful thinking   I think [the Packers] are going to invite him for this week.   11/3/87

Jim McMahon   I don't have much respect for Coach Gregg and I don't have much respect for some of their players. I think they used to have a real good organization. It just seems to me it's kind of gone downhill the last three or four years, and I think Forrest Gregg's got to be part of that.   11/3/87

When asked if he expected trouble in Green Bay, Ditka replied   I doubt there will be any extracurricular activity. There might be. If there is, we'll handle it the best way we can when we come to it.   11/4/87

ON THE CHARLES MARTIN INCIDENT _____

Forrest Gregg   That was certainly something I didn't like. It really reflected on all of us. We really had not a leg to stand on.   11/5/87 *Chicago Sun-Times*

I've defended myself enough in this case. If [the Bears] want to continue to talk on this, let them. Because they're really very good at that.   11/5/87 *Chicago Sun-Times*

THE RIVALRY, 1987 _____

Forrest Gregg   The Bears are a great team, and the fact that we can play them close has to help our guys. When you've got a lot of young people, they don't know what they can do.   11/29/87 *Chicago Sun-Times*

Dave Duerson, Bears Safety   They have a talented club, a lot of athletes. The problem is, they don't play clean. When they decide to play professional football at a class level, they'll give a lot of teams trouble.   11/30/87

Dave Duerson, after the Bears beat the Packers 23–10 at Soldier Field
We attempted to play this game clean. Mike Ditka has made it clear to us. He tells us every week we play the Packers that he's not going

to have any cheap shots coming from us. If we start anything we're going to get fined. And he means that. So we've played it within the rules. But we're concerned because we've lost a number of players in the Bears-Packers rivalry. Not because of great defense or great hits, but because of cheap plays.   11/30/87

18

DITKA FROM THOSE WHO KNOW HIM

MIKE DITKA'S WIFE, DIANA

I don't think he is an underdog. He is very confident in everything he does. But maybe he's trying to prove things to himself.   11/17/85

MIKE DITKA'S DAD

I'll tell you something. I've seen him when he was very pleasant company. You couldn't ask for better. I've seen him when things weren't going right and I'll tell you what, he wasn't fit to talk to.   11/17/85

FORMER BEARS TEAMMATES

Mike Pyle, Center, 1961–1969   Bears players always have been taught they are supposed to win. And now, Ditka is teaching them all over again.   11/10/85

Doug Atkins, Defensive End, 1955–1966   Unbelievable. It really is, the way each week they keep on rolling. Seems like they're so well balanced. I always thought Ditka was a good coach. He was schooled under good people.   11/10/85

Fred Williams, Defensive Tackle, 1952–1963   This team is so good I'm going all the way to Dallas from Tennessee to see them next week. Tell Ditka I'm available, I'll be glad to be his chauffeur and I won't touch a drop while I'm driving.   11/10/85

Johnny Morris, Wide Receiver, 1958–1967   It's as if Ditka has personally stamped each and every Bear with his own personality and competitive zeal.   11/10/85

Rudy Kuechenberg, Linebacker, 1957–1960   I love Mike Ditka. I'm the biggest Mike Ditka fan around. Before the 1984 season, HBO called to talk about my picks for the upcoming season. They asked me, "Who is your surprise team?" and I said, "The Chicago Bears."   1/12/86

Ronnie Bull, Running Back, 1962–1970   The rest of the country may be surprised at the job Ditka has done. But it's no surprise at all to those of us who knew him as a teammate and competitor.   11/10/85

George Blanda, Quarterback, 1949–1958   I'm just so pleased. I've always been a Mike Ditka fan. I'm so happy he has made believers where some of them were skeptical four years ago. I think the Bears are going to be good for a long time.   11/10/85

Dick Butkus, Linebacker, 1965–1973   I remember when I first came to the Bears in 1965, and we're playing the Rams, I think, at some place in Tennessee, I think. It's only an exhibition game, but here he is, standing by the doorway to the field, yelling it up. He's never changed, and it looks like all these guys [the Bears] have that feeling now. 12/24/85

BEARS ALUMNI

Bronko Nagurski, Fullback, 1930–1939   It took Mike Ditka a long time to get there and get straightened out. He was his own worst enemy for a couple of years. He's gotten himself straightened out and he's doing a good job now.   11/10/85

George Conner, Tackle-Linebacker, 1948–1955   A lot of people thought the old man was senile when he named Buddy Ryan and Mike Ditka. But Halas wanted to give back something to the Bears and the fans, and he gave them Ditka.   11/10/85

Sid Luckman, Quarterback, 1939–1950   This is, without a doubt, the finest Bears team I've seen in my lifetime. Ditka has instilled his own personal spirit. Coach Halas told me he anticipated that within three years, Ditka would win the Super Bowl. You can't count the strike year [1982] so this is the third year.   11/10/85

FAMOUS NFL PLAYERS

John Mackey, ex-Baltimore Colt Tight End   My idol was Mike Ditka. I used to study the way he did things. Ditka gave this one guy a physical beating like I've never seen before. He was all over the field. From that day on, I wanted to be just like him. Ditka had a mean streak in him. He didn't accept punishment, he dished it out.   9/8/85

Roger Staubach, Dallas Cowboys Quarterback   Mike Ditka is a fantastic coach. Mike wants to win very badly. Mike will not let anything come between [him and] winning. Hopefully he can bring that focus back.   2/10/87

Bob Griese, ex-Miami Dolphin Quarterback   I read the papers and I'm amazed at some of the things that are said. My relationship with Don Shula was a very close one, to the point where if I didn't like plays from the game plan, we wouldn't run them. From what I read, it's 180 degrees different in Chicago. Words back and forth, "I don't care what he thinks. I'm going to do this." I don't know. Maybe it works better that way. And Chicago has always been a little different anyway. 11/14/86

John Brodie, ex-San Francisco 49ers Quarterback   Only one thing you have to know about Ditka—that he'd just as soon knock your head off as look at you. The old man [Halas] ought to like that.   11/27/84

RECENT BEARS

Jim Osborne   At first the players didn't know how to accept Mike Ditka. He came across very hard with us at the beginning, but he was entirely different one-on-one. Behind closed doors, we found he was easier to talk to.   11/27/84

Jim Osborne   Abe Gibron was my first coach. Great guy, but you'd have to question his ability to be head man. I don't think, though, that he had what he needed to survive. Jack Pardee was next, and that's a period I'd like to wipe out altogether from memory. No personality at all. I remember once a bunch of us were taking a sauna on a cold day, coaches and all, telling jokes. It was packed, then somebody left and Pardee came in. One by one everybody got out. I was the only one left. The guys took it upon themselves to get to the play-offs in 1977, but Pardee got most of the credit. Could never talk to him about anything but ball. Neil Armstrong was a fine a person as I've ever met, but certain guys took advantage of him because he was so nice. Now Mike Ditka, nobody takes advantage of him. First couple of weeks I was thinking "Here we go again. This guy is gonna kills us." But Mike, he's the kind of man if you've got a problem at three in the morning, he's the guy to call. That's the kind of spirit he's instilled in the Bears. I've never seen it this good.   1/4/85

Brian Baschnagel   I've been around very emotional coaches. I know how to deal with it. It might bother you if he yells and screams, but you have a responsibility to do your job and if you fall short, you've got to forget about it. One of Mike's biggest assets is his ability to motivate. I've never seen him yell and scream and then hold it against someone.   10/16/83

Bob Parsons   I've been here 10 years and we never were criticized. But look at our record. It's about time we were criticized. When Neil Armstrong was here, they said we didn't win because he was too nice.   10/16/83

THE DALLAS ORGANIZATION

Tom Landry   When he started with us, I didn't think Mike had the poise and all that was necessary to be a head coach. But he has matured greatly through the years. When he left, I was confident he would be successful. He wanted to coach the Bears so bad.   11/14/85

Dan Reeves   We hit it off right away. I had a picture of him in my mind but the picture was totally different when I got to know him. He's extremely competitive. If he gets beat, he doesn't want to quit. There are no gray areas for Mike. Either a guy's a player or he's not. Mike is always going to look for the guy who's highly aggressive. He's never cared about what a guy ran [in the 40] or how big he is. Mike makes people play hard, or he'll get somebody else.   1/22/86

Dan Reeves, when Ditka lost a card game to him   He picked up his chair and threw it. All four legs stuck in the wall. I said, "Man, this guy hates to lose.   11/17/85

Jim Myers, former Ditka Coach at Dallas   No doubt about it, Mike is a rough-tough guy who identifies with the character of the Chicago Bears. And I think he'll transmit that to the players. Mike wouldn't go for a drinking, brawling team today. He's picked up a lot of polish from the Cowboys . . . Mike will be tough. He'll demand conditioning and discipline. But he'll also recognize the sophistication of the modern player. And he does know football. The important thing is, he'll be going where he thinks he belongs.   1/24/82

COACHES AND OTHER FAMOUS PEOPLE _____

Bill Parcells, Head Coach, New York Giants   Mike and I are similar in what we believe it takes to win football games. It's hard work. Play tough, and make the other guy know that you're there.   1/3/86

Jerry Glanville, Houston Oilers Coach   It's a credit to Ditka that they keep growing in their attack. It's all there; the number of different runs, formations, motion, shifting. Everybody would like to be able to do that.   12/21/86

Abe Gibron, former Bears Head Coach and former Tampa Bay Buccaneers Head Coach   The Bears reflect the way Mike played and the way Halas coached. We tried to do that, but we didn't have the personnel. The Bears take no prisoners. They play good, legitimate, hard-nosed football.   11/10/85

Weeb Eubank, ex-Head Coach, New York Jets and Baltimore Colts   I don't expect the Bears to play with the same intensity for the next two or three years. Things will happen that Ditka, or anybody else, won't be able to handle. It's human nature.   8/25/86

Joey Meyer, Coach, DePaul Blue Demons, on radio callers on a sports talk show ripping Ditka   The guy wins the Super Bowl, goes 14–2. What the guy's done for the city—I couldn't believe they were ripping him. I know I don't have to stick up for Mike Ditka. He can handle himself pretty well. I'm just saying what he's done. It's incredible what he's done. And I think that's a good example for our players. It comes and goes and you can't worry about it.   1/7/87

George Steinbrenner, ex-Northwestern University End Coach and New York Yankee owner, on Ditka being tough with his players   They might cuss and moan, but they want discipline. That's why Ditka is a winner. To me, he exemplifies all the things I think are great. I could take Mike Ditka and put him into baseball and win the World Series with him.   2/29/87

John Madden, former Raiders Head Coach   The best thing a coach can do is be consistent. You can copy ideas, but not personalities. Mike Ditka, for example. Mike Ditka gets on his players, and people wonder how his players take it. It's his consistency. He does it to everyone. That's him. That's what Mike Ditka is. And that's the thing. You have to be who you are, what you are, all the time. Dick Vermeil. He was the same all the time. The ones you worry about are the ones who don't talk to players one week, then want to be their friends the next week. Then the players don't know who they are.   1/8/88

19

DITKA AND THE MEDIA

On mistakes in strategy   Hold the coaching staff accountable. You're going to anyway.   11/8/83

THE PRESS VS DITKA

Was the end of the first half the turning point?
  No. Next question.
Did you want a time-out called?
  Yes. Next question.
Did you want the ball thrown out of bounds on third down?
  Yes. Next question.
Why did you run two running plays right before that?
  Because we thought we wanted to.
Why did Walter Payton run only four times in the third quarter?
  No kidding? I don't know.

Did you want the pass at the end of the half thrown into the end zone?
   No.
Why not?
   Why would I?
The clock ran out.
   So what?
Here Ditka was asked again about the turning point.
   What turning point? The first time we touch the football we fumble and they kick a field goal. We take it down and score, they take it down and score, we take it down and score, they take it down and score. You tell me where the turning point is. Maybe the turning point was last Tuesday. Maybe it was last year when they scheduled it. Who knows?   10/1/84

Were the Bears' expectations at the end of the 1985 season too high? Ditka sarcastically replied   I'm really sorry it's all come down to this, such a disappointing December. The expectations will not be known until January 26 [the Super Bowl game].   12/10/85

On press questions before the Super Bowl   We have no control over the types of questions. By the time it's over, they have written everything you do from Grade 1 to 12 and that you probably stole a car in high school.   1/16/86

A LITTLE ANIMOSITY?

You're the same people who tell Spud Webb he can't play basketball and Wally Backman he can't play second base and Len Dykstra he can't hit a home run. We also have a quarterback who is 6 foot with a bad eye. You guys think you can't come out of the ghetto and be president. That's what you guys think. But Flutie isn't asking anybody to put him on stilts.   10/23/86

You guys keep on telling them [the Bears] they're good. Don't do that. You say negative things about me. You can find negative things about them and use them.   10/14/86

I don't want to say too much now because last week you got a couple geniuses in the media in Chicago. They were offended when I said we didn't play good last week. I only speak the truth. I don't bullcrap people. Today we played great. We just got a couple of bad breaks. If that's what you want to hear, you're talking to the wrong person. You're dealing in fiction. I don't deal in fiction. I deal in reality. I've been around the game 25–26 years and I know what good and bad is. I know what execution is, and I know what lack of execution is. And I don't need anybody in the media to tell me what it is.   10/20/86

Holding up a newspaper at a press conference   See this? I read about [Flutie] in the newspaper. I believe everything I read in the newspaper. No, I just liked everything I'd seen about him and everything I'd heard about him, characterwise. And then, I guess, when people tell me that he's not the answer, then I think more he is the answer.   12/28/86

DISH IT OUT, MIKE

Jim [McMahon] and I have a mutual admiration society. Now how are you going to headline that one?   8/14/86

At the start of a local post-practice press conference, to a T.V. cameraman   Give me a break on those lights. I had a pimple and it was showing the other day.   10/1/87 *Chicago Sun-Times*

One reporter repeatedly asked about the Fridge's weight. Ditka's response   You're the only overweight guy in this room and you keep asking about Perry's weight.   8/2/87 *Southtown Economist*

An old friend sent an essay he wrote about Ditka years ago, as a freshman in college. Teased Ditka   He wrote an essay on me 30 years ago when he was a freshman at New Mexico. I had never seen it. He got an A on it. If you guys are good, I'll let you have the essay. You'll sell a lot of papers.
It's a true story. What life is all about. You start at the bottom and

work your way to the top. Even though it refers to me, I forgot about it. I forgot about those days 30 years ago. It's interesting.   11/22/87

Early one week Ditka said that the Bears defense stunk. Then the Bears beat the Lions. Reporters asked if the Bears responded to his criticism of the defense. Ditka's reply   I don't know. You guys responded. You all wrote it. That's all that counts. You guys have no imagination. I have to tell you what to write and then you write it.   11/23/87

GENIUSES

After the play-off loss to the Redskins, the media played up the idea that major changes next season were certain.   You're making like we have to clean house here. We have to make a few changes, not wholesale changes. There's no need for that, despite what you experts write and broadcast. You geniuses.   1/12/88

Some of the media and some players criticized Bears playcalling. Ditka's solution   [Have the media call] the first play of each quarter and have the players call the rest of them.   1/12/88

There's a lot of ways you analyze. But until you know what you're talking about, players and media should keep their mouth shut.   1/12/88

After telling several reporters he had no comment on rumors that Wilber Marshall would leave the Bears, he later told another reporter   You got a better "no comment" than they got before.   3/18/88 *Chicago Sun-Times*

If there was no pressure there would be nothing to gain. I mean, what if we only played against high school teams? Pressure is not the problem. We've spoiled our fans. I've seen it happen in Dallas. I've seen it happen in a lot of places. You have to live with it. That's part of life.   3/20/88

20

WINNING AND LOSING TO SUPER BOWL XX

1982

The pre-Mike Ditka Bears They didn't like losing, but it seemed to be a way of life, so they accepted it. You find ways to blow games. You find a way to blow a last-minute game in Minnesota just because those sons of guns have purple uniforms on. That's bull. I don't believe in that. 11/17/85

In one of Ditka's first interviews with the press, a reporter asked Ditka if he thought the Bears, who were 6–10 the previous season, could win their division with him as coach. George Halas, who was at Ditka's side, couldn't resist breaking in with, "Come on, now," but Ditka enthusiastically answered, "Yes, yes!" He went on Now what were the Bears? Six and ten, right? That's only three games. And the one they lost to us in Dallas by one point on Thanksgiving Day—well, no one could accuse them of playing with little intensity. The Bears aren't that far from turning things around. 1/21/82

It's got to be a physical, intimidating football team.   1/24/82

After a 10–0 loss to New Orleans the day before the 1982 strike began We struck yesterday. If they strike, we're right in tune. We're a day ahead of schedule.   9/21/82

After the New Orleans loss, Ditka was particularly angry.   I believe some don't take it seriously enough, when you're supposed to pull on a run and you don't, or pull on a pass block and you don't get there on time, or you run the wrong pattern, your head isn't in the game. It takes total commitment. We have guys who haven't totally committed to what we're doing.   9/20/82

Robin Earl told reporters that after the New Orleans loss, Ditka said all players would have to reapply for their jobs.   He said the door will be open and anybody who wants to play should see him. If anybody doesn't want to play or wants to be traded, he'll be willing to oblige. He said a few changes will be made.   9/20/82

Later in the season, the Bears lost to Seattle 20–14 on a quick kick, which Ditka described as "a high school play." Seattle coach Mike McCormack took offense. Ditka's response   I never said they were inferior. Basically what I said is we beat ourselves with bad field position, and I said the quick kick was a well-designed play. There's nothing wrong with high school plays. If Mike McCormack finds that offensive, that's his business. I'm not going to worry about what anybody says. I said they aren't a great football team because they're not. 12/15/82

After his first season as Bears head coach, Ditka was optimistic.   It's like if you have a nice-looking apple and you have a little bad spot. You have to peel it off. It's not a cancer that has to be removed, just a few blemishes we have to change around.   1/4/83

1983

It's just a matter of some teams knowing how to win, some don't know how to win. We're going through that right now. We hope we are finding out how to win. Teams like Dallas and the Raiders know how to win. They find ways to win. They believe they can win. They never believe something's not going to happen.   10/14/83

As the Bears lost to the Detroit Lions 38–17 in a home game, an angry Bears fan threw a drink at Ditka.   I had earphones on most of the time, which is really maybe a godsend because I didn't hear what they were saying. I had a drink thrown, but if that's the worst thing that happens to me, I got it made.   11/1/83

In the middle of the 1983 season the Bears owned a dismal 2–5 record. As they embarked on their next game in Philadelphia, Ditka took a hard line.   I told them [the players], "Don't get on the plane if you don't want to play." I didn't care if I went on the plane with 15 players. If you don't want to bust your ass stay home. Get out of my sight. We won 7–6 and it wasn't pretty, either. And we lost the next two games. But I felt with the Philadelphia trip they started to understand what we were trying to do here.   12/31/84

1984

Ditka saw the 1984 season, his third with the Bears, as pivotal.   The Bears have now got a foundation they can build on for years, and if they keep drafting as well as we've been fortunate enough to draft the last couple of years and not be afraid to play people, I think they have a chance to do really good things.   7/10/84

On November 25, 1984, the Bears defeated the Vikings 34–3 in Minneapolis to win their first championship since 1963. Characteristically, Ditka spoke of George Halas' confidence in him.   This is for the 49 guys in there [the locker room] and for the guy who hired me [George Halas]. Somewhere, he's smiling pretty good right now. 11/26/84

The worst thing is to compare this team to 1963. This is a great defense. That was a great defense, too, but look at these statistics across the board.   11/26/84

I hope the players see what I'm trying to instill here. When I came, too many guys were in football just for a paycheck. You can't live that way. I don't care if the players like me now. I just hope they respect what I'm trying to do. I'm sure they still look at me sometimes and think, "Who is the jerk on the sidelines?" But, you know, football isn't all x's and o's. It's people.   12/4/84

Our guys just don't take any crap. We don't like to be bullies, but we don't like to be bullied either.   12/23/84

Play-off football, Ditka-style   We don't want to limp into the play-offs, we want to run in.   11/26/84

There's nothing to save it for. No holding back. You gotta let it all go this week.   12/30/84

The Bears played their first play-off game in Washington, against the Redskins.   We have our work cut out for us. I don't think anybody understands what it's like to play in R.F.K. [Washington's Stadium]. It's tough. They only get 52,000 people, but you got no friends. None. It's tough. We have to concentrate, play our game, forget the fans; don't play the scoreboard, play the opponent. If we can do that, we can be effective.   12/25/84

The Bears defeated the Redskins 23–19. The next Bears opponent would be the San Francisco 49ers.   If I'm Montana [49ers Quarterback] watching today on T.V., I gotta be prepared to throw that ball in a hurry. With our defense today, Joe Theismann [the Redskins quarterback], he had to get rid of it in a second. They were fabulous. I'm not surprised . . . This is some football team here.   12/31/84

Ditka felt confident prior to the 49ers game.   Nobody awes this football team. I still like our chances.   1/4/85

The thing that is in our favor is that even though they know more about our defense than they did a year ago, they've still got to defeat it. 1/6/85

The confident Bears lost to the 49ers 23–0 and were eliminated from the play-offs. It hurt, particularly because the Bears really felt they would win.   I apologize to our fans and to the team. We'll be back. The 49ers are a better football team than us right now. They just beat the butt off us, that's all.   1/7/85

We have no excuses. We were beaten soundly by a good football team [the 49ers]. I am disappointed for the players and for the fans in Chicago.   1/7/85

At the end of the game, the 49ers placed a lineman in the backfield, further humiliating the Bears. Ditka was calm. Little did anyone know that this would be the catalyst for the Refrigerator's debut one year later.   I've got to give them credit. How many guys would think of putting a guard in the backfield? Plus you got the best quarterback in football, and you put him out as a flanker. I think Bill [Walsh] was ready for this one. They taught us a lesson.   1/8/85

I thought we'd handle the 49ers. Maybe I was part of the problem. The players may have felt like I did. We didn't seem as urgent as the first game [against the Redskins].   1/8/85

1985

You're only as good as your last game, and our last game wasn't very good.   7/21/85

The most important thing for this team to realize is that what you do one year has nothing to do with what you'll do the next year. Everyone has a tendency to say, "Well, you were successful in '84 so therefore you automatically have to be successful in '85. That just does not hold water unless you are willing to pay the price." 7/21/85

We are not going to surprise anybody. Teams know the kind of football we are capable of.   9/4/85

We are not San Francisco, we are not San Diego. We are not Miami. We are the Bears. I like that. Being the Bears is not too bad.   9/4/85

Before defeating the Vikings 33–24, Ditka commented   This game is what football is all about.   9/17/85

If you can stay away from key injuries, you've got a chance, if you're a good football team. Our schedule is tough. Evidently we've got two good teams in our division [Minnesota and Detroit at the time, 3–1 on the season]. We have a great rivalry with Green Bay. We play an excellent Miami team on the road, and an excellent San Francisco team on the road, and an excellent Dallas team on the road. The Jets look like they know what they're doing, and we've got them on the road. When you look at our schedule, that's why I say it's going to be tough. 10/6/85

The main thing we try to talk about is, we don't have any control over two weeks from now. We have a lot of control over three hours on Sunday.   10/6/85

Prior to a rematch with the 49ers in the 1985 season   What if we both don't show up? They're the best team in football. Most intimidating defense I've ever seen. Most innovative offense that's ever been coached.   10/10/85

Not surprised at the 8–0 start   I'm not saying that to be conceited or cocky or otherwise. I'm just not surprised, because I'm not going to deal in negatives. If you had speculated before this year, it would be pretty far-fetched. But I think we've legitimately won them all. To go 16–0 would be a little far-fetched, also. But stranger things have happened.   10/28/85

If people want to say we play good offense because of McMahon and Walter Payton, that's fine. I don't care. If they say we play good on defense because it's Buddy's defense, that's okay. They're all working for the Bears. I don't want the credit, I just want the wins.   11/17/85

After the Bears lost the only game of the season to the Miami Dolphins   We had a Bears football team, and we lost that in the last few weeks. All of a sudden we just had a defense. We had a perfect defense. Our Bears defense is perfect when the offense is capable of scoring and the special teams are capable of getting us field position.   12/4/85

More on the Miami loss   I made a statement to the team that I believe. Nobody has beat us yet. We beat ourselves.   12/4/85

1985 Play-off preferences   I have no preference at all. We've played hard enough and earned the right to get into the play-offs and play at home. Now whoever we have to play will have to come in here and it just doesn't matter. They're all good football teams.   12/22/85

The Bears played poorly in the 1985 late season victory over Detroit, shortly before they won the Super Bowl.   We'll be the underdogs, no question about it. Maybe we're doing too many Super Bowl Shuffles . . . . Say I'm concerned. Say I'm terrified. Anything you want . . . We couldn't beat a play-off team today. We would have been eliminated.   12/23/85

How to win the Super Bowl   Put a chip on your shoulder in July and keep it there until January.   1/26/86

The Bears defeated the New York Giants in the play-offs. Ditka looked forward to playing the Los Angeles Rams.   We're a better team than we were last year. Our determination has been good all year. If you have watched us play, we play hard. That's all you can ask.   1/12/86

There's a poem that says something about we've come many miles, but we've got many miles to go. I don't want to sound like I'm not happy about what happened today, but we're on a mission and it won't be finished until we're finished in New Orleans.   1/13/86

Ditka feared that the Bears might be too happy going to the Super Bowl.   That's the worst thing you can be. A lot of teams are happy to be there the first time they go. You can't go that way.   1/14/86

SUPER BOWL! _____

Dan Hampton   He told us to have fun. We shouldn't try to inhibit ourselves. The media has a job to do. It only becomes a distraction if we make it a distraction.   1/21/86

Ditka   When you get this far, if you can't concentrate on football, you better get another job. We're just going down to play a game. The Patriots will go down and do the same thing. Everybody will enjoy it, and then we'll go on with our lives.   1/16/86

It's not life or death. It's not going to be World War III. But it will be interesting. 1/19/86

The Bears defeated the New England Patriots 46–10 in Super Bowl XX

21

THE 1986 "ARE YOU SATISFIED?" SEASON

TURNED HEADS

Mike Ditka's motto for the 1986 season was, "Are you satisfied?" He gave golf shirts to his players with the motto stenciled on it, hoping to inspire the Bears to another Super Bowl season. It became apparent early in 1986 that motivating his team could be difficult. Their heads should be turned. I want to emphasize that. They accomplished a lot of things. If they want to take a few bows, that's okay. But I guarantee you when we go to Platteville, I would say our tempo will be better than last year. We're going to have some new faces on this club. I'll guarantee that. 5/25/86

The Bears' first preseason game opened in London, England against the Dallas Cowboys. The last Bears-Cowboys preseason contest had been described as a fight with some football in between. Ditka alluded to this in anticipation of the 1986 game. It won't be like soccer. It might look like boxing, but it won't look like soccer. 8/3/86

The Bears handed Dallas a 17–6 defeat in London, but Ditka was unimpressed with his team's performance. He told the press Fellas, I know what it takes to win, believe me. We'll have it. But we don't have it now. So many of those guys [rookies and players trying to make the team] don't know how to win, what to do. We need people, such as the receivers, to start jumping up at us. Now's the time to step to the front. I'm not jumping up and down about what we did Sunday. We won, but we did a lot poorly. But for the first game, that's not unusual. The effort didn't displease me. But we need better blocking technique and some smarter quarterback reads. We're a ball-control team and the more we have the ball, the more games we will win. We're not a home run team. We have to hit the open guy rather than try for the home run.   8/5/86

After defeating the Pittsburgh Steelers and Baltimore Colts in preseason games, Ditka was more upbeat about this team.   I'm proud of the way they play. The guys play hard.   8/14/86

The Bears opened against the Houston Oilers with a 5–0 record. Some observers were concerned that games were too easy for the Bears to win. Ditka replied   Our team is not complacent.   10/12/86

The Bears defeated Houston 20–7, but Ditka was angry at the way his team played.   We were horsespit.   10/13/86

He was especially hard on the media, whom he accused of pumping up the Bears' egos too much.   You guys pat them on the back and tell them how good they are. But we're not good enough.   10/13/86

. . . we're not going to measure ourselves against the Houston Oilers or the Eagles or Minnesota. We measure ourselves against ourselves. 10/14/86

LOSING THE EDGE ⸻

One week later Ditka's fears were realized. The Bears seemed distracted by the acquisition of Doug Flutie and Jim McMahon's criticism that the Bears organization was disloyal to back-up quarterbacks Mike Tomczak and Steve Fuller.   I didn't see us playing as a team Sunday. We didn't pick up one another as well as we had to. I don't know if it was caused by last week's sequence of events or not. I don't have all the answers. I'll listen to anyone, coaches or players, anyone who has a helpful suggestion to make.   10/21/86

We are no longer head and shoulders above anybody.   11/5/86

I don't think anybody ever thought we were invincible, because we're not. Last year we played hard and won a lot of games. Now we're playing hard and we've lost a couple. I don't know if that's the invincibility factor. I know if I played on another team against the Bears, I wouldn't think they were invincible. I never thought the 49ers were, the Raiders, the Redskins. Other teams that play us love royally to kick our butts. That's a fact. Period.   11/5/86

With the loss of Jim McMahon, Ditka rallied the Bears around the notion that no one was indispensable.   One person didn't make us Super Bowl champs. We can overcome anything.   11/30/86

Bears critics pointed to an easy schedule as an obstacle to winning Super Bowl XXI.   You go tell our opponents that we have an easy schedule. They're ready to play us. Tell Green Bay, Pittsburgh or any of those clubs they aren't a lot of competition. It's been a dogfight all year. 1/3/87 *Des Plaines Daily Herald*

Overconfidence is the biggest thing. And maybe an aura of self-importance, [a feeling] of how important the individual was, instead of how important the team was.   1/2/87 *Chicago Sun-Times*

LOSING THE GAME _____

The Bears lost their first play-off game to the Washington Redskins, 27–13 at Soldier Field. Ditka tried to downplay the disappointment. You can't take away what we did. We lost the battle, but we didn't lose the war. We're still a young team and still learning. Maybe we're learning as coaches, too. I was confident we'd win the game, but we weren't up to the task. My dreams didn't come true this year.   1/4/87

A lot of guys will feel bad sitting around the TV watching the Giants, because we should be there.   1/6/87

Two weeks later, brooding over how winning a Super Bowl changes a team   The thing that changes, I think, is not so much the people as it's maybe your incentive for getting [to the Super Bowl]. The importance of it, maybe that's what I'm trying to say. It doesn't seem as important. Once you're in the Super Bowl, the game can never be what it's built up to be. The other day I read the great Duane Thomas quote, "If it's the ultimate game, why is there going to be another one next year?" That struck home. There's gonna be one every year and we're gonna be back in it.   1/5/87 *Des Plaines Daily Herald*

We played a very undisciplined game all the way through. That's why we lost the game. We just didn't do things we were capable of doing, offensively or defensively. We completely forgot to play defense in the final series when Washington had the ball. Everybody tried to do it individually rather than play team defense.   4/19/87 *Des Plaines Daily Herald*

22

PREPARING FOR THE 1987 SEASON

THE DRAFT, 1987

Prior to the 1987 draft, Ditka felt that the Bears had plenty of quarterbacks. We have quarterbacks we can go to the Super Bowl with. 4/26/87

I've heard stories we're going to draft a quarterback. I think that would be a silly draft. I'm really not in favor of drafting a quarterback. 4/29/87 *Chicago Sun-Times*

Jim Harbaugh, Michigan's quarterback, was the Bears' no. 1 selection. Ditka's reaction We did a great job for our offense, we confused everybody and ourselves. 4/29/87 *Des Plaines Daily Herald*

I'm satisfied. Believe me. Time will tell. 4/29/87

After the Harbaugh pick, many observers felt that the Bears would keep McMahon, Flutie, and Harbaugh, cutting Fuller and Tomczak. Ditka did not agree.   It's foolish to assume Tomczak and Fuller will be gone. There's a lot of scenarios. If Jim can't play and we're down to four quarterbacks, who do you keep? I'm keeping the three best. I won't play favorites.   7/21/87

A DIFFERENT SEASON IN 1987

I think next season we can look forward to the kind of football our fans will really enjoy. I'll guarantee we'll be ready to play and we'll play the kind of football that'll make people proud.   1/5/87 *Des Plaines Daily Herald*

Ditka apparently felt the Bears were distracted by a number of events during the 1986 season, particularly the acquisition of Doug Flutie. We're going to play great football in 1987, and the fans are going to be tremendously proud of the players and what they accomplish on the football field, and we're going to keep all the other stuff out of the newspapers.   1/20/87

We need the discipline to put the team first. When any team wins, be it the Bears, the Giants, or the Lakers, there comes a point [where] some individuals think they become more important than the team. And in part, that's true, because everyone is the reason for success. It is the team that makes it happen, though, and the problem comes when someone says, "You can't win without me."   7/21/87 *Des Plaines Daily Herald*

The biggest change our fans will see in our offense is that we don't fumble as much or throw the ball away or trip ourselves or not score from inside the 40-yard line. That will be the biggest change.   7/21/87

My job is to find a way to get [young halfbacks] Neal Anderson and Thomas Sanders on the field. We're not going to diminish the effectiveness of Walter Payton. We're going to enhance it.   12/28/86

The comfort zone is over. There becomes a thing called the comfort zone with some players. They think they have been here, and so they always are going to be here. That's not true. We've made significant player changes. Look at the team pictures up on the wall, and see how many players we've changed. We can make the changes again that will enable us to win the Super Bowl. It's not a threat. It's a fact. I think we stood pat a little too much last year, but with good football players and good guys who worked their rear ends off. Now I wonder if we don't have guys with more talent at some positions, and maybe a little younger guys, and we'll have to make those moves. There's no more comfort zone.   7/21/87

CAMP

I want it to be like it was in '84 and '85, where we had to scratch and claw a little bit. We played reckless, with a chip on our shoulder. We challenged people. I want to go back to challenging people. No more Mr. Nice Guy. We had a couple of people play us like thugs the last couple of years. We're going to play any way they want to play.   8/2/87 *Southtown Economist*

We're the sleepers in the National Football Conference. We went to sleep for a year. We're back.   7/26/87 *Chicago Sun-Times*

We're not the world champions anymore. That's the difference from when we came in here last year. It's not that you're ever invincible, but we had a great feeling of strength. Now I think that's all out the window. We've got to prove that again. I think this will be a bigger challenge than last year was.   8/3/87 *Chicago Sun-Times*

There's a lot of disappointments. I'd rather stay off of that until we either release them or trade them.   8/21/87 *Chicago Sun-Times*

We have no second group to protect the quarterback. So after our first group left the scrimmage, we just got beat up . . . . Our protection is absolutely atrocious, with a few back-up people. You can't blame the quarterbacks or anyone else. It's a shame. It's hard to evaluate anybody in those situations.   8/10/87

After weeks of tough two-a-day practices, the players were grumbling.   I refuse to take the shortcuts they want to take. We have guys who don't even want to practice in the rain. They're mad at me and I like it. We're going to work hard and gripe and get mad at the coach and call him bad names and then we're going to play better. 8/19/87

Concerned about the lack of experience on special teams, Ditka hinted that he might use linebackers there.   We have a luxury here we just can't afford. We've got to get better help on our special teams.   8/27/87 *Chicago Sun-Times*

After losing 20–16 to the Cardinals   We've got a lot of work to do before we play the world champions.   9/1/87 *Chicago Sun-Times*

The Bears beat the L.A. Raiders 20–17 in an exhibition game.   I don't know what the game proved except our back-up people got it in on their back-up people. One of our sloppier games.   9/6/87

THE QUARTERBACK SITUATION ⎯⎯⎯⎯⎯⎯⎯⎯

It's especially tough to have injuries at the quarterback position. Go in with a plan that says this guy is going to be here, and when he's not around you have to start switching around. We'll know right off the bat if Jim's well. If he is well and gets hurt, I still think the preparation going into the games will be better for the people who are behind him at quarterback, and we'll be a better team.   7/22/87

I'm looking at everybody right now. And nobody's jumping out at me. We're having a hard time completing passes. Every once in a while we're doing something well. But we're just not doing it consistently.   8/7/87 *Chicago Sun-Times*

With Steve Fuller injured and out of camp and Jim McMahon assured a spot, competition focused on Mike Tomczak, Jim Harbaugh, and Doug Flutie. After an intersquad game   Mike did a pretty good job. I thought [Doug] had no pass protection at all, period. Jim runs like a back. He made things happen.   8/9/87 *Chicago Sun-Times*

The quarterbacks are a little erratic right now. But I'm not worried about it. Sometimes they throw real good, sometimes not so good. That's going to happen with young quarterbacks. 8/12/87 *Chicago Sun-Times*

The Bears defeated Miami 10–3 in the exhibition opener. Ditka complimented Harbaugh, Tomczak, and Flutie.   Our quarterbacks handled it well. We kept the offense tight. That's the way we have to play football. It's no secret we're not fancy.   8/18/87

There are quarterbacks who probably don't play in the preseason who start the regular season, but that's not what I like to have happen. [Jim McMahon] hasn't had work at it. He has to have work against defenses.   8/26/87

You have to understand we're a pretty good team, regardless of who sits under center.   8/28/87 *Chicago Sun-Times*

With Fuller hurt early and Jim McMahon going on injured reserve, Ditka was asked if he would keep Tomczak, Flutie, and Harbaugh.   I'll meet with my staff. But yeah, I guess I am. They just gotta realize that they can't all play as much as they might want to.   9/6/87

Ditka felt Jim McMahon helped Tomczak, Flutie, and Harbaugh to develop during camp.   This year he knows he's not ready to play. And I think they understand that.   9/13/87 *Chicago Sun-Times*

I'm looking at the possibility of cutting people who were major football players here for a long time. That's part of life.   9/2/87

OPENING AGAINST THE GIANTS _____

As if by fate, the first game of the 1987 season matched the 1986 Super Bowl champion New York Giants against the Bears, in Chicago. Ditka was asked how he felt about it.   It doesn't matter. You have to play somebody. Nobody can say we're limping into the season. We'll be diving right in.   4/12/87

We don't measure ourselves against the Giants; we measure ourselves against ourselves.   3/19/87

I bet not one son-of-a-gun in Russia is watching. It's not a global conflict and it's not the ultimate game.   9/14/87

You have to remember the Giants lost their opener last year on a Monday night in Dallas and came back to win it all.   9/14/87

Who will the Bears' punt returner be in the Bears–Giants game?   This will probably come as a shock, but that is the last of my worries right now. My main job is to make sure we make sure they punt the ball.   9/8/87 *Chicago Sun-Times*

Neal Anderson and Wilber Marshall were made wideouts on the punt coverage team.   We've got to put our best people on the field.   9/12/87 *Chicago Sun-Times*

I doubt if this game will be as good as people think.   9/14/87 *Chicago Sun-Times*

Once the Giants get the upper hand and the pressure goes on, it's like being caught in a vise. You can't get out of it. That's why you've got to keep on an even par with them. If we end up with a lot of pressure, it's going to be a long night.   9/14/87 *Chicago Sun-Times*

THE GIANTS–BEARS GAME

It was one of the hardest-hitting football games I've ever been around. But the greatest thing about this is, we can get on with the football season now.   9/15/87 *Chicago Sun-Times*

How were the Bears able to neutralize Lawrence Taylor?   Even if you don't do a good job blocking him, you distract him . . . . We ran at him more than away from him.   9/16/87

Lawrence Taylor hasn't been beaten to the corner by a fullback ever, but he was beaten by this kid [Neal Anderson].   9/16/87

We just wanted to play the game. Not that we're a better team than the Giants. That doesn't matter. But we play with great intensity, and when you do that, sometimes good things will happen to you that maybe shouldn't happen.   9/17/87

Why was Walter Payton reduced to low yardage by the Giants?   [We] didn't do a good job of picking off the Giants' inside linebackers running up the middle.   9/17/87

We had something to prove. All we proved is we won one game.
9/17/87

It was interesting [studying the film before the game]. Because when I went back and looked at films after we talked about it and saw how many people do play them with a lot of zone, I saw how many plays they hit on the zone. We just tried to make it tougher for [Simms] to throw the ball in there.   9/16/87 *Chicago Sun-Times*

THE BEARS VS THE BUCS _____

After the Bucs defeated the Bears 20–3   That's a good football team. They make it awfully tough for us to get our job done. Our defense again was outstanding.   9/21/87

STRIKE _____

I'm sure a lot of people in Chicago don't care what the Bears are doing, but there's a certain amount of joy people derive from a winning team. If you take it away, I don't know if that's right. If you take it away, I wonder if people will keep coming back.   9/18/87

I think I would give them [the owners and the union] common sense, but that's not my role. Determined people working together can overcome anything there is.   9/20/87 *Chicago Sun-Times*

I don't know about anybody else, but I assume there is going to be no disruption in our football season. For me to sit here and say that there would be a disruption, I think I would be doing a disservice to myself and the fans and players. I can't do that. If there is a disruption, it's something I know nothing about and I really don't care about it. I just don't want to be involved in that aspect of it.   9/10/87 *Chicago Sun-Times*

We've worked very hard as a team to put ourselves in a position to do something. I would hate to see that snatched away by those who care nothing about the Chicago Bears. I'm not sure if they care about the individuals concerned. It's just tragic to me. 9/18/87 *Chicago Sun-Times*

I leave [the strike] to the geniuses of life. I know nothing about it . . . . Evidently they [the owners and the union] don't know a whole hell of a lot about it either. 9/18/87 *Chicago Sun-Times*

Ditka's father, Michael Ditka, was the former union president of the Transport Workers Local in Aliquippa. Mike Ditka had a suggestion for reporters. I wish he was [in Chicago] to see this and talk about this. I think you'd have to call him on the phone and talk to him. That would be interesting. 9/22/87 *Chicago Sun-Times*

Michael Ditka wasn't too happy with this idea. Mike is big enough to answer for himself. What the hell's the matter with him, telling people to call here? I don't need the publicity. 9/22/87 *Chicago Sun-Times*

He did give an opinion, however. I have yet in all the years I've been involved in these activities seen a strike settled without people sitting down. We would sit down around the clock in that position, even if we were angry. A couple of sensible people can hammer anything out. I've never seen a strike yet where both sides are a winner. 9/22/87 *Chicago Sun-Times*

Mike Jr.'s view It happens in all walks of life. I was raised in a steel mill town. My dad went through one of the longest strikes in the steel industry. I don't know what it accomplished. Evidently, they thought it accomplished something. 9/20/87

Free agency is THE issue. 9/22/87 *Chicago Sun-Times*

Gary Fencik, speaking before a luncheon gathering in a Chicago hotel You might wonder why me or Walter Payton or Jim McMahon or the other top-paid players are even going out. I look back to when Mike Ditka first became head coach. He told us we were not a defense and an offense, but one team. He said, "Until you start doing things as a team, you won't win." And that has a lot to do with the solidarity we have today.   9/23/87

When told the striking Bears would be conducting their own practices, led by Mike Singletary, Ditka was skeptical.   You ought to find out where they're practicing and you ought to see if there's 45 out there every day. I'll bet you there aren't. On any day. Are we talking about togetherness? Unity? Don't give me that crap. Because there's no discipline involved in it. We live in a world of discipline.   9/24/87
Chicago Sun-Times

23

1987:
THE STRIKE SEASON

THE SPARE BEARS

*The football owners' decision to field non-union teams created much
controversy. On the first day of practice, Ditka was philosophical.*
We're all part of the American dream. I'm just happy to be working,
believe me. There's enough coaches out of work now. We don't need
the ones working out of work. I don't feel like somebody's pulling the
rug out from under me. For one day I felt that way, then I realized
life goes on. I'm kind of happy.   9/25/87 *Chicago Sun-Times*

*When asked if he would treat his non-union players differently from
the real Bears*   The only thing I'll do different is, I won't yell at
anybody. I'll say "please" a lot more and fear that somebody will walk
away and not come back.   9/22/87 *Chicago Sun-Times*

The first day of practice for the non-union Bears brought back distant memories   I really have a visual realization now of what my high school coach saw when he first saw me as a sophomore. Is this kid going to kill himself or what?   9/25/87 *Chicago Sun-Times*

Scabs?   I don't use the word. I don't understand what scab means. It's kind of a silly word.   9/25/87 *Chicago Sun-Times*

Immortality for the non-union Bears   Forever in history their names are going to be written down in the Bears yearbook as players on the team. You might have to put an asterisk after it, but they put an asterisk after Roger Maris' home run record and it's still there.   9/25/87 *Chicago Sun-Times*

Non-union Bear Mark Rodenhauser   Basically [Ditka] just talked to us and told us as long as we wear Bears uniforms we are Bears and we need to present ourselves as such.   9/27/87 *Chicago Sun-Times*

It's hard to take seriously. It's going to be hard to do the job. I think we will do it. I think we've got great coaches. We'll try like heck, I'll guarantee you.   9/23/87 *Chicago Sun-Times*

The Bears organization took a new team picture of the non-union Bears.   I just hope we have Christmas cards this year so they're on there. I want copies of this picture to go up on my wall. This is part of history. This is nice.   10/1/87 *Chicago Sun-Times*

Describing the difficulty of fielding a non-union team   You got to realize you take kids for 10 days and try and give them an offense, a defense, and special teams. I don't know what you can expect. But they're a good group of kids. They work hard, they keep their mouths shut, and they're appreciative. That in itself is different.   9/29/87

I forget how our regular players play. I haven't seen them play in so long.   10/5/87 *Chicago Sun-Times*

The kids have been "Yes, sir" and "No, sir" and "I want to do it" and always looking to get better. You've got to be proud of that. You've got to be excited about it.   10/5/87 *Chicago Sun-Times*

Using non-union players   Maybe it's a step backward. But maybe it's a step forward in a lot of other ways.   10/5/87 *Chicago Sun-Times*

This is a real work ethic group, a bunch of lunch bucket guys. No Gucci shoes in this outfit, gang. No Guccis.   10/13/87 *Chicago Sun-Times*

There are a couple of players right now who are turning my head at a couple of positions. There will definitely probably be room for them on this team regardless of who comes back.   10/4/87

Saying goodbye after the strike   It won't be easy. Things are never easy for me. You don't make associations and friendships and get attached to people and all of a sudden say, "Goodbye, I'll see you," just because somebody else has a whim that they want to come back and play football.   10/6/87 *Chicago Sun-Times*

THE STRIKE SEASON BEGINS _____

Eagerly awaiting the first non-union Bears game against the Eagles I'm really into it now. If this isn't fun there's no such thing as fun.   10/1/87 *Chicago Sun-Times*

On the Eagles–Bears game   It could be the highlight of my career or the most embarrassing moment of my career. Who cares? Win, lose, or draw I'm going to hold my head up high.   10/4/87

Experience only counts if they can play. If they can't play it doesn't matter. If they have previous NFL experience and they're not playing in the NFL right now, there's a reason for that, too.   10/4/87

Will Reggie White, star defensive lineman for the Eagles, play in the first non-union game?   I just hope Reggie White doesn't go in at Philadelphia. We'd have to get a gun to stop him.   10/1/87

Non-union Bears favored over non-union Eagles   It must be the uniforms. I don't know. How could anyone put a line on these games? That doesn't make any sense. I have no idea what Philadelphia has. They don't know what we have. I'm not sure they know what they have. And I'm not sure we know what we have until we play.   10/4/87

On pickets outside Philadelphia's stadium   What are those people doing out there? This game was going to go on. All they're doing is wasting gas and energy. That's silly.   10/5/87 *Chicago Sun-Times*

Bears officials reportedly discussed the possibility of crossing the picket line in Philadelphia.   I expect the police will help us get through. If police are in the picket line, we're all going to have problems. I'm not going to take a gun out there; it's not that important. If they have guns, I'll tell you what: I'll be long gone.   10/1/87

Diana Ditka on the Philadelphia game   Mike said he'd rather I not go [to Philadelphia] because they expect a lot of problems.   10/2/87

GOON SQUADS

Ditka was particularly angry at the scuffles and violence outside Veterans stadium in Philadelphia between pro-union picketers and fans.   They use the word scab. The word I'd use for those people is goons. Goons on the picket line. Goon squads. That's basically what they are.   10/6/87 *Chicago Sun-Times*

On beating the Eagles 35–3   We just had better players, especially at quarterback [Mike Hohensee].   10/5/87 *Chicago Sun-Times*

Ditka gave every non-union player a game ball after the victory.   That's something they'll remember forever. This is a special thing, regardless of when it ends. They're special to me anyway. 10/5/87 *Chicago Sun-Times*

On the problems fans, players, and stadium workers experienced in Philadelphia before the Eagles–Bears game   This is America. I thought this was the land of the free and the home of the brave. Now is it just the land of the brave? Do you have to be brave to come on the field?   10/5/87 *Chicago Sun-Times*

Mike McCaskey on beating the Eagles   I can't compliment Mike Ditka, Vince Tobin, and Ed Hughes enough.   10/7/87

THE BEARS VS THE VIKINGS _____

Before the Vikings game in Soldier Field, the non-union Bears were introduced over the stadium public address system.   At the beginning of the game when those guys were introduced, that was the loudest I heard people cheer for guys being introduced in a long time.   10/13/87

On pickets at Soldier Field   If people want to stop people, we have a totalitarian country. Fans have a right to go and watch a game in peace without being cajoled, shoved, spit at, or called names. If it ever becomes any other way, we're living in the wrong country. 10/15/87

In contrast to the 1986 play-off game with the Washington Redskins, in which Ditka remained calm and collected, during the non-union Vikings–Bears game he raged the sidelines.   I got into that game more than I've gotten into a game in a long, long time. If I'd been into the Washington game like I was in that game, we might have won. Somebody might have believed something I said.   10/13/87 *Chicago Sun-Times*

The non-union Bears defeated the Vikings 27–7.   We had people we didn't think could help us that much come on the field and play pretty darn good. I take my hat off to them.   10/12/87 *Chicago Sun-Times*

I don't think anybody has an advantage now on our football team. We're very confident after winning two games. You better not tell them how good they ain't, you better prove it. They think they are pretty good. Geez, they played hard. 10/13/87

On the non-union Bears having 20 quarterback sacks in two games That'll about get you in the *Guinness Book of World Records* somewhere.   10/12/87 *Chicago Sun-Times*

Ditka assigned a pet name to the new non-union Bears.   Remember when we were kids growing up? They used to call them clodhoppers— little black shoes. They had steel things on the toe and heel. I used to wear them and you could play football all year in them. They'd last you two or three years. We've got a lot of clodhopper guys.   10/13/87 *Chicago Sun-Times*

THE BEARS VS THE SAINTS

We're playing a better team on the field than we are. It'll take everything we can do to win the football game. They have better people.   10/18/87

This should be a special game for these guys and they all know that. I think they'll play with a lot of heart.   10/18/87

Mike Hohensee decided not to start against New Orleans because of a bad knee. Said Ditka He saw fit not to play, and that's his prerogative. He got hit in the knee last week, but he practiced all week on it and practiced last night. We thought it was a bursa sac; it might be a cartilage. He thought it was giving out on him, so he opted not to play. We respect his option.   10/19/87

Mike Hohensee I told them Saturday I didn't know if I'd be able to go because the knee was giving out on me just walking around the hotel.   10/19/87

When I got my shock [that Hohensee couldn't play] a half-hour before the game, that was big-time. Then you know you have to have a trick up your sleeve to win. Now I sympathize with the guys who didn't have quarterbacks.   10/20/87

Forced to alternate between quarterbacks Sean Payton and Steve Bradley, Ditka explained his strategy in the New Orleans game.   I was trying to save their lives. I thought maybe with one guy not taking a steady pounding we had a chance.   10/19/87 *Chicago Sun-Times*

We had a lot of laughs about a lot of things. We laughed at ourselves and laughed at the situation. Yet there was a lot of pressure on everybody to try to make it as good as we could make it, to not blemish the record. We just couldn't quite make it. So the record's blemished. I didn't want to get it blemished this whole year, but it's blemished. Hopefully, with the veteran players we can pick it up and not let it be blemished anymore.   10/19/87

Helping out quarterbacks Payton and Bradley We had the plays numbered 1 through 50 on the back of a towel. That didn't work quite so well.   10/19/87 *Chicago Sun-Times*

SAINTS 19, BEARS 17 ⎯⎯⎯⎯⎯⎯⎯⎯⎯⎯⎯

I wished everything could have been worked out where they [the union Bears] played this game. For their sake, the league's sake, our sake, for everybody's sake. Mostly for them. But I don't make the rules. I follow them.   10/17/87

I take every game in football seriously. Maybe their counterparts on strike don't think it means anything. But it means a lot to the young men who are out there playing. We instill that in them and we're proud of that. We're proud of being the Chicago Bears. We're proud of what the game stands for and what it will always stand for. We're not about to go around bitching and griping about things that don't make any difference. These kids don't gripe about anything. We hauled them out at 5 o'clock in the morning Sunday and they were there and they went into the locker room and went to sleep. They got up, went up-stairs, and ate a pregame meal. All unusual circumstances. And they loved it. Then they went out on the field and played like hell. Our defense looked the same to me. If you take the names off the jerseys and change the numbers around, you'd never recognize the difference. 10/6/87

DITKA ON MIKE HOHENSEE ⎯⎯⎯⎯⎯⎯⎯⎯⎯⎯

Mike Hohensee's a pretty darn good quality football player all the way around. He's food for thought, is what Mike Hohensee is.   10/5/87 *Chicago Sun-Times*

I think Philadelphia might even have had an edge in receivers with size and speed. But the key in these games is the quarterback [Mike Hohensee]. We had a decided advantage.   10/6/87

Offensively we're getting better. Hohensee was outstanding Sunday at handling the offense, moving people around, reading the defenses, getting rid of the ball when he had to. I like his nerve, his guts, his composure, his arm.   10/13/87

On keeping Mike Hohensee   Well, I can get rid of one of our quarterbacks immediately and keep him. What's the problem with that? There's no problem at all.   10/6/87

After Doug Flutie was traded to New England, Ditka was asked if he would keep Mike Hohensee.   I don't know if I'd be willing to put Mike through the problems that would occur. I think you have to consider every avenue. He's an excellent young man, but I'm not going to put him out there as a sacrificial lamb for anybody.   10/17/87

Mike Hohensee   I hope he doesn't base a decision on that. I'm willing to go through it. If they [the regular Bears] want to make my life miserable, that's them wasting their time.   10/17/87

GLENN KOZLOWSKI

Glenn Kozlowski caught 5 passes for 65 yards in the Eagles game. Ditka was impressed.   Kozlowski was working on a construction crew up until Thursday. He flew in Friday and practiced Saturday morning. He was the last receiver cut, and it makes you kind of think maybe we cut the wrong one.   10/6/87

He's a hell of a kid, a special guy. He's got a big heart. He's my kind of guy.   10/12/87 *Chicago Sun-Times*

ANTHONY MOSLEY

Mosley's our best running back.   10/12/87 *Chicago Sun-Times*

JIM ALTHOFF

In the Eagles game, non-union Bears player Jim Althoff scored 42 points on the Bears defensive rating system. The season high had been 34 points, scored by Wilber Marshall in the Giants game.   I've been here a long time and I've never had a defensive lineman score 40 points on this point system—not even near 40. Althoff was all over the field. I don't care who he was playing against.   10/6/87

ON ALTHOFF AND HOHENSEE

Hohensee probably played as good a first half as we've had played by any quarterback. Don't ask me why teams overlook people like this. Why I didn't know Jim Althoff, I don't know. Maybe because he's not 6-foot-5, but a little shorter for a defensive lineman. But his heart is bigger than most. Don't ask me why I didn't know about Mike Hohensee. Pretty sharp kid. Both he and Althoff are pretty good examples of what we like Bears players to be. They're quality people.   10/6/87

MIKE HOHENSEE ON DITKA

He was very patient with us the first day. But that only lasted the first day. At least when he yells at you, he tells you why.   10/4/87

On telling Ditka he couldn't play just before the last strike game   I would have been out there if I could have. I've played with a broken wrist, a busted sternum, and just off arthroscopic surgery. I have no problem being injured and playing, if I could help the team. But [Ditka] is thinking negatively of it, and I don't feel my chances are very good of being kept. He'll probably release me, and maybe I'll be picked up by another team. If not, it's on to Arena Football.   10/26/87

On November 3, Mike Hohensee was released by the Bears. He confirmed that Ditka was upset about his missing that last game.   He pretty much told me I'd never play for the Bears again and that he wouldn't recommend me to anybody.   11/23/87 *Chicago Sun-Times*

I still think I can play in the league. But [Ditka] was disappointed because I didn't play injured and he's a little bitter about it right now.   11/23/87 *Chicago Sun-Times*

I know it caught him by surprise, but I had no reason to want to sit out. I knew if I could play, it would help my chances of staying. I know in my heart I made the right choice, but if I hadn't maybe I'd still be there.   11/23/87 *Chicago Sun-Times*

I played my heart out. The most unfortunate thing is that I don't think Coach Ditka knows me as a person. I've never sold anyone out. 11/23/87 *Chicago Sun-Times*

When asked what he told Ditka after being cut   I thanked him for the opportunity.   11/23/87 *Chicago Sun-Times*

ANTHONY MOSELY ON DITKA ⸻

He wants to win no matter who's playing. That's what it takes in a coach. They have to push you, and he's a perfectionist.   10/12/87 *Chicago Sun-Times*

He came in and kind of apologized to everybody. He said, "I'm out there ranting and raving and throwing a fit, but I want things done right and I want you to be the best you can be.   10/16/87

MORE NON-UNION BEARS ON DITKA ⸻

John Wojciechowski   Coach Ditka came in and told us, "We're going out and practicing and playing a game as far as we know." But we went to practice with mixed emotions. It was difficult to go through. You don't know if it's your last practice, or what.   10/16/87

Greg Fitzgerald   The coaching staff made us feel welcome. They never made us feel this was a joke. They took everything we did seriously. We played with the pride of the Bears because the coaches believed in us.   10/5/87 *Chicago Sun-Times*

Glenn Kozlowski   I think [Ditka] means I give everything I can. When I go out there, I do everything I can to win.   10/12/87 *Chicago Sun-Times*

OTHER SECOND CHANCES

The strike opened options for players the Bears had not signed on the non-union roster. Some speculated NFL rosters would go from 45 players to 49 players after the strike, allowing teams to carry an additional four players. Eric Jeffries   Coach Ditka had good things to say about me, and I truly believe I'd have still been on the Bears if there was room for me. Now with the chance for an expanded roster, I think I can come back and show them again I can play for them. 10/7/87

John Duvic, who played for a week before being cut   Without question it was worth it. Just to see Mike Ditka get so excited. It's not like this was a job—it's a sport, it's fun. That's what it's been to me.   10/5/87 *Chicago Sun-Times*

Jon Norris, who resumed his job as a part-time bartender in Milford, Conn., after the strike   The biggest pain in the butt is working in a bar, because everyone asks the same questions, beginning with, "What's Ditka like?" I tell them he's a great guy. Around here, they only see him yelling and screaming.   11/23/87 *Chicago Sun-Times*

24

1987: REFLECTIONS ON THE STRIKE

STRIKE FRUSTRATION

You feel frustrated. Everybody talks about how they've been betrayed.
I feel like I've been betrayed. I feel like the coaching staff, the
organization, has been betrayed. I feel like George Halas has been
betrayed, 63 years of history has been betrayed. Why? I don't know.
I haven't heard an answer yet. I've heard our players talk about it,
management talk about it, union representatives talk about it. And I'm
still not sure what anyone is saying. Is the game important or isn't it
important? Everyone says it's based on togetherness and solidarity.
Maybe that's another word for greed. It's always that last-second
syndrome, thinking you're going to scare somebody into doing something
they don't want to do. Nobody's going to scare anybody in this deal.
Both sides are unscareable. It could well go down to . . . maybe there
will be no football as we know it, only football as we see it out there
in practice.   9/29/87

Dan Hampton   It's tearing him up not to be coaching the best talent in the NFL. For him to be coaching inferior talent . . . well, that's why he's saying all the things he has said.   10/7/87

Diana Ditka   He's very frustrated. He's really anxious to get the players back. He's having a good time with these kids, but it's not the same, even though these kids are playing their hearts out. Mentally, it's wearing on him. It's tough—I think he thought the players were going to come back this week.   10/12/87 *Chicago Sun-Times*

Diana Ditka   He would give everything if he could have the real team on the field, but he's just taking it one day at a time. Sometimes he's really frustrated and other times he's fine.   10/2/87

Diana Ditka on the annual Bears' wives luncheon   He approached the wives at the luncheon and he was like a caged lion. He was very emotional and he said, "Go back and tell your husbands that I love 'em and I miss 'em and that I want 'em to hurry up and come back."   10/12/87 *Chicago Sun-Times*

Mike Ditka's view   In this whole thing, everybody is hurt, including fans and coaches. But the players are hurt tremendously because it's their source of income and it's what they do, what they enjoy. They miss it more than anybody has really said.   10/17/87

I want these games to count. I'd be very disappointed if the [NFL] Management Council backed off on that. It'd be a cop-out. The games were played by professional people.   10/6/87

What would happen if we win? Do you understand what would happen to the whole structure if we keep winning? Someone will have to turn around and say, "We did a lousy job of scouting, of evaluating personnel."   10/13/87

After a certain number of games, Ditka predicted that the owners would have to go with the replacement teams for the entire season.   I just assume it'd have to happen. I think the league is going to say that past a certain time you're playing the hands you're dealt, go with it. 10/13/87

Would loss of pay for striking players end the strike?   I don't know if it'll help end the strike. It gets to the point where I don't have any opinions anymore. You quit caring about it. I don't worry about it anymore. I've been in this position before where we were a lousy football team. In 1982, we were. People forget about that. We weren't very good. Now we don't know if we can be good or not—until we play.   9/29/87

On rumors of a possible breakthrough in the strike negotiations Yesterday, there was a possibility. But one of our coaches summed it up well when he said, "This is the last time I'm going to get on the rollercoaster." He's right. There's no use getting up and down. Whatever happens, happens, and you go with it. We've resigned ourselves to that. These kids will try. I don't know if you get any accolades for that. But they'll try.   10/15/87

All I know is this [the strike] shouldn't happen in our business. 10/12/87 *Chicago Sun-Times*

On the coaches' role   We're just gadgets on the machine, trying to do our job.   10/11/87

THE STRIKING BEARS

There can be strength in unity, but there can also be stupidity. How much do you think [Bears] players get along together? You think they get phone calls every night from their teammates saying, "Why don't you come over and play checkers?" Once they leave here, how many of them talk with each other? We have guys who don't talk to anybody. So what difference does it make? I don't see these guys socializing much. A few guys get a beer together, but other than that, they all scatter. 10/6/87

Of the striking Bears, Ditka explained that he had only talked to Payton and Suhey.   I know they're trying to do the right thing, trying to help the team together.   10/6/87

Who are the real Bears?   The Chicago Bears are the people who played yesterday [the non-union Bears]. And the Chicago Bears are the people who'll play next week—whoever that may be.   10/6/87 *Chicago Sun-Times*

On the real Bears practicing   Last week would have made sense because they were going to play someone. Now that they're not going to play, I wouldn't practice. I'd be like those eight guys [who didn't show]. 10/1/87

They are all big boys. But to do something for the sake of other people doing it is foolish because two wrongs do not make a right. Twenty-seven wrongs don't make a right no matter how you do it. There can be strength in unity. There can also be stupidity in unity.   10/6/87 *Chicago Sun-Times*

When told his prediction that some of the Bears would fail to show for the impromptu practices [33 of 45 practiced] was correct   We have some of the laziest guys who are non-motivated in the world. They get a lot of credit, you know, and that in itself should show a lot of players who do show up—they don't really care about them. There's no togetherness. It's all for themselves. The egos rule. We have a tremendous amount of egomaniacs. And the only way you control egomaniacs is with discipline. The better word in the dictionary calls it prima donna. She don't dance on this field. She don't sing in this theatre. But she's around, if you let her be. My frame of mind right now is not good. I wonder if the coaches in the NFL should tell them [the players] to stick it. Of course, the players don't need coaches. We all know that. They can play without us. You know how well they played here for years. They're super without coaching; they can do whatever they want.   9/29/87

Dave Duerson on egomania   To be a pro athlete, you have to have something that Mike Ditka had, too, and that's a tremendous ego. But you have to have something else, and that's pride.   9/30/87 *Chicago Sun-Times*

After making controversial comments about the striking Bears, Ditka addressed several striking Bears' wives at a luncheon.   I get stubborn at times and say things. But still that doesn't affect my feeling for those football players who aren't here. I respect them. They're making a decision that's not easy for them.   10/8/87 *Chicago Sun-Times*

I hope my players know what I think of them. I respect them tremendously. They're fighting for a cause they think is right. I don't know who is right or wrong anymore.   10/12/87 *Chicago Sun-Times*

THE FANS

Explaining that he didn't expect problems in Chicago like those encountered by fans and football personnel in Philadelphia   We're a little more orderly in this city.   10/8/87

If the fans boycott Soldier Field   If our fans feel that's what they want to do, more power to them. We're going to play the game whether we play in front of 40,000 or 5,000. So it doesn't matter. They're going to miss a good game, is all.   10/6/87

It's up to the so-called fans whether they want to come Sunday. They came out and watched us in 1982. What the hell, this team we're playing with now is a better team than we had in 1982. In every area. Let's be realistic.   10/6/87

Some ticket-holders took advantage of the Bears front office policy of providing refunds for the non-union game. Ditka's response   If I owned the club and they turned their tickets in, I wouldn't give them a ticket next year. Seriously. I don't care if people like it or not. It's not any reflection on the Bears ownership. This is me talking. To me, if you turn it in, I'd find somebody else to give the tickets to. That's the way I am. I think Mr. Halas would have played hardball like that.   10/6/87

Every time I say something, it seems to be wrong. We appreciate the people who appreciate us. Those who don't appreciate us, we're sorry we're not as good as they want us to be. But we appreciate anybody who appreciates us. We try to do the best we can. It's just an unfortunate situation.   10/12/87 *Chicago Sun-Times*

Later in the week Ditka's attitude toward those fans who asked for refunds was less harsh.   The ones that turned their tickets in, they certainly have a right to.   10/8/87 *Chicago Sun-Times*

You get frustrated and say things, and you don't always mean them. In the true sense of the word it's not who WE accept, but if the fans accept us. The guy who pays all the tickets in life is the fan. What I said about the fans last week certainly wasn't right. I said it in a fit of anger. They have a right to do whatever they want.   10/13/87

25

1987:
THE STRIKE ENDS

On October 15, the players' strike officially ended. Ditka was elated. You know my feelings. It's the best thing in the world they're coming back. *10/16/87 Chicago Sun-Times*

Should the Bears play on their first Sunday back? I'm not one of the experts, I'm the Clodhopper Kid. What's my opinion got to do with anything? *10/17/87 Chicago Sun-Times*

When told the NFL Management Council would not allow striking players to play on the Sunday following their return to work Is it written in stone? *10/16/87*

When asked if the league would make up any non-union games played, Ditka responded They're not going to make them up, you watch. You

can bet on it. There will be an announcement made in the next couple
days. The games we play are going to count.   9/29/87

We just finished a morning practice with the replacement team. They'll
go to their hotel and, hopefully, rest with the Saints dancing in their
heads. In will come the regular team for an afternoon practice. Then
we're going down to the corner of Kedzie and Cicero. Want to see if
we can find a team we can practice with tonight.

Those streets run the same way? Gosh darn. That's why I get lost
all the time.   10/17/87

WE'RE READY

*Immediately after the strike ended, the Bears players, led by Mike
Singletary, met at Halas Hall and expressed their desire to return
immediately to prepare for Sunday's game. That evening the Bears
practiced under the lights at Soldier Field. Just prior to the practice,
Mike Singletary explained*   The coaches don't feel we'll be ready. We
feel we're ready. We'll practice tonight, tomorrow, Sunday, whatever
it takes. Hopefully, we'll be playing Sunday.   10/16/87

The first practice after the strike, Ditka was pleased.   The practice
was exceptionally good. Upbeat. Everybody worked. Everybody knew
what they were doing. Everybody executed outstanding. It was a joy
to see. I'll be the first to say I'm amazed and pleased. I didn't feel,
with the three-week layoff, they could pick it up as fast as they did.
We didn't run that much. All we did was run plays. But I feel most
are in pretty darn good shape. I haven't seen anything that looks out
of line. I haven't put each guy on the scale yet. But I haven't seen
anybody that looked different than they looked before. I talked to Tom
Thayer and I thought he looked heavier. But his weight is right on the
button at 278, or 275, which is what he was when he left. Some guys
even looked thinner to me.   10/17/87

REPLACEMENT BEARS AS REAL BEARS? _____

Mike Hohensee   The coaches here made it better for us than probably any other team in the league. They treated us like professionals. 10/16/87 *Chicago Sun-Times*

Ditka   Even if we sign some people to a future contract, that's important. I realize, when you do those things, a lot of people are going to say this and that. But you have to look at developing people. Sure, you'd have to practice these guys together with the regular team. If that came about, you'd have to hope for the best. It would fall on me and the coaching staff to control the situation. It's controllable, I think. But then, I'm an optimist.   10/17/87

We have some kids we'd like to develop. We have to find out how they mix in, and if they don't mix in, then we'll make a decision. 10/19/87

You take strawberries and bananas and put them in a blender and they mix up pretty good.   10/23/87 *Chicago Sun-Times*

Throughout the entire strike the Bears stuck together as a unit. Ditka was impressed.   They've taken a stand and, by God, they stuck to their guns. Our guys were outstanding. What happens from here on out, that's up to us. We'll do the best we can to get back on track and get back the spirit we had. I think that will happen. The other things will be resolved by people more powerful than us. In a court of law. Whoever wins or loses has to accept it.   10/17/87

The hard part is not what's past; it's what's coming.   10/19/87

You can't expect everybody to come up and be buddy-buddy, especially with me. But with each other, they're probably together more now than when they went out on strike. Yesterday afternoon and last night

I talked with them about some things. But talking is not the answer. You can talk until you're blue in the face. Those guys don't want to hear me talk. They've heard me talk enough. It's a matter of doing and feeling and understanding what it's going to take. The road ahead, it's not like it's insurmountable. This is an excellent team. They've come back with an excellent attitude, from what I can see.   10/17/87

NO SCABS

Dave Duerson   The decision of our group is we can win the Super Bowl without the need of scab players.

Mike Ditka   You never know, that might be the advice we follow. 10/20/87

If problems occur between the replacement Bears on the roster and the regular Bears during practices   I'll take into consideration the people who caused it to occur and we'll ask them to leave. We're not going to put up with anything.   10/21/87

We're not going to put up with it. This is law and order, this is America.   10/21/87 *Chicago Sun-Times*

THE VOTE AND THE VETO

Ditka let his regular players vote on whether the non-union Bears could become regular Bears. It was reported that the vote was 44–1 against the non-union Bears. Ditka rejected the decision.   I let them vote because I thought they'd be realistic about it. If someone could help our team, I thought they'd let them. But they saw fit not to do that. The only thing I worry about is winning games. I'm not in a popularity contest. A lot of those guys made a lot of decisions the past four weeks. I'm the boss now. I make the decisions and I live with them.   10/21/87

You know what President Reagan does? He vetoes. I vetoed. That's my power.   10/21/87 *Chicago Sun-Times*

Bill Tobin   He didn't think it was right and he overrode the players' vote. So the decision has been made that these replacement players will integrate with the players who were on strike.   10/21/87

Asked how his players reacted to the veto   I don't know and don't care.   10/21/87

If I'm a bad guy and they think that, God bless them. But there are five guys [replacement Bears] out there who think I'm a pretty good guy.   10/21/87 *Chicago Sun-Times*

FAMILY FEUD

Dennis McKinnon   The family got vetoed. It doesn't make any difference what we say. We found out we had no power. The family structure holds no water. We're 45 guys who are gonna go out and win. We're gonna do our best to win the Super Bowl. And this time it will be a player who will be carrying the Super Bowl and not management. 10/22/87 *Chicago Sun-Times*

Jim McMahon   At the time Mike [Ditka] said we'd vote, Michael McCaskey turned around like he was surprised. It probably wasn't the smartest thing to do. At the time it was, "If you guys don't want them, we won't keep 'em. It's as simple as that." Well, I guess it's not. 10/22/87 *Chicago Sun-Times*

Ditka   This probably has done a great thing in bringing people very close together.   10/25/87 *Chicago Sun-Times*

Ditka   They're tired of practicing and they're ready to play. They've got a lot of frustrations they want to get out of them and they can only get them out Sunday on the field.   10/23/87 *Chicago Sun-Times*

Jay Hilgenberg   Everyone is just thinking about football. If we're mad at Ditka, we're foolish. We have more important things to do, like get back to the Super Bowl.   10/23/87 *Chicago Sun-Times*

Ditka   We're so fortunate we've got three quality quarterbacks right now, and I would not feel uncomfortable with any of the three. I could go with Jim Harbaugh and feel comfortable.   10/23/87 *Chicago Sun-Times*

John Matuszak, former Raiders lineman   The Bears are the Raiders of the 80s and I love 'em. I loved it when Mike Ditka let his guys vote on the replacement players and then he overruled a unanimous vote. I'm partial to mean and nasty teams. The Raiders are still mean and nasty, but you gotta win. The Bears do.   11/5/87

26

1987: THE REAL SEASON BEGINS

THE BEARS AT TAMPA BAY

Our problem this week will be Tampa Bay. We didn't exactly blow them out of the bleachers the last time we played them. 10/20/87 *Chicago Sun-Times*

Ditka was upset at the officiating at the Tampa Bay game. On one play Todd Bell was tackled by a Buccaneer player. Their tight end tackled Todd Bell on that play when Todd jumped up and down. One of the great takedowns. Hulk Hogan would have loved it; that's how bad it was. 10/27/87

The call on Jay Hilgenberg was not holding. The call against Maurice Douglass on Dennis Gentry's long kickoff return was not a good call. He hit the guy in the side, and all the referee saw was the end of the play. You cannot make the call if you don't see the beginning of the play.   10/27/87

We're known as Peck's Bad Boys. Maybe I have to keep doing it [complaining about the officiating] and you [reporters] have to keep writing it and finally the people in New York will say, "Hey, wait a second. The Bears aren't bad guys just because they play tough." 10/27/87

Jim McMahon came off the bench and with 2:44 to go engineered an 85-yard drive to beat Tampa Bay 27-26 in the final seconds of the game. Jim McMahon did it. He called the plays by himself on the final drive. He's a tough son-of-a-gun.   10/26/87

Maybe they got too conservative. If you play zone against that guy [McMahon], he'll kill you.   10/26/87

KANSAS CITY AT CHICAGO

They're wounded right now. I'm worried about teams that are wounded.   11/1/87 *Chicago Sun-Times*

Once again, Jim McMahon, with the help of key plays by special teams and offense, scored late in the fourth quarter to beat the Chiefs 31-28. Ditka felt the Bears were becoming too predictable. We have to take a look at what we are running. We're getting stereotyped there. Kansas City was guessing with us, and they guessed right a few times. We're going to have to start running some counter-plays.   11/4/87

We're getting very tell-tale about what we're doing defensively. 11/3/87

We're going to have to change the nature of who we are. We just can't keep running the ball on people all of the time. So we might have to throw it more. It doesn't matter to me how we win. 11/4/87

We've won a lot of different ways, but basically we've won with great defense. Today the defense needed help, from the offense, from the kicking game. I think after the last two weeks, we all have a better understanding that this is a team, the Chicago Bears TEAM. 11/2/87

After two last-minute victories over Tampa and Kansas City We'll be okay. It's kind of like coming out of camp again. 11/2/87

BEARS AT GREEN BAY

We have to practice better. We have to give the defense a better picture in practice. They have to concentrate a little better, too. We don't put any pressure on our defensive line in practice. It comes time for the game and they go up against a line like Kansas City and it's not all so easy. We have to come up to a thud tempo. Not live, not all-out, but a pretty good tempo so we can figure out what we're doing. We've done it in the past. We'll be all right. 11/3/87

For the third week in a row the Bears needed fourth-quarter heroics, this time a 52-yard field goal from Kevin Butler with no time left, to beat the Packers 26–24. We've won three football games in a row that really defy explanation. Except I know we've got a lot of guys who are very committed and believe they can win and they aren't going to give up for anything. 11/9/87

We probably have used up our allotment of miracles. 11/9/87

Otis Wilson and Dan Hampton were injured in the Packers game. On Otis Wilson's injury It was a leg whip. The rules are, you're not allowed to leg whip. It should be called as a clipping penalty. The head official [referee Fred Silva] was standing right there. And he looked at it. And he didn't call it.   11/10/87

When asked why he didn't file a report with the league office about the officiating, Ditka replied I'm tired of filing reports.   11/10/87 *Chicago Sun-Times*

On losing Wilson and Hampton They're all-pros and we'll miss them. But the other guys know what their job is. They've been waiting for a chance, and this is their chance.   11/12/87 *Chicago Sun-Times*

Back in Chicago, Ditka and his coaches reviewed the game films with the team. Ditka left halfway through the film. I don't think I've ever done that since I've been here. I was upset looking at the films myself. I didn't feel comfortable with them, so I went upstairs to my desk. It was a good decision. I thought I might have said some things that would have bothered some players.   11/10/87

How does he feel about the state of the Bears team? Perplexed. That's the word. That's a good word. Our staff here always has given credit to the players. We win because we have good players, so we have to take some of the blame for what's happening now. Our record is 7–1, and I'm happy about that. But our attitude, our intensity is more like 4–4, and that bothers me.   11/10/87

THE BEARS AT DENVER _____

Coach Dan Reeves of the Denver Broncos and Mike Ditka were assistant coaches together at Dallas, and still are close friends. Prior to the Bears–Broncos game both coaches reflected on the strike and its effect on players throughout the league. I've talked to Dan in Denver. He feels the same thing. There's a hollow feeling, a closeness that wasn't there. I guess it's all over the league, and we're more fortunate than others. We're 7–1, not 1–7 like the Rams, and our guys are trying hard, and they're 5–0 in the regular games. You can't knock that.

But we had all our priorities in order, our goals, for that New York game. And now I have trouble capturing the spirit of the thing. I say, "Let's win this game for the organization," and it's like they're saying to me, hell with the organization. Where players used to look forward to the start of a practice week, it's almost like you have to pull them out on the field now.

There are two ways to look at practice. Either as something that can be productive, or as boring, like you're disgruntled. I see a little lackadaisical attitude, like everybody's pulled back. I might be wrong. I hope I'm wrong, but this strike thing really seems to have taken something out of us. If the Chicago Bears hadn't have gone out, there would have been no strike, because nobody else would have gone out. That's how respected these players were, and still are.

I suggested that to them. Keep playing and demand that it be settled by such-and-such a date. But they went out anyway. And it hurt us bad, not because we were so far ahead of everybody else, but because we knew what we wanted. And now I'm more part of the other faction than ever. I'm management. I used to maybe yell at them and get them mad, but they'd go out and play like hell on Sunday anyway. Now I don't know whether to criticize them, offend them, or what.

It's almost like when I talk to them, they don't really want to hear me anymore. You tell them something during practice and they nod. Yup, we understand. And then on Sunday, they play like they don't understand. Things we've been doing for a couple years, they don't understand. We aren't playing well. You have to stop saying everything's okay and prove it's okay. We're so ruthless, teams can't wait to play us. We weren't the Monsters of the Midway Sunday. It was us who got slapped around like teddy bears in Green Bay. I'm trying to smile, even at 7–1, but I'm not having a real good time.   11/10/87

It's going to be a challenge at Denver. We haven't played our best football, and Denver has had a little struggle. It's an important game for both of us. We've had some good practices, some not so good. Today was a good, spirited practice. I think we're ready. We've been sitting back and waiting. It's almost like we're waiting for bad things to happen. But that's not the way we built this club. We went out and challenged people. We concentrated better today in practice than we have. There was an importance, an urgency, to what we were doing. Before, that wasn't there, maybe because of who we were playing and because we didn't think it was that important.   11/12/87

Ditka emphasized that the key to beating the Broncos would be stopping Denver quarterback John Elway.   You're not going to stop him; you know that. You just hope he doesn't have one of those fantastic nights. You try to keep him from scrambling, but you're *not* going to keep him from scrambling. You try to keep him in the pocket as much as you can and try to do some coverage downfield by mixing up the defenses, whether or not you're right when you play zone or right when you play man-to-man. We have to mix it up on him and hope we can create a little indecision for him and cover the receivers enough to get a pass rush on him.   11/15/87

Containing John Elway meant that the Bears' pass rush and secondary would have to play better. Examining the secondary in the three previous games, Ditka concluded   We don't play zone so well. It's no secret.   11/15/87

DENVER 31–BEARS 29

After taking an early 14–0 lead and driving to score, a mix-up on an attempted handoff to William Perry at the goal line cost the Bears an opportunity to go up 21–7 at the half. Denver quarterback John Elway eventually completed 21 of 40 passes for 341 yards, with three touchdown passes, giving the regular Bears their first defeat of the year. Later, William Perry explained that he was surprised to get the ball, prompting McMahon to give his assessment of what happened.   If we would have scored there it would have been 21–7 and a totally different ball game. It was a stupid play on my part.   11/18/87

Mike Ditka on Perry's fumble   It was a perfectly designed play by a great, great football coach. Don't you ever forget that. What usually happens when you fake to Perry? A bunch of people go to Perry. There is only one guy outside and he has his choice of taking the quarterback or Payton. He probably would have taken Payton and Jim would have walked in. Lest you people forget, it was the identical play that we scored on in the Super Bowl. Very well designed and thought out, almost to the point of being excellent, but executed terribly.   11/18/87

I give credit to John and the Broncos. I really do. But there's a lot of discipline lacking on this team. What we've built here, we've lost. We've lost the will to excel.   11/17/87 *Chicago Sun-Times*

WHAT'S WRONG HERE?

We can't stop anybody on third down. We've just been killed. Two weeks in a row we have given up touchdowns at the end of the half. That's like scoring a goal in hockey in the last two seconds. We were in a three-deep zone when we gave up the third touchdown to Denver. That should never happen, never.   11/18/87

Offenses have caught up with us. We've had so-so cornerbacks in coverage. We have no pass rush at all without blitzing. When we do get pressure, we don't cover anybody. We haven't had a sack from the defensive line since last spring.   11/18/87

Who do we have who is a good pass rusher? Richard Dent? C'mon. He's not disciplined. He was offsides half the time. He hurt us more than he helped us. And William Perry's not a good pass rusher. 11/17/87 *Chicago Sun-Times*

We had seven offside penalties on defense. Two of them turned out to be free plays that went for 30 yards and for a touchdown. We aren't executing. If you can't execute what's called, it doesn't matter what's called.   11/18/87

A lot of guys, this is very important for them, winning, playing for the Bears. For a lot of guys, it's not. I still subscribe to the philosophy that football is not a right. It's a privilege. A lot of guys think it isn't a privilege, it's a right. Rights don't last very long. Privileges you'll cherish and make the best of it. It's a way to spend eight hours, get a paycheck and go home. That's about it.   11/18/87

We stink. Period.   11/18/87

DETROIT AT CHICAGO _____

Before the game   What I told them today is, the most important thing in life, football, business, and success is all a matter of attitude. You are what you think you are. If you go out doubting, then you can't do it, or you won't do it effectively. That's a big part of our problem. There's been a little indecision. We're not sure we can make the plays that we can make.   11/20/87 *Chicago Sun-Times*

Ditka inserted Maurice Douglass and Shaun Gayle into the line-up in an attempt to shake up the Bears secondary before the Lions game. We'll look at any combination we can to get it right. We want a group out there that plays with confidence. That's all this thing is, is confidence. If you're struggling, it's hard to be confident.   11/21/87 *Chicago Sun-Times*

Detroit is probably licking their chops.   11/22/87 *Chicago Sun-Times*

We're not going to worry too much about what Detroit does.   11/22/87 *Chicago Sun-Times*

BEARS 30–DETROIT 10 _____

For the first time since the strike ended, the Bears offense, which gained

*over 500 yards, and the Bears defense, which held Detroit to one
touchdown, performed up to expectations.* We're 8–2, and nobody
else in the NFL can say they're any better. Last year, we were playing
dynamite defense and getting by by the skin of our teeth. Then the
play-offs came, and we didn't do so well. Maybe it will all come together
at the right time this year. Eight more in a row and I'll be happy.
11/23/87

*Several offensive linemen played injured. Ditka complimented the
line* I'm proud of the offensive line. They played their butts
off. 11/23/87

This is the way we've got to play ball. We've got to control the ball,
play tough defense, score some points, and take time off the clock. We
know that people can't run on us. All we've got to do is be smart about
our pass coverages, and we'll be all right. 11/23/87

Al Harris But it's not like we're mad at Ditka for what he says. We're
madder at ourselves than anybody. If we think we've been playing well,
we'd just be lying to ourselves. 11/23/87

Ron Rivera We have been a little tentative. We haven't been cutting
loose like we can. Maybe some feelings were hurt here by things that
were said during the strike, but I'm not complaining. I agree with
everything Mike has said, except that we've lost what we had and won't
get it back. We have lost something, but I believe we'll get it back.
11/23/87

Mike Ditka If you think I'm gonna start shouting off the highest
building, "Everything's OK," you're wrong. We've got to get better.
We are moving in the right direction. 11/24/87 *Chicago Sun-Times*

After we beat New York and played good early in the year, everybody said, "This is it. Get your tickets ready." Don't get your tickets ready until we keep proving it. But we're doing a lot of things better. 11/24/87 *Chicago Sun-Times*

My statement two weeks ago that the defense stunk was not a good statement to make. I didn't mean it the way it was said. All phases of the defense weren't playing bad, but some were. The area I was talking about was mental mistakes. My motives are always good but my methods sometimes aren't as good as they should be.   11/26/87 *Chicago Sun-Times*

GREEN BAY AT CHICAGO: BEARS 23, PACKERS 10

Once again the Bears defense held the opposition to one touchdown. Kevin Butler, the hero of the previous Packers game, kicked three field goals while suffering from an injured leg. Ditka's view of the game   We're not where we want to be yet. But we're getting better. I saw a lot of good things. The Packers have been playing very well the last couple of weeks. We caught them on a day when they did a lot of things well, but we won.   11/30/87 *Chicago Sun-Times*

THE BEARS AT MINNESOTA

Playing at home in the Metrodome, the Vikings were a two-point favorite over the Bears. At stake was the Bears fourth straight Central Division Championship. Commented an excited Ditka   This is a make it or break it situation for the Bears, and also make it or break it for the Vikings, so we like that.   10/1/87 *Chicago Sun-Times*

I would like to win it [the Vikings game] more than any other game of the season.   12/1/87 *Chicago Sun-Times*

Prior to the game, Ditka grabbed media attention by referring to the Vikings' domed stadium as the Rollerdome. Some observers speculated that Ditka was doing this to draw attention away from his players' preparation for the game.   I'd like to play them on a neutral field, but we don't have that opportunity. We've got to go up to the Rollerdome.   10/1/87 *Chicago Sun-Times*

When you get into these Rollerdomes, they're all the same. My God, they ought to be outlawed. Indoor domes should be used for roller rinks. Football was meant to be played outside on grass. Domes have no place in sport, none. Unfortunately people spend a lot of money building them.   10/1/87 *Chicago Sun-Times*

A Minneapolis radio station suggested Ditka wear roller skates to the Rollerdome. His reply   I might. It's not out of the question. How about roller skates and a tuxedo? I'll carry a whip, too. 12/3/87 *Chicago Sun-Times*

Viking General Manager Mike Lynn sent a pair of skates to Mike Ditka, who was later seen roller-skating down the halls of Halas Hall. Lynn explained   He said something about me being too cheap to buy our cheerleaders roller skates. So I sent them with my good wishes, and I hope he wears them in our Rollerdome. I wanted to prove I wasn't cheap.   12/4/87

Ditka graciously accepted Mike Lynn's gift, but couldn't resist getting the last shot.   Mike Lynn sprung for them. That might refute everything I've heard about him from his players.   12/4/87

I have my reasons for everything. You'll find out in life usually when I say things, they bother people who listen a heck of a lot more than they bother me.   12/3/87

BEARS 30, VIKINGS 24 _____

For the fourth time in the season, the Bears scored a touchdown with only 40 seconds remaining in the game, wrapping up their fourth consecutive NFL Central Division title. With an injured Jim McMahon on the Bench, Mike Tomczak engineered a 98-yard scoring drive culminating in a 38-yard touchdown pass to Dennis Gentry. A key series of plays was the Bears defense stopping the Vikings four straight times late in the fourth quarter from the 1-yard line. The goal-line stand was incredible. I've been excited, but I've never felt this way. Every cliche you teach your kids about never giving up, they proved.   12/7/87

Ditka had told Dennis Gentry all along that he would be the star of the game. Gentry's clutch 38-yard touchdown catch and run with 40 seconds left stunned the Vikings and their fans. Unbelievable. They proved they had the guts to do it. I said all week Dennis Gentry was going to be MVP. Don't ask me why.   12/7/87

We have a spirit again. I was worried about that. I thought we lost it. We played hard together as a team.   12/8/87

During the fourth quarter the Bears bench was assessed an unusual 15 yard unsportsman-like conduct penalty. Two days later, it was rumored that Ditka had spit on an official. Ditka confirmed It really didn't have to be called. It could have been left out. I'm wrong. I'm not always right. Fortunately we overcame it because it would have been a classic example of stupidity if we couldn't have overcome it. It was something that shouldn't have been done.   12/9/87 *Chicago Sun-Times*

Apparently not much spittle hit the official. It was a pretty weak effort.   12/10/87 *Chicago Sun-Times*

Steve Kazor, Bears Special Teams Coach He didn't spit at anyone. He had tobacco juice slobbering down his face. I was standing right next to him. I did not see him spit at an official. He was misjudged because he is an amateur tobacco chewer. He was yelling at the official and so was I. Everybody thought the penalty was on me.   12/10/87

After the victory over the Vikings, Emery Moorehead expressed awe at Ditka's motivational techniques.   I don't know where he thought of the Rollerdome. He thinks of something brand-new every week to get the people excited. It's amazing. He's such a tremendous motivator and publicity guy—he gets everything done.   12/9/87 *Chicago Sun-Times*

However, even Moorehead began to wonder when Ditka purposely urged the Vikings fans to boo as the Bears came onto the field.   At that point, I was wondering if he had all his marbles.   12/9/87 *Chicago Sun-Times*

THE BEARS AT SAN FRANCISCO _____

After clinching their fourth straight Central Division Championship against the Vikings, the Bears and the 49ers had 10–2 records, the best in the National Football Conference. The next Bears game, against the 49ers in San Francisco and televised on Monday Night Football, would be crucial to determine which team would have the home field advantage in the play-offs. With several injuries to the offensive line, and Hampton and Wilson not at 100 percent, Ditka was concerned.   We're beat up physically. But sometimes it works to your favor. People play harder and things work out. Guys pull for other guys. But we've lost a lot of talent on the field that's not gonna be there when we go up against the team with the best record in football.   12/8/87 *Chicago Sun-Times*

With a pulled muscle in McMahon's upper thigh, Ditka was concerned about the health of his quarterback.   I don't think it looks good for this week, I really don't. He will be very doubtful.   12/8/87

I don't know how we're going to stop Jerry Rice and Joe Montana. No one else has stopped them. What would make you think we would?   12/8/87

We've got to have inside and outside pressure on Montana. He gets rid of the ball so quickly. If we pressure him, it'll be something to write home about, because he gets rid of it in a hurry. The 49ers are an excellent team, really good. They're beat up, too, but we're really beat up. Sometimes it works in your favor. Guys pull together and play hard.   12/8/87

After describing Minnesota Stadium as the Rollerdome and receiving a pair of roller skates from the Vikings, Ditka was asked how he would describe San Francisco's Candlestick Park.   A den of wolves.   12/10/87
Chicago Sun-Times

PREGAME NICETIES

Bill Walsh, 49ers Head Coach   They're a great team [the Bears], not only with great talent but with great coaching. They're football at its very best.   12/9/87

Bill Walsh, comparing himself to Ditka   There are a lot of similarities between Mike and me. We both have high expectations. We both demand a lot. We both give a lot of ourselves. We both have a bottom line and don't look for ways to explain failure. We don't prepare our teams for the likelihood of failure; we're not looking for downsides. The thing about Mike is he's always willing to go after it. I think I'm in that category, too.   12/10/87

Keith Fahnhorst, 49ers tackle, on Walsh and Ditka fluffing   They are in their fluff mode right now. He [Walsh] has always taken that approach. Even in our first Super Bowl against Cincinnati, he talked about how we had our worst practices of the year at that time. It's just his way of pulling us together, and it works. But it's the same as what Ditka does. We know how it is before a big game, and everyone takes it for what it's worth.   12/9/87

In the two previous games against the 49ers, the Bears won. Ditka explained   The two times we beat them, we kept [the 49ers offense] off the board.   12/14/87

Running is a good idea if you can do it, and I don't see any reason why we can't.   12/14/87

Ditka on the team of the 80s   I would like the Bears to be the team of the 1980s, like the Steelers were of the 1970s and the Packers of the 1960s.   12/13/87

Bill Walsh responded   If you name a team of the 80s, which is a little absurd to be honest—not from Mike's standpoint, I know just what Mike's thinking—but for the press to start talking about a team of the 80s? It's 1987. We still have 1988 and '89 yet.   12/13/87

R. C. Owens, former 49ers star   They've always been interesting games between the two teams. Of all the teams I've played against in the league, I always felt different against the Bears. Their helmets looked funny. They didn't look like football helmets to me. They looked like helmets for monsters from Mars, and guys like Mike Ditka and Dick Butkus fit that image proud.   12/14/87

Ditka's last thoughts before the game   I know one thing—and I found that out in Minnesota—we'll play hard, we'll play long. And if we're still standing at the end, we'll have a chance. That's all I can say. 12/14/87 *Chicago Sun-Times*

They keep putting people in there that I never heard of, and they keep making it work. Because I really think that [Coach] Bill Walsh, when it comes to offensive design of attacking defenses, nobody can touch him.   12/14/87 *Chicago Sun-Times*

He [Joe Montana] does what he's supposed to do. He knows when to run, when not to run, when to get rid of the ball, when to throw it away, when to take a sack.   12/13/87 *Chicago Sun-Times*

49ERS 41, BEARS 0

With both Jim McMahon and Joe Montana out with injuries, reserve quarterbacks Mike Tomczak and Steve Young took over for the Bears and the 49ers. In the first half, Tomczak threw four interceptions and the Bears fumbled twice for a total of 6 turnovers. At the half, the Bears were losing 20–0. In the second half, rookie quarterback Jim Harbaugh started but was unable to engineer a Bears score. During and after the game, the Bears and Coach Mike Ditka were subjected to verbal abuse and showered with debris from the 49ers fans. Mike retaliated by throwing a wad of gum into the stands, which hit a woman in the head. The 49ers fan promptly filed charges with the San Francisco Police, who kept the wad of Ditka's gum as evidence. When asked if the Bears' poor performance may have been a result of the players trying to make the Pro Bowl I won't lose any sleep over it. I'm not worried about that. If they're worried about that, they're on the wrong team, because we're trying to make the Super Bowl. There might be a few guys who have an ulterior motive for playing this game, but I doubt it.   12/15/87 *Chicago Sun-Times*

Ditka discussed the Bears' recent loss with the Seattle media, in town the following week for the Seahawks–Bears game When you lose like that, you start to question a lot of things. Nothing looks very good. Hopefully that won't create a hangover for our players. We've got a lot of pride and character, they'll bounce back.   12/19/87 *Chicago Sun-Times*

THE GREAT GUMBALL CAPER _____

San Francisco police officer George Pohley filed this report about the incident.   As I was escorting Coach Ditka from the playing field, he stopped and looked at the people sitting in the pullout seats. He then took a piece of gum from his mouth and threw it at victim-reportee Ornelas, striking her in the back of the head. Coach Ditka then flipped the bird with his left hand and exited the field.   12/16/87 *Chicago Sun-Times*

Ditka responded   Any time anybody throws something at me, I'm going to throw something back.   12/16/87 *Chicago Sun-Times*

Steve Kazor, Bears coach, said he was hit by a ball of ice wrapped in tape.   That was probably aimed at Mike.   12/16/87 *Chicago Sun-Times*

Diana Ditka on the incident   She [the woman] was lucky Mike didn't have a bat in his hand. He'd have thrown it.   12/16/87 *Chicago Sun-Times*

Mike Rodenhauser [Bears Center] commented on the unbelievable nature of the whole incident, especially booking the gum as evidence.   That's ridiculous. What are they gonna charge: assault with a deadly gumball?   12/16/87

During breakfast in the hotel restaurant the morning after the game, Ken Valdiserri [Bears publicist] approached Mike and Diana Ditka. Diana Ditka repeated their conversation   Kenny told Mike there was a group of reporters wanting to speak to him about the gum thing. Mike said, "What for?" Kenny then told him the lady was planning to press charges. That's when Mike blew up, and why not? I see she's changed her mind; she's not going to carry this dumb thing any further. All she wants is some sort of apology, I guess. Well, what about Mike and our players? Don't they get an apology for the way they were treated? They were like sitting ducks out there Monday night. The fans are right on top of you in that park, and they throw everything. Does this lady admit she threw a cup of ice at Mike as he was leaving the field after the game? Of course not. But she's gotten her name in the papers and her face on TV, so that's all she cares about. Those fans are awful out there. There were cops on horseback on the field after the game, and still the fans came out of the stands. Imagine what would have happened if the 49ers had lost.   12/17/87

Diana Ditka   Mike doesn't even chew green gum. And I've never seen him chew Trident, either. He likes that cinnamon stuff, or that Red Man. What they probably did out there in San Francisco is pick up the first wad of gum they could find after this fan called the police over. It's ridiculous. The whole thing is stupid. It really is.   12/17/87

In the week after the 49ers game, the 49ers announced that action would be taken against individuals who harass visiting teams. Also, Bill Walsh telephoned Mike Ditka to apologize for the behavior of the fans.   Mike was a gentleman about it. Mike minimized it to me; I maximized it to him.   12/21/87

SEATTLE AT CHICAGO: SEAHAWKS 34, BEARS 21

The Seattle Seahawks defeated the Bears 34–21. Walter Payton scored two touchdowns and ran for 79 yards, during what was possibly his last home game. Once again, turnovers were costly to the Bears, and allowed the Seahawks to score 13 points. Of special concern was the Seahawks' last touchdown drive: with a little over five minutes left in the game, Seattle ran with the ball 55 yards for the touchdown.   They ran it down our throat when they hadn't run worth a nickel the whole game until there. We take for granted we can do this and do that, and yet when it comes time to make the play, we don't make them. 12/21/87

On offense, the mistakes are alarming. The fumbles are alarming. The penalties are alarming. Everybody looked like they expected everybody else to make the play.   12/21/87 *Chicago Sun-Times*

Ditka predicted that Mike Tomczak would rise above the San Francisco game.   We've won a lot of games with [Tomczak] and we think he'll win a lot more.   12/19/87 *Chicago Sun-Times*

Prior to the Seattle game, Ditka stressed the importance of the Bears winning their last two games against the Seattle Seahawks and the L.A. Raiders.   The main idea the last two games is to improve going into the play-offs with a little bit of momentum. Right now, we don't have very much, but it can come back in a hurry.   12/19/87 *Chicago Sun-Times*

GUM-THROWING AFTERMATH _____

After the loss at San Francisco and the media interest over the gum-throwing incident, Mike Ditka was unusually noncommunicative to the Chicago media. Ken Valdiserri, Bears publicist, issued the following statement.   Mike [Ditka] has decided to decrease his accessibility to the media because of an increasing disgust with the media treatment over what he perceives are very trivial incidents that have occurred over the last couple of weeks.   12/17/87 *Chicago Sun-Times*

After Mike Tomczak's poor showing against San Francisco, Mike Ditka had some words of encouragement for him. Tomczak repeated the advice.   He was telling me he still has a lot of confidence in me and to get back to my style of play, and if you cut down on the turnovers and stupid mistakes, you can do a lot for this team.   12/19/87 *Chicago Sun-Times*

In keeping with his boycott of the Chicago media, Ditka told Seattle writers before the Bears–Seahawks match that the Bears' running game and the Seahawks' run defense were both suspect.   It will be two suspects meeting each other in a dark alley.   12/19/87 *Chicago Sun-Times*

Ditka on the Bears' tough image   I don't know that we scare anybody right now. As a matter of fact, I think we're playing a little bit scared ourselves. I mean we're afraid to make mistakes.   12/21/87 *Chicago Sun-Times*

To be realistic, we are a good football team. If we weren't, I'd say we weren't.   12/21/87 *Chicago Sun-Times*

We may have to go back to the drawing board.   12/21/87

THE BEARS VS THE L.A. RAIDERS _____

Ditka's frustrations before the game   We have certain individuals who do not feel urgency to get things done. They worry about how high their socks are, if the white shows a lot, whether they got their shoes on right, decals painted on right, little wrist bands, a little eye black. They forget to play football, but they look good.   12/22/87

Our tackling has stunk for two weeks. There's not any purpose to it, not any madness about it.   12/22/87 *Chicago Sun-Times*

As a result of back-to-back losses to San Francisco and Seattle, Ditka indicated that the Bears would be making changes in the lineup.   I want to see if I can find a better chemistry than we have out there right now. If it works, fine, we'll probably go into the play-offs leaning that way. If it doesn't, we'll go back to the way we were. We can't be worse for it.   12/22/87 *Chicago Sun-Times*

The following day Ditka made several lineup changes. Otis Wilson and Neal Anderson were out of the starting lineup because of injury. Todd Bell, Mike Richardson, William Perry, Tom Thayer, and Paul Blair were taken out of the starting lineup in an effort to find the right team combination, as the Bears looked ahead to the play-offs. It's not like I'm mad at anybody. I'm groping, and when you're groping you're going to do some different things. I think we fool ourselves sometimes when we don't play all the people we have, especially when there's not that much difference in the talent.   12/23/87 *Chicago Sun-Times*

BEARS 6, RAIDERS 3 _____

The Bears defense held the Raiders offense to less than 200 yards. Mike Ditka singled out the play of Maurice Douglass, Al Harris, and linebackers Rivera, Singletary, and Marshall as exceptional. It was one of the few times all year the Bears managed to create three turnovers. Another key to the victory was the play of the Bears special teams, who blocked three Raiders field goal attempts. Ditka on the Bear victory I don't know how prettv it was; I really don't care.   12/28/87

I thought we played with a lot of discipline. We looкed like we were organized. It looked like everybody was doing what they were supposed to do instead of individuals doing what they wanted to do.   12/29/87 *Chicago Sun-Times*

27

THE REAL SEASON ENDS

THE PLAY-OFFS: WASHINGTON AT CHICAGO

We'll probably go into the playoffs as a weak sister. We're letting people think what they want to think about us.   12/28/87 *Chicago Sun-Times*

The Redskins are one of the teams picked to do it; we're one of the teams not picked to do it.   1/5/88

I think we'll win it all. Because it's our team, the Bears, because we expect to win. We don't expect to lose to anybody. In general, this team plays with a lot of pride, with a big chip on the shoulder. We're one of eight teams that can win it. One play can make or break it. This is the bigtime. This is what you dream about when you're a kid. This is what you can tell your grandchildren.   1/8/88

What has happened in the past means nothing. The Vikings proved that. Get hot in the play-offs and you can win. Get cold and go home. 1/8/88

Redskins lineman Dexter Manley allegedly called Ditka a bum as a result of the gum-throwing incident in San Francisco. Ditka's response The one thing you have to understand is that Dexter has the IQ of a grapefruit.   1/5/88

Dexter Manley   I have said nothing about Mike Ditka. I'm not getting into fighting words with Mike Ditka. Whatever Mike Ditka says. 1/5/88

Tom Haivers, sports psychologist   I grew up watching Jim Taylor with the Packers. Not great ability, but intense drive. Came to the stadium in a beat-up old Ford. Same with the Bears' coach, Mike Ditka. Now these players come to the stadium in limousines. The gifted athletes on the Bears, unfortunately, have been put on a pedestal by other players, friends, family, and the media and are not overestimating their self-importance. The bottom line in sports, no matter how gifted you are, is that the state of mind of the performer determines the performance.

The state of mind that results from overestimating your talents is not conducive to optimum performance. The Bears are football players, but now they are selling us tires and sandwiches and hair spray. Their minds have become scattered, and much as Mike Ditka tries to motivate them through fear, which used to work, it doesn't work anymore. He made some lineup changes, which are good, because a guy like Gary Fencik has made it on desire all along. But Richard Dent? Ditka can't humiliate him into playing better by calling him Robert. It's a different era. And the economic gain from going to another Super Bowl isn't that great.   1/10/88

REDSKINS 21, BEARS 17 _____

The Redskins eliminated the Bears from the play-offs. Turnovers and the inability to capitalize on opportunities led to the Bears defeat, their third defeat in the last four games. At the end of the game Walter Payton, playing for the last time, sat dejectedly after all the players had left. Ditka   I want to congratulate the Redskins and wish both teams (Minnesota also) the best of luck. They've worked hard and they both deserve it; they earned it. It's a credit to the Minnesota football team and to the Washington football team. I think very simply, in a nutshell—I won't belabor the point because I don't want to be up here very long—we ain't good enough right now, gang, it's that simple. We had a number of opportunities, but when we have to stop people, we aren't capable of stopping people. And when we have to score or block people, we don't do a good enough job. Of course the inconsistencies and turnovers hurt us again, and we had some key opportunities to make some big plays and we didn't make 'em. We just are not good enough right now with the people we have or the way we're playing. So something's got to be changed.

We'll all evaluate ourselves, coaches and players, and I think that's where you go. It's not a dismal year; I mean it was a good year if you consider a lot of things that happened. There were a lot of good things. But when it goes two years in a row that you end up in this same position [losing the conference semifinal], it's not very much fun. I don't want to be in this position again. So it's about that simple. There's not much else to say. Our guys played hard. It wasn't a matter of wanting to; it wasn't a matter of being ready; it wasn't a matter of being stale. It was a matter of not being able to make the plays when you have to. They made a play on special teams and we didn't—it's that simple. It was a close game and I thought it would be.   1/11/88 *Chicago Sun-Times*

Ditka's view of the loss   When it happens to you two years in a row, it's not any fun. I don't want to be in this position again. If we can't do it with the people we have or the way we're playing, something has to be done.   1/11/88

Next week we'll be watching the Vikings and the Redskins in Washington and saying that should be us out there. No, it shouldn't. We just aren't good enough.   1/11/88

On Jim McMahon playing hurt in the Washington game   Half the guys in the country wouldn't even have been playing, the way Jim felt. 1/11/88

I've got to get somebody to protect my quarterback if we're going to throw, so he's not killed back there on the three-man rush—where he's actually almost killed.   1/12/88

Dexter Manley   What's their excuse now? Is McMahon too tall? Last year they blamed the loss to us on Doug Flutie because he was 4'11". Here they were talking about this short guy all week and he isn't even on the team anymore. So is McMahon too tall? We kicked their butts and I ain't afraid to say it. I may have a big mouth, but at least I can back it up. All you guys from Chicago media, you just go ahead and tell Mike Ditka that.   1/11/88

Mike Ditka   Any time the national anthem is being played and he puts on the show he put on during the national anthem, it's a disgrace. If that's all the respect he has for his country, then I'll say what I think I have to say. You're taught from the time you're in 5th grade what you do during the national anthem, if you have any respect. He never even stood still. He ran up and down behind the rest of the guys on the sideline. Had his head in the heater. And I'm crazy for inciting him.   1/12/88

He might be right about me being foolish and stupid. I wouldn't argue that with him. The thing about people like Charles Mann and Dexter Manley is that it's okay for them to say something, but it's very unbecoming for a coach to retaliate. In my position, a lot of coaches wouldn't retaliate. All I'm saying is somebody asked me a question about what [Manley] had said and I made a statement about grapefruits. That offended him. But that's my true opinion of him.   1/12/88

DENNIS McKINNON ON DITKA _____

It happens every year, never fails. If we win, he [Ditka] takes credit.
If we lose, then we get the blame. That's how it is.   1/11/88

When you get on the field in big games like this, he [Ditka] has to take
control. He has to run it the way he wants to run it, as opposed to what
the opposition is giving you. McMahon knows what's happening. He
should be in control of the game. When we won the three of four times
at the finish of games [after the strike ended], Ditka said Jim basically
called the plays in the fourth quarter. Why didn't Jim do that today?
Today [Ditka] called the plays that didn't make sense.   1/11/88

We have a lot of different philosophies, offensive and defensive, that
work every now and then. But they aren't totally consistent. If it wasn't
for our athletes, we wouldn't be in the postseason any year. Once you
get to the postseason, you have to let them play. I don't understand
it. You practice hard all week and then you get to the game and the
coach starts calling all the plays. It was the same scenario as last year.
Only Bambi [Doug Flutie] was here then, and he had all the plays on
his wrist. Ditka decided to go with him instead of Mike Tomczak or
Steve Fuller, who had the experience. All Washington did last year
was bring everybody [on a blitz] so Flutie would have to step up to
throw and couldn't see. He didn't see and he still threw.   1/11/88

I'd rather play on a team where I feel I'm going to be utilized instead
of sitting around doing nothing and letting some rookie take my spot.
1/11/88

A lot of guys should be playing who aren't. We have a lot of guys playing
because they've been there or because of who they are. We've got too
much talent not being used, and maybe some other team in the league
would be glad to have us. We have better offensive talent than
Washington, but we have a run-based philosophy and it doesn't get
used like it should. We knew Jim couldn't run today because of his injury

and we told the offensive line all week, "Give him four seconds to find the open man and throw the ball." Then we don't do that.   1/11/88

In 1985, giving the defense a 14-point lead like we did today would have been like giving candy to a baby. Not this time, though. We've changed a lot from 1985 and I'll keep bringing it up until we get to another Super Bowl.   1/11/88

DITKA RESPONDS TO McKINNON _____

I don't want to talk about Dennis McKinnon, believe me. I read where we are supposed to throw the ball 60 times a game. McKinnon said the Bears should have thrown that much against the Redskins because their defense was vulnerable to the pass. We didn't get to be a winning team the last four years by throwing the ball 60 times a game. But that shows you the mentality of some people. That's just not the answer. I don't want to hear about the system. You make it happen. The guys who are talking, catch the ball and hold on. Give us a chance. I don't care if it's a miracle play. I don't believe in miracles. Let's not talk about the system. The system's good.   1/12/88

THE PLAYERS SPEAK OUT _____

After the Bears were eliminated from the play-offs there was speculation that Otis Wilson would be one of the first players to go. Otis responded I'm not even going to go into that. I just want to play football. I don't know what's going to happen. I don't think he [Ditka] knows what's going to happen. Everybody's upset right now. We're all men, we're all professionals in what we do. And we'll have to make adjustments.   1/11/88 *Chicago Sun-Times*

Otis Wilson He [Ditka] said he would evaluate and let some people know whether their face is good around here. No doubt about it, I enjoy it here in Chicago. I want to play here in Chicago, but I don't want to be unhappy in Chicago. When he makes this decision, I'll make mine. 1/12/88

On Otis Wilson's and Dennis McKinnon's criticism of the Bears organization and Mike Ditka   It's imperative to be happy wherever you are, and I don't think they're very happy men.   1/12/88

Richard Dent   I don't think we have an attitude problem at all. We just couldn't make the plays when we needed to make them.   1/11/88 Chicago Sun-Times

Dave Duerson   We are a good team. We have a winning attitude. When I first got here five years ago we were happy to finish 8-8. Now we aren't pleased unless we get to the Super Bowl. It's not Mike Ditka's problem. It's not Vince Tobin's or Ed Hughes'. It's each of the players on the field. We have to make things happen. We have to reach within ourselves.   1/11/88

Duerson   Until you know what you're talking about, you should keep your mouth shut.   1/12/88 Chicago Sun-Times

CHANGES FOR THE 1988 SEASON _____

I'm tired of the lack of discipline, tired of people who think they have better answers and solutions because all of a sudden we win a few games. There are people who consider this drudgery, no fun to be around. That wasn't the case two years ago. It was fun to be here. My God, if you consider it drudgery, then don't do it. Do something else and see if we can make that kind of money doing something else in society. We can't.   1/12/88 Chicago Sun-Times

I've been in this game 27 years as a pro, and I know what it takes to win. The difference now is we have 50 experts instead of a couple. 1/12/88 Southtown Economist

What are the implications of losing highly talented but unhappy players? Time goes on. The difference between the guys who are playing and the guys who aren't in most cases is minimal. All the guys who are playing for us now, that's how they got their start. They were behind someone, they got their chance and made the most of it.   1/12/88 *Southtown Economist*

It's very hard in the league to trade, especially in the first round. Nobody is going to let you move up. It can happen. But I'd rather not give up draft picks. I'd rather try and gain some. If our talent is as good as we've analyzed our talent to be, and if other people look at it the way we do, they should be willing to talk about some of our people.   1/12/88

Where do the Bears need help from the 1988 draft? We need a cornerback, an offensive lineman, and maybe another defensive lineman. Tight end. Fullback. They're all things you can look at. The main thing we want to do as a coaching staff is evaluate personnel before we make any comments. We want to establish a philosophy on what we want to do offensively, defensively, and special teams. Sometimes we do too many things, and that makes it hard to concentrate. I read where we're supposed to throw 60 times a game. We didn't get to be the winningest club in football the last four years by throwing 60 times a game.   1/12/88 *Southtown Economist*

I just have no desire in calling plays anymore. I've done it my way, now I'm willing to back off and do it another way because we haven't won the big games lately and it bothers me.   1/12/88 *Chicago Sun-Times*

Our defensive unit is not good enough. Something is missing that was there even early in the year.   1/11/88

I have total confidence in the coaching staff.   1/12/88

We have to get back to the offseason conditioning program that we had in here a couple of years ago when people thought it was important to work out. All of a sudden we're a bunch of individuals that all have their own gyms in their own house. They all work out at home—maybe they do, maybe they don't.   1/12/88 *Chicago Sun-Times*

You don't get healthy in Platteville. You get healthy in April or March. 1/19/88 *Chicago Sun-Times*

28

MIKE DITKA —
BACK IN 1988

In late December there were rumors that Mike Ditka would leave Chicago and coach the Dallas Cowboys when Tom Landry retired.
No, I wouldn't go there. I'm not Dallas, I'm really not . . . . You don't follow legends [Tom Landry] and have much success.   12/28/86

I'm not Dallas. I'm Chicago, Pittsburgh, Buffalo, Cleveland, teams like that.   12/28/86

There are a lot of ways you can leave a mark in football and society. Coaching is one of them. Ownership, part of front-office management—I just think there's different ways, and I think somewhere in life you start thinking about them. Not right now, but someday.
1/2/87

AFTER THE FIRING OF JERRY VAINISI—
A CONVERSATION ON THE STAIRS _____

Ditka: Yeah, I'll go to California to play golf next month. I'll relax
a little, then one more year.
Man: One more year 'till what?
Ditka: 'Till I retire.
Man: Retire? You're not going to retire?
Ditka: Watch. You watch.   1/16/87

Of course, I mention a lot in the heat of emotion and anger.   1/20/87

If Mike Ditka is here or not, the Bears will survive.   1/20/87

On leaving the Bears   If I did, a very big part of my life would leave
also. For a long time I've dreamed about [being the Bears' coach] and
when it happens you kind of get to love it and you don't want to just
walk away from it. But I've learned to walk away from other things
in life and if it came down to that, I probably could do it.   1/20/87

I can work with anybody. I just can't have my legs cut off, that's
all.   1/20/87 *Chicago Sun-Times*

I feel I'm a tremendous part of a great thing that's happened here and
I would like it to stay that way. I just don't know what events are going
to come up that might change it, that's all.   1/20/87

I think it would be silly of me to give up something I love dearly, which
is the Chicago Bears and coaching, just to follow Jerry [Vainisi] just
because he's my good friend. At the end of this season [1987], I'll
reevaluate the situation, but I think I would like to put the Bears back
in another Super Bowl—not that I'd do it, but I think the players want
to do it.   1/21/87 *Des Plaines Daily Herald*

On Vainisi being fired   I think you're always hurt when you lose a good friend and you don't understand the reason behind it.   1/21/87 *Des Plaines Daily Herald*

When you're hurt, you say things. But when you re-evaluate, my whole life revolves around the Bears. I have no dreams of working on Wall Street or coaching in another city. When Mr. Halas gave me the opportunity, it meant a lot to me and it meant a lot to repay some of the confidence he had in me.   1/21/87

Did Ditka tell McCaskey he wouldn't be back in 1988?   No, I didn't. 1/20/87

PREDICTING DITKA'S FUTURE _____

Johnny Roland, Bears Offensive Coach   He'll be back for 1987. What he's talking about is after that.   1/20/87

Ed Hughes, Bears Offensive Coordinator   Once things have a little time when the harshness wears off, Mike's always been a Bears man. I think he likes it here. I don't see any reason why Mike would move on.   1/20/87 *Des Plaines Daily Herald*

Players have asked if my heart was in it. Yeah, it's in it.   3/19/87

I'm just happy to have a job. I don't worry about it. Look at all the guys with contracts who get fired. You guys [reporters] are more secure than coaches, and you don't have contracts. I guess Ann Landers has a new contract. I just don't think that far in advance. I'd like to believe I will be back.   3/19/87

So, if I don't have a contract agreement by the first game of the regular season, I definitely won't have one until the season has ended. I don't use an agent, and once football starts, I'll think of nothing but football. Period.   7/21/87

Would he be coaching the Bears after the 1987 season?   Probably. I'm not smart enough to do anything else.   1/21/87 *Des Plaines Daily Herald*

THE 1987 SEASON

McCaskey on Ditka's contract   What is a problem is how much the Bears can afford to pay, and I intend to stretch just as far as we possibly can because Mike Ditka has been a very fine coach for the Bears and we want to see that continue.   8/2/87

We've been talking for a couple of months about it and there's a good chance we'll be able to resolve it before the start of the season.   7/29/87 *Chicago Sun-Times*

We're trying to form a team that is as strong as it can possibly be and get back to the Super Bowl. With Mike as our head coach, I like our chances.   7/29/87 *Chicago Sun-Times*

Sure, we're joined together by a business, but we've been through some wars together, too. While we're not tight friends, there is, on my part at least, a sense of concern about Mike Ditka, the person. He's done a lot for the Bears. There have been some tough spots, but we've come out of them OK for the most part.   8/6/87 *Southtown Economist*

He may make more money than any coach in football [with endorsements, commercials, etc.]. If he, in his own thinking about what is a fair amount for him to receive, took into account the terrific opportunity he has had and continues to have for making money because he is the head coach of the Chicago Bears, then it would make it easier to reach an agreement. It's something Mike Ditka has to decide.   8/2/87

DITKA ON HIS CONTRACT _____

I want to coach here. I think it's a matter of time until these things are worked out. 7/31/87 *Chicago Sun-Times*

I don't anticipate anything being done before the season. I haven't thought about it. I don't worry about it. I haven't lost one bit of sleep about it. 8/10/87

I don't think anything will be done . . . ever. That's the way I feel right now. I've never been told I'm wanted. 8/21/87 *Chicago Sun-Times*

JERRY VAINISI ON DITKA _____

Would Mike Ditka, in his opinion, coach in another city? Maybe, Dallas, to pay a debt. But Tom Landry just signed a three-year deal. And Mike is as much in love with the city of Chicago as the city of Chicago is in love with him. If it doesn't work out in Chicago, Mike doesn't want to go anywhere else. 8/9/87 *Chicago Sun-Times*

On the Ditka-McCaskey relationship They're doing a pretty good job [of working together]. They all seem to be on the same page. And Mike says he's working pretty well with [McCaskey], which everybody would have been surprised at. I don't know how much of that is Michael trying to show Mike [Ditka] they can work together, to soften him up for his own contract negotiations. But Ditka's contract ought to have a very clear statement of who has responsibility for player personnel and the draft. 8/9/87 *Chicago Sun-Times*

Lions Coach Darryl Rogers, replying to speculation that Mike Ditka would replace him at the end of the season Mike isn't going to be lured away from Chicago unless the Bears are nuts, and I don't think they are. 8/9/87 *Chicago Sun-Times*

To Jeanne Morris, reporter for WBBM-TV Chicago, Ditka remarked that coaching was only one facet of his life. Matter of fact, I'm thinking more and more about it . . . Who knows? I may be one of these guys who try to sail across the Pacific Ocean or something . . . You have to look around and say, "Do I have a value or don't I?" If I don't, fine. Get somebody else. 8/23/87 *Chicago Sun-Times*

MIKE DITKA IS SIGNED

On 8/30/87 Mike Ditka and the Bears agreed to terms. Ditka's new contract was estimated to be around $650,000 per year for three years as a base salary. There are a lot of higher contracts, and a lot of lower ones. The opportunity I have in Chicago is second to no opportunity in the United States—not New York, not Los Angeles, any other place. That's evidenced by the support we have in this city both as a team and individually. It's evidenced by the outside opportunities to make money. That's all I'll say. 8/30/87 *Des Plaines Daily Herald*

We talked about length of contract. I don't think it's fair to saddle me or the organization with a contract beyond a certain period of time because if I wasn't doing the job, it could become a burdensome thing. Three years is fair. If we had argued for a while, it could have been longer. 8/30/87 *Des Plaines Daily Herald*

I intend to be here and finish my coaching career here, the good Lord willing. Money doesn't matter. I was the lowest-paid coach when I came here and we've done all right. Maybe [after the contract expires in 1990] it will be time for me to step aside. I intend to be around for a while. My health is good, unless something freakish happens. I never intended to coach in this league 20–30 years. There are young people very qualified to do the job, and if it's time to step aside, I'll do that. I've had my day in the sun, that's for sure. 8/30/87 *Des Plaines Daily Herald*

Did he ever really consider leaving? It never crossed my mind. I was mad last week about other things. 8/30/87 *Des Plaines Daily Herald*

MIKE McCASKEY ON DITKA'S CONTRACT _____

There couldn't be a better head coach for the Chicago Bears.   8/30/87
Des Plaines Daily Herald

I'm sure as I'm standing here that this gives us the best chance of getting
back to the Super Bowl.   8/30/87 *Des Plaines Daily Herald*

PLAYER REACTION TO SIGNING MIKE DITKA ___

Dan Hampton   Now Mike can concentrate on getting us back to the
Super Bowl. This is something we need to put our minds to rest,
knowing the Bears will be in Mike Ditka's hands for the next few years.
Not many good things happened in Chicago until he showed up. Since
then, we've been one of the premier teams. I don't see any reason why
we can't continue that.   8/30/87 *Des Plaines Daily Herald*

Jimbo Covert   I think it'll have a positive effect on him and on the
team.   8/30/87 *Des Plaines Daily Herald*

Mike Bortz   I think it's great for the city of Chicago. I think he belongs
here because of his personality and because of the personality of the
city. This is one less thing we have to worry about. The players can
concentrate on football.   8/30/87 *Des Plaines Daily Herald*

Dave Duerson   Give credit where credit is due. Talent wasn't the
question here, but he's the one who put it together. The Bears never
had the kind of team unity where the offense and defense communicate
on and off the field.   8/30/87 *Des Plaines Daily Herald*

Otis Wilson   I'm glad he got it, but I hope he didn't get it all [the
money from the Bears]. He deserves it. He can buy champagne instead
of wine.   8/30/87 *Des Plaines Daily Herald*

Walter Payton   I might have a hard time stealing him away now [if Walter receives a football franchise].   8/30/87 *Des Plaines Daily Herald*

MIKE DITKA ON HIS SIGNING _____

Many people wondered if Ditka was serious about leaving coaching at the end of the season.   It depends on how many offers from Hollywood come in. I check the mail every day, but nothing's going on right now.   10/20/87 *Chicago Sun-Times*

I just don't want to be put in a position where everything I say, somebody's offended by it. I came here six years ago, and I said some things six years ago, and a lot of guys who were offended by it aren't here anymore. That's all right. I'm still here. But I'm just tired of trying to mend a bridge everytime I say something.   10/20/87 *Chicago Sun-Times*

Would he still characterize some players as egomaniacs?   I don't retract that, and they should know that. If they want to hold a grudge, fine. I don't hold grudges against anybody.   10/20/87 *Chicago Sun-Times*

After the strike ordeal, Ditka was not so enthusiastic about coaching. To Chicago TV reporter Johnny Morris   I mean what I said. Right now, it's not fun. They key thing is right now. I might turn around and say, "Boy is this great." You know how I am. What do they call me? Sybil. Wait till I change my dress.   10/20/87

VOLATILE MIKE _____

Diana Ditka   He's just fine. Mike's volatile, but that's one reason he's such a good coach. And before he changes, he'll get out. He's talked about how it isn't as enjoyable as it used to be, and I don't doubt for a minute that he means what he says. It's hard to imagine him not coaching, but there's so much about the job that's not fun. Because it's not football.   12/17/87

Michael McCaskey—on the 1987 season   It's been a tough year and presented all of us with novel challenges that no one in football has ever seen before. As each week went by, something else popped up, and I think Mike and the rest of the coaches have responded well.   1/1/88

When asked if some Bears players quit believing in Mike Ditka, McCaskey reportedly responded   Yes.   1/1/88

Did relations between Mike Ditka and some of the Bears players have a negative effect on the team in the 1987 season? McCaskey's response   It's within the organization. It's a scab that's healing. If we talk about it a lot, we're picking at it. The best way for it to heal is for everybody in the Bears organization to let it heal. We need some time for that. It's not just Mike Ditka, either. There's a lot that happened in the strike. Things that were said. Hopefully, the great majority of that is behind us.   1/1/88

Jim McMahon, commenting on McCaskey's remarks   McCaskey said we don't trust Ditka anymore? Well, I don't think it's big news that we didn't appreciate some of Ditka's remarks during the strike. Even Ditka knows that. But that stuff shouldn't affect how we play and how much we want to win. Heck, two years ago we weren't the happiest team in the world and we lost one out of 19 games and won the Super Bowl by the biggest margin ever.   1/4/88

PREDICTING THE FUTURE _____

On reports that Ditka might resign in 1988 though he signed a 3-year contract   There's a lot of things that are going through my mind right now, but I'd rather not talk about it. It has been a difficult year. You

lose your sense of value, what the heck's important. That's what bothers
me. And then when I do some things that aren't the way I want to
do them, it bothers me. It's been a tumultuous year. Is that a good
word? Sounds like a milkshake.   1/5/88 *Chicago Sun-Times*

It's been different this year. I'm not going crazy. I've still got all my
facilities, contrary to a lot of public opinion. You lose your sense of
value of what the heck's important. That's what's been bothering me.
When I do some things that aren't the way I want to do them, it bothers
me. I have to live with that and that hurts me a lot. It's been a
tumultuous year. Last year was kind of fun. It was a challenge. This
year was fun for a while.   1/10/88

If I thought retiring was in the best interest of the Chicago Bears, I
would retire. I don't think there's anybody better suited in America
to coach the Chicago Bears than me. I say that with no ego involved,
just pure fact. There have been many others who have stepped to the
fore and tried who haven't done it. We've done it because we know
what the hell we're doing, period.   1/12/88 *Chicago Sun-Times*

*Jerry Vainisi, commenting on the end of Mike Ditka's contract in
1990*   I'd look for him after that to look for new horizons to conquer.
But if he stays in coaching, I firmly believe it will be in Chicago.
Nowhere else. But the intensity with which Mike coaches, there is a
burn-out factor involved. I can't see Mike being a 25-year head coach.
He lives hard, works hard, and plays hard. I think the John Madden
TV role for Mike would be a natural. Mike's going to want to try
something different in a few years. He'll have had nine years as a head
coach in 1990 . . . and if he wins the Super Bowl in the next three years,
I'd say he definitely would get out of coaching. Go on to television.
2/4/88

Ditka's view   I have things to accomplish in the next three years, but
I want to accomplish them with a team, not individuals.   2/8/88

I really haven't decided what I want to do. I know one thing. I never set out with the ambition to coach 20 years. My ambition was to bring the Bears a winner and instill pride back. We've done some of those things, but I still have some goals for this team.   2/12/88 *Chicago Sun-Times*

Anybody can predict anything. Somebody can predict I'm going to coach one year and go into politics for the next presidential campaign, too, but that's not fact. I appreciate what people say, and Jerry's my very dear friend, but I haven't thought that far ahead. My goals are more for the team than they are personal. Personally, I've been very fortunate. But I've got some team goals I want to see fulfilled. When they're fulfilled, if I still feel like doing it, I'd do it. But if I didn't, I wouldn't be reluctant to say, "It's been great. I enjoyed it," and turn it over to someone else.   2/12/88 *Chicago Sun-Times*

When I turn this team over, I don't want to turn over a team that's old. I think that's what we've got to go through now. We've got to make sure we know our course of direction and start following it.   2/12/88 *Chicago Sun-Times*

29

THE 1988 SEASON

OFFENSE 1988

We almost bit on a few [offensive linemen] that we like. But there is nothing the matter with our offensive line that, hopefully, a few surgeries didn't cure. Covert, Hilgenberg, and Van Horne, and even Thayer had that knee surgery. We had four guys who got nicked last year, but I like our offensive line.   5/1/88

You must change personnel. When you have to go with one back, two tight ends, and two receivers, you go to it. When you have to go with one back, no tight ends, and four receivers, you go to it. You have to try to get mismatches, and you do that by changing formations and moving around.   4/25/88 *Chicago Sun-Times*

You've got to realize this is no longer a team that's going to be dominated by Walter Payton. I don't know that we're going to run that kind of offense anymore. We're going to try to run an offense that can utilize whatever people we have so [defenses] won't know when we're going to pass, when we're going to run.   4/25/88 *Chicago Sun-Times*

ANALYZING 1987 _____

I didn't feel close to the players at all [in 1987], and they didn't feel close to me. I totally disagree with what they did [in striking]. I totally disagree with what the American athlete is doing. Football is good for everybody. When you've got to rape the game, you've got a problem. Everybody talked about how they felt betrayed. I felt betrayed, too. I shouldn't be saying this now, but something should be said. Whether I'm close or not, it's important to have a great amount of respect, and maybe that's what wasn't there on either side.   2/8/88

We blitzed 30 percent of the time. We were beat 24 times for touchdown passes and 18 were versus the blitz. You tell me what to do. We're going to make a couple of changes but nothing earth-shattering. Some of the wounds will be healed because of a parting of the ways. Some players won't be around. Other than that, a lot of wounds are because players are not signed. We'll try to do the best we can.   2/8/88

We're going to change some things on offense, and I want to be more involved with the defensive coaches—not that we're changing, because what we're doing is right.   2/8/88

People sometimes forget why you win. You win because you're a team, not because you're a collection of 49 individuals needing a new contract. When you start thinking you're the main reason we win, then you have a problem. That was a major part of our problem.   2/8/88

With the percentage of turnovers we had, we worked a miracle. That is, our players worked a miracle. It was amazing we won. And we won in a lot of different ways. We won with McMahon and we won with McKinnon and we won with Gault. And Payton. We didn't have the big plays from the defense last year that we had in the past. And that hurt.   4/10/88

I don't consider the Redskins above our level at all. I don't consider a lot of teams above our level. Yet there are teams with better records than us. It comes down to how you play the game. 4/10/88

We didn't have one guy on the offensive line who was really as healthy as he was the year before. 4/10/88

When you set a record for fewest points allowed the year before and you don't match that, of course you feel like you're falling off. We did fall off defensively, but the biggest and most important area we tailed off in was that we did not create turnovers. We weren't a team that intercepted the ball and created fumbles. 4/19/88

I don't think that what we are doing is wrong. We have the right approach, but it is only as good as the people playing the defense, and if they are not playing it well, then we will have some problems. We had very poor execution in some areas. We have to take the bull by the horns in a couple of positions and challenge people. 4/19/88

Our record indicates we're a good team. What we've failed to do is win the game that was important to win. In the last two years it didn't come down to the other team beating us as it did our beating ourselves. Of course, a lot of people don't like to hear that, but I'll say that and live with it. We beat ourselves. We didn't make the plays when we had the chance to make them. We had a number of opportunities to score. We had a chance to cover a punt that we didn't cover well. But I take nothing away from the opposition because they played very well. 3/12/88

We would have been a tough team to beat last year if there hadn't been a strike. But there was a strike. We didn't even know where to go sometimes on defense. We just weren't concentrating. The intensity level was not nearly what it was after the strike in practice or in games. Don't ask me why. I don't know the answer to that. If I had known the answer I would have changed something last year. 3/20/88

We seemed to be sitting back on our heels a lot, waiting for bad things to happen. We started giving a big cushion [between corners and receivers], and the more we gave a cushion, the more the ball started being thrown in front of us and we seemed to lose confidence.   4/8/88 *Chicago Sun-Times*

We were playing with guys who were all beat up in the play-off game. An All-Pro center in Jay Hilgenberg, who played darn good, was banged up. And Covert, who was also beat up, is as good a tackle as there is in football. Keith Van Horne played the whole year hurt and never really said anything about it. Thayer had surgery after the year, and I never knew he had a cartilage injury. Bortz had a pinched nerve all year. We didn't have one guy that was really as healthy as they were in the years before.   4/20/88

CHANGES IN 1988

Everybody thinks they've got a way with their suggestions. But what we've done for six years has been right. We've got more fans in the last six years than a lot of teams in the league. Anywhere you go, people talk about the Bears, even when we get our butts knocked out in the first round.   2/8/88 *Chicago Sun-Times*

We have to put football and the team first. For those people who aren't willing to do that, maybe they'll have to get out of it, or I'll have to get out of it.   2/8/88 *Chicago Sun-Times*

There are so many nagging things in your mind. If this. If that. Can we do this better? Should we have done this? You drive yourself goofy. I'm not going to do that anymore. But yet there's the anguish of knowing the team that won everything is the team we had completely in control and let it get away. This year, I did not have fun. I don't know how many coaches had fun. If every year was like this, then I would say I wouldn't last very long.   2/12/88 *Chicago Sun-Times*

We have a few guys who gripe a lot, but everybody gripes in life. We may have a few guys who may not be as enthusiastic as others. If everybody concentrates on the team concept and forgets about who's making the sack or getting credit for the tackle, we won't have any problem. I think incentive clauses should be based on what the team does instead of the individual, and that would end a lot of the griping.   3/20/88

We're lean on back-ups. That's where we're dead. My God, we wonder why we don't cover well on punt teams. We only have two linebackers on our whole team covering on punts. They are back-ups and they certainly aren't the best athletes we have. That has become a problem with us.   3/20/88

Whether I change the way I act on the sidelines or wherever I'm at, that really doesn't matter. We're going to go out there the way I've always envisioned the Bears playing. Not that we haven't done it the last two years. I just think the consistency has to be greater than it was a year ago.   4/10/88

I think you win with defense. The offense can be good at times. We have to get back to where it was prior to the strike. On defense, we've got to create turnovers. We've got to look at the individual techniques played within the defense. We have to show more discipline in practice and do the things the way they have to be done so they will hold up in game conditions.   4/19/88

THE 1988 DRAFT

This is a key draft for us because, they say, in football you go through cycles. Everybody has an "up" cycle and a "down" cycle. If you can keep the supply of players properly, you can create the competition at certain positions that you have to. Hopefully, we can bring that back to where it was. I think that's my job.   4/10/88

We're going to try and get everybody signed and happy and playing the way they did in 1985 and 1986. But we're still going to look hard in the draft at cornerback. 4/18/88

Can you draft tight ends? I don't know if you can draft great tight ends. You must develop them. But if we can find one who can block well and catch well, we'd sure love to have him. 4/19/88

Is drafting Perry's brother a possibility? You need two tackles, so it wouldn't bother me to have two brothers on the team. 3/12/88

We're looking hard right now at what we can get in the draft in the way of help in the defensive secondary. The first thing we talked about as a staff was getting help as back-ups on defense. This has become a specialists' game. We have had a lot of players playing well on the defensive side for a long time and we're not getting any younger. We've got to start getting some good back-up people in there to replace them. I mean, Hampton is not going to play forever, and McMichael. And even Singletary or Otis [Wilson]. None of those guys. We're not getting any younger. We'd like some help at cornerback. We need another rush man. We need an offensive lineman. We need another linebacker. We need a tight end. We're happy with our receivers and we're happy with our running backs right now. 3/12/88

I just hope we never get the first pick. I think that would be the day I'd be gone anyway. 3/12/88

THE DEPARTURE OF WILBER MARSHALL

I think any coach who bases his philosophy on one player is making a mistake, whether it's a quarterback or a running back or what. I think teams that win don't always have the best players, but they have the best team. It's how they play together. 3/18/88 *Chicago Sun-Times*

When Wilber Marshall signed with the Redskins   I'm not going to jump off any high buildings.   3/19/88

I don't think that our defense equates their talent to anything that Wilber does. I think our guys have a lot of pride, just like Wilber had a lot of pride. They will go out and play hard and do the best they can. In my mind, it's a big loss because we drafted Wilber No. 1 [in 1984], and we knew he was a heck of a football player. We were right. But he's not a part of our team anymore, and we just have to go on from there and find somebody to replace him. I think we will have people who will play awfully hard, and I'm very optimistic we will accomplish the things we want early to be ready for our first game against Miami.   4/17/88

There are a lot of good players in the league. Lawrence Taylor is an outstanding football player, one of the most dominant defensive players I've ever seen in the game. Carl Banks is outstanding and maybe one of the most dominant linebackers I've seen in the last 10 years. There are a lot of good football players . . . . I don't know how you explain [$1.2 million] to people. That's all I'm saying. If that becomes the going price, then the game is done. Our game is done. I mean, it just can't last. I don't begrudge anybody anything. I'm not saying what's right or what's wrong. I don't know. It's just a tough situation for everybody. I don't begrudge the player because it's an opportunity of a lifetime. 4/17/88

Building a successful team is similar to putting pieces of a puzzle together. We've got a missing piece, but a lot of capable talent to fill the void. It will be a good challenge for our management, coaching staff and players to put this behind us and continue to be one of the best teams in football. We wish Wilber well. 3/19/88 *Chicago Sun-Times*

OFFENSE 1988

On Dennis McKinnon   I have no problem with Dennis McKinnon.

He's a fine person, a fine football player. I have great respect for the way he plays the game. I admire him. He talks sometimes and he probably regrets some of the statements he made. We all make statements in our youth.   4/6/88 *Chicago Sun-Times*

On John Wojciechowski   We played him last year at tackle, but I think he's a guard. When I watched him at guard in the replacement games, I saw a lot of good things. A lot of fluid movement. He's not a real fast, pretty kid, but he's fluid.   4/20/88

On Tim Wrightman   I'm sure Tim's going to come back and try. We'll just see what happens.   4/6/88 *Chicago Sun-Times*

On Jim McMahon   He's playing racquetball. He's working out some here [in Halas Hall]. Maybe not as much as he did a couple years ago, but he's playing golf, so it [McMahon's shoulder] can't be too bad.   4/6/88 *Chicago Sun-Times*

On Willie Gault   You cannot measure his value by the number of balls he catches. He also improved a great deal in the blocking area.   4/22/88

On injuries   Jim Covert is a key concern, and Hilgenberg. Hilgenberg has to have another surgery on his elbow. The surgeries we've had so far have been successful. Van Horne had the latest surgery, and hopefully he will recover from it.   3/12/88

On Anderson and Sanders   I would say that Neal Anderson will be a better running back from the tailback position than he was from the fullback position. First of all, he's going to hopefully be healthier. With the proper use of Thomas Sanders, I think he can spell Anderson. 3/12/88

No More Payton   I think our kids will perform. There aren't any Walter Paytons out there. I think they understand their role is not to be Walter Payton. Their role is to be themselves and do the best they can.   3/12/88

DEFENSE 1988

On Todd Bell   Todd really hasn't asked to be traded. We just talked about some possibilities.   4/6/88

On Otis Wilson   To me, it would be foolish to take Otis off the left side, where he has lined up for years, and move him to the right side. He's so acquainted with that side. I'm not saying that he can't play the other side, but I think you want to keep him comfortable.   4/17/88

On Mike Richardson   He played well in 1986. Then he missed mini-camp and training camp last year, and when he came back and started playing, he pressed and tried to make big plays. You have to play the defense that's drawn up.   4/17/88

On changes in technique   Some of the techniques are going to change. I want to put our corners in more of an attacking position, where they are confident and feel like they can get up and bump people if they want.   4/17/88

THE 1988 SCHEDULE

On the Central Division   I think Minnesota is a heck of a football team and I think Green Bay will be much better. Tampa Bay has shown tremendous improvement. Detroit will also be a lot better. I think our division will be a lot better. Minnesota has now turned the corner and they now know that they can win.   3/30/88

On division games late in the season   I'd like to have them earlier.
4/8/88 *Chicago Sun-Times*

We really don't play any tougher teams than the ones in our division.
But there's a silver lining around strong late schedules. If you're playing
good football, it'll make you better for the play-offs. If you're not, you're
going to find out anyway. We had a few chinks in our armor [last year].
We found out we weren't playing as good as we could have.   4/8/88
Chicago Sun-Times

If it did come down to the last game, it would be good for the Central
Division. But we would hope that that didn't happen. We hope to win
the Central Division before the last game. I'm sure they're saying the
same thing up in Minnesota.   4/10/88

1988 DRAFT OUTCOME

On Brad Muster, fullback, Stanford   We considered trading up for
this guy. When we figured he would fall and come to us, we got pretty
excited. We've been real fortunate.   4/25/88 *Chicago Sun-Times*

He's a nice guy, clean-cut, his mother is from Chicago. He's got a lot
of good things going in there.   4/25/88 *Chicago Sun-Times*

But can he block?   The kid's got some tools, but we've got to find out
if he can block like Matt [Suhey] and Calvin [Thomas].   5/1/88 *Chicago
Sun-Times*

On Wendell Davis, wide receiver, LSU   We didn't draft Wendell Davis
to put pressure on Willie Gault or anybody else. He just happened to
stick out like a sore thumb.   4/25/88 *Chicago Sun-Times*

He's courageous. He'll catch the ball inside and go up over the middle with a block. He'll fit in very well.   4/25/88 *Chicago Sun-Times*

I think you just bring him in, line him up, let him compete, and see who's the best out there. I think this guy is a talent.   4/25/88 *Chicago Sun-Times*

Davis impressed Ditka in a LSU vs Mississippi game.   They got behind. They threw the ball to this kid eight times in a row. He caught every one of them. He scored a touchdown. They went ahead and won the game. Everybody in the stadium—including me, the coaching staff, everybody—knew the ball was going to him, and he still got open and caught the ball. So I think you're talking about an exceptional football player.   4/25/88 *Chicago Sun-Times*

On Jim Thornton, tight end, Fullerton State   He's an interesting guy. We liked everything about the kid except we wish he was 6'5". He's 6'2", but the son of a gun can run. He's strong. He'll put his nose in and block you. He can go deep.   4/25/88 *Chicago Sun-Times*

The Bears picked three players in the draft from the University of Oklahoma: Caesar Rentie, tackle, Dante Jones, linebacker, and Troy Johnson, linebacker.   These kids from Oklahoma are smart, they're alert. They know what is going on.   5/1/88

All in all   I'm not saying we had the best draft or the worst, but we're in there favorably. I thought Jerry [Vainisi] did a great job for Detroit. They got some good football players. And, of course, Minnesota got some good players. And Green Bay and Tampa Bay got some players they can get the ball to. Our division is going to improve.   5/1/88